limited language: rewriting design

responding to a feedback culture

Colin Davies, Monika Parrinder

limited language: rewriting design

responding to a feedback culture

Birkhäuser
Basel · Boston · Berlin

Layout: Oskar Karlin

This book is set in Monotype Grotesque (captions and references), Berling
(body text) and Monoikos (all headers). Oskar Karlin designed Monoikos specifically for
this book. The typeface is based upon Monaco in 10pt which was used on the original
Limited Language website.

Cover image: Luna Maurer + Kristin Maurer
De Zee naar Harderwijk (The Sea at Harderwijk)
www.dezeenaarharderwijk.nl
Commissioned by SKOR Foundation Art and Public Space.

The Dutch coastline at the Oosterscheldekering in Zeeland is streamed live (with sound)
to patients at the St. Jansdal Hospital in Harderwijk, The Netherlands. Every five minutes
a film still is archived online and patients receive a weekly postcard of images shot during
the previous week.

Technical realisation: @Xit
Courtesy SKOR/Photography: Teo Krijgsman

Library of Congress Control Number: 2009934863

Bibliographic information published by the German National Library.
The German National Library lists this publication in the Deutsche Nationalbibliografie;
detailed bibliographic data are available on the Internet at http://dnb.d-nb.de.

© 2010 Birkhäuser Verlag AG
Basel · Boston · Berlin
P.O. Box 133, CH-4010 Basel, Switzerland
Part of Springer Science+Business Media

Printed on acid-free paper produced from chlorine-free pulp. TCF ∞

Printed in Germany

ISBN: 978-3-7643-8934-5

9 8 7 6 5 4 3 2 1   www.birkhauser.ch

For Loukia, Joseph and Christian

For Mia and Eve

Acknowledgements

Thanks,

To everyone who has contributed to the Limited Language project
over the years.

For publishing the book
Birkhäuser Verlag
Robert Steiger, Commissioning Editor
Daniel Morgenthaler, Editorial Assistant Architecture & Design

For the design
Sofia Andersson, assistant designer
Amalie Borg-Hansen, assistant designer
Oskar Karlin, Web and book concept and overall design
Luna Maurer, for her generosity in discussions over the cover

For sub-editing the text
Emma Angus
Michael Clarke

All the kind colleagues who have helped with reading,
advising and recommendations to the publishers
Jeremy Aynsley, Jess Baines, Adriana Cerne, David Crowley,
Adriana Eysler, Ian Horton, Joel Karamath, Joe Kerr,
Dene October, Rick Poynor, Sarah Temple, Tony Todd

For research funding and research leave
in the preparation of this book
London College of Communication
Royal College of Art
University of the Arts, London
University of Wolverhampton

Everyone who has so generously supplied image copyright

Finally, from Colin,
Monika (for her endless patience), my children (again),
Mum and Dad, and Emma.

And from Monika,
Ben, Beth and Lynne for discussions about the book, and everything.
Matt, Mum and Dad, for everything.

In memory of
Alice Swanson who died on 8 July 2008.
Ben Kinsella who died on 29 June 2008.

The Limited Language project

The original idea, which ignited the Limited Language project, was to create a brand that used the Web as a platform for generating writing about visual communication. The idea of the brand in this context was a deliberate conceit – to explore how words, like images, are commodities.

Cutting, pasting and recycling are all properties of contemporary image culture and are present in the way we generate ideas. Thoughts and conversations are cut and pasted from one context to the next, taking on a new signicance in each. Limited Language aims to capture this as a working process for new writing.

Anyone can be part of Limited Language by responding to trigger articles. We encourage people to recycle comments in their own research, as we collage them into our own writing. Any comment eventually used is credited.

We began writing under the guise of Limited Language in London in 2005, as two lecturers/practitioners in visual culture and theory. We were searching for a way to engage with visual culture, largely one in which image is read as text. We were aware that the words we wrote with, in many ways, shared the same outcomes as images. To us, words and images have the same systems, same structures, same fetish and commodity value: you can buy and sell words, ideas and criticism as you might a Picasso, a bag of chips or pornography. Sometimes, of course, that's a Citroën Picasso.

What we became increasingly conscious of was the way that, although some might talk of the possibilities of language as unlimited – of the procession of images, simulacra, as unending – to us, Language is Limited in two respects. First, the vocabulary of postmodernism; its flattening of critical positions into an atonal mantra of relativism – where high and low culture lose their magnetic North and become one and the same. The second is in the visual realm, where increasingly our worlds are shaped by sound bites, lists made up of top tens, anthologies, page layouts – communication concertinaed into byte size representations via sms messaging, the looped voice mail, a scrolling message board, or the chat room – where text and image are brought together in an online stream of emoticons and fcuk©ing abuse.

From this starting point, we decided that our subject should be *process*. And, if we were to write about the creative process, then we should at least explore how processes from within design culture (a culture of recycling and mash-ups etc.) inspire collaboration and cross-media/cross-disciplinary practice and by extension new ways of generating and distributing writing about process.

Limited Language is an attempt to weave these modes back into a framework – a narrative to be used, re-used and again recycled. Not, we promise, just another rehash of the remix though – a cop out, to fill media space – but here we re-use and recycle as a deliberate technique because to revisit concepts in different contexts, at different times is to enrich, expand and hopefully capture the serendipity of creative process.

On the website, designed by Oskar Karlin, we decided to invite practitioners and critics to post essays on subjects from their area of discipline or expertise, with relevance to issues of 'process'. The aim became to explore how ideas and processes transfer across disciplines. This idea informed the Web design, whereby we run three concurrent articles at once, allowing readers to read/comment across debates.

The articles posted on the site are not intended to be 'finished' (although many are) but rather, provide ideas and questions which allow responses to integrate with the original text. These responses often take on a life of their own: existing articles may divide and multiply... paragraphs from one topic may be isolated to generate new thinking elsewhere. Our remit always intended to go beyond a traditional design blog, where discussion is an end in itself.

The Web here – immersive, responsive, collaborative – becomes a useful mode of facilitating research. In turn, this becomes synthesised and redistributed through print publishing: from journal articles, published lectures to this book. (But the book is a starting place, every article ends with an URL for the conversation to continue!)

Our writing on one topic migrates from the Web to print, via lecture halls, and back again. It is an ongoing 'collaborative' process. Just as walking down the street is as much about the mutterings and the conversation that you hear as it is about what you see, we use this feedback culture to construct our critique. This critique focuses in particular on the process and experience of design, visual culture and the everyday. In Photoshop you can't save to print unless you have 'flattened' the layers. We don't aim to flatten, but to produce a lamination of outputs, a composite for use and resale.

Book methodology

Which design audience?

We started out by looking at visual communication but any demarcation between practice disciplines was soon corrupted and the site came to occupy the in-between space of process and practice: how we craft/create/discuss/think/reinvent.

We write about art, design, architecture, sonic and visual cultures and practitioners from all these disciplines have contributed writing to the site too – some of which we have included in this book.

What is feedback culture?

Feedback culture is one of the cultural spin-offs of the Web 2.0 inspired velvet revolution in cultural agency, where design increasingly facilitates, rather than simply providing bounded social practices in communication.

Whilst many get themselves into (post-modern) knots discussing the true benefits of these cultural changes; websites such as Twitter and Facebook are changing how the world is perceived and how we perceive ourselves within it.

Increasingly the image has been side-stepped by 140 digit tweets and downloaded MP3s – screen based culture is fast being eclipsed by touch-screen tactility.

Everyday, through screens, keyboards, wireless networks and Bluetooth accessories we are performing agents in a feedback culture.

We have taken the responses from the Limited Language site as our starting place. Sometimes it has been a simple passing-of-the-baton where we write on a subject and the responses have carried on in the same vein – maybe fleshing out more detail or giving a more mappable path – but equally tied to the original writing or response.

We do not agree with everything written by others under the Limited Language banner but, rather, enjoy the serendipitous path it might inspire us to follow.

Many of these journeys can be found in the writing in this book.

Structure of the book

The book is organised into chapters which do not follow disciplinary lines but coalesce around certain themes that have emerged as recurrent concerns over the years. The book layout is divided into two columns. The first, in black, is a starter article which has already appeared on the Limited Language website or elsewhere and which has tended to frame some sort of question or provocation. The second column, in colour, is our reflective response. This reframes the question in relation to some of the feedback received on the site (whilst taking into account its new context and changing events since originally posted).

The starter articles comprise both our own writing, and writers and practitioners we asked to contribute to the Limited Language site. The book can only cover a small proportion of the writing published on the site over the years and we are equally indebted and inspired by those not appearing within these pages.

We had no absolute criteria for selecting material for the book but have tried to choose the articles that captured certain themes and investigations regarding practice and process. In the end it can only be an arbitrary selection to try and give a feel of the ongoing Limited Language project.

The responses to the starter articles are not only re-realised in our own writing but we attempt to explore the thinking process through the practical work, which has always inspired us (although the work is never physi-

cally represented on the Limited Language site: each article in the book ends with an URL for you to return to the Limited Language site.

We decided upon a text only website to provide a focus on words (and thinking) as apposed to image/colour/text: the predominant blog format is image/text...image/text etc.

On the site we have made use of hyperlinks to allow readers to go off elsewhere to feed the need for images and the physical realm!

As design historians, this book seeks to revisit old work as much as new, and to explore how it materialises, and focus on its making. To this end we show sketches where possible, to try and capture work in progress.

We're interested in what designers are doing and try to make sense of it in a wider context: its relationship between disciplines is as important as its cultural ramifications.

Beyond the book... the Limited Language Web-platform will capture how our reflections here coalesce in a feedback culture: readers of the book can post onto the Limited Language website – providing a point of departure for new discussions in an on-going process.

Each chapter's opening spread includes keywords that we have identified as critical moorings to the proceeding essays. In brackets, we have shown their Google hit rates when added to the word 'design'. This is of course ever changing, but it gives an idea of what is out there.

Table of contents

Critical moments

The problem with design / What voice can design have?
Design in crisis / Too much history
Patronising Prada / Critical effects
Love/hate / Base and superstructure
Shock and awe: the politics of production / The process of consumption
Multiverso / Embodied information

This chapter explores how design can have its own voice:
from politics to violence; methodology to consumerism.

Keywords
History (217,000,000)
Marxism (550,000)
Problem solving (10,800,000)
Violence (24,300,000)

Keywords and their Google hit rate in conjunction with the word design.

The problem with design

What voice can design have?

In *Fear of Small Numbers: An Essay on the Geography of Anger*,[1] Arjun Appadurai comments on how the West is increasingly dominated by a fear of the lone bomber with explosives strapped to their chest. Surely, a more rational fear would be the panic of spotting the lone designer with a portfolio, packed with high problem-solving principles strapped to their chest.

Problem solving, the methodological bedrock of design, is the semantic key to a designer's belief that they are in a position to change society. Social problems and design form a symbiotic relationship, something politicians and cultural commentators alike find alluring.[2] The 'designer as cultural-mediator', has an established history in Britain: from the *Great Exhibition* in 1851 to the *Festival of Britain* in 1951.[3] During this period, the designer's role as cultural mediator has evolved into the 'problem-solving' or 'social-engineering' conception of design we witness today.

The trouble with problem solving is its contingency. The problem could be anything: global warming, social housing, over-consumption or even 'the Jewish problem'. Indeed, the scar of the Holocaust is incised, in part, by the work of designers who (often unintentionally) created the blueprints for mass killing; drew up plans for the work camps, rationalised and set the train timetables and so on. Today, it should be remembered that one person's problem is another's home or fight for freedom or means of transport.

Much contemporary design has taken on the role of cultural beautician or plastic surgeon, providing a global parlour plied with consumer goods, manicured with good intentions; all plucked from a repository of modernist thinking. It's like 1980s Alessi[4] with a social conscience. In *Wallpaper*[*5] magazine, Dieter Rams (the influential designer for the German consumer electronics manufacturer Braun), listed the Ten Commandments

The original article took issue with the figure of the designer as already expert problem-solver with their oft-quoted claims for social responsibility. Design and social responsibility aren't directly linked. They are part of a matrix of historically situated relationships between people, contexts and media in which design is embedded. An ironic (?) take on this thinking can be seen in a T-shirt that says *Design will save the world.* A counterpoint to this thinking was on show at the Compostmodern 09 conference hosted by AIGA, the professional association for design in America, with its aim to 'connect the dots' on design and social responsibility. Here, inventor Saul Griffith's presentation started with the image; *Design won't save the world. Go volunteer in a soup kitchen you....*

Replies on the Limited Language website, to *The problem with design*, were less polemic, more ponderous than the sloganeering above; the equivalent, perhaps, of answering the question 'What voice can design have?' with more questions. This has provided us with the opportunity, here, to explore what's at stake in the shift from design authors and outcomes to design process.

This isn't to deny design a voice, but re-cast it as one process, amongst others, of asking questions about the world. If, as Nigel Cross suggests, there is a 'designerly way of knowing',[1] then what would be a designerly way of asking questions?

An alternative to the black-clad designer with his problem-solving principles of grids and typographic layouts comes from Michel de Certeau in *The Practice of Everyday Life.*[2] From the top of the World Trade Center, where the viewpoint that transforms the city into a rational layout is an illusion, De

T-shirt by Osika LLC for
Artefacture (2008).

Text from a presentation by inventor Saul Griffith at the AIGA
conference Compostmodern 09, as it appeared on several
Internet blog sites in Spring 2009.
http://bit.ly/saul_griffith
http://bit.ly/compostmodern09

of good design: at number 4, 'Good design helps a product be understood' and at number 6, 'Good design is honest'. Here, fashionably repackaged, is the old Modernist dichotomy: design's raison d'être of moral instruction alongside its decorative, consumptive self.

Pick at the stitches and you find the dilemma for all design: its relationship to commodity and the dialectical tensions between use and life-function. Every design will add to the flow, creating an ever-greater distance between actual use and the symbolic order it falls within: an upturned box, a picnic table, an IKEA table, a Habitat table, a John Lewis table, a Heal's table, a Marcel Breuer table etc. The list expands to become a series of eBay 'tags'. Likewise, non-branded trainers and anti-globalisation T-shirts validate the system they intend to critique.

In a modern capitalist world, where the route to social influence is pock-marked with the fallout of political spin and unrealistic assumptions of design's public impact, design's dilemma is this: what voice can design have?

Design needs to go beyond the rhetoric of manifestos (which have become the bored patter of fingertips on the table while you wait for the next big idea to come along). Design needs to be a series of small ideas – mini explosions, eureka moments – which atomise and settle in unexpected places. A few immediately come to mind such as the paradigmatic and well publicised work of architectural collectives like British FAT (which stands for Fashion, Architecture and Taste) and muf (a group of architects and artists) and product designers like Dutch Droog design. One could also add Swedish Front Design and graphic designers like the French M/M (Paris). Altogether, they present work of different and often opposing stances as to how design should live in the world. All their work is more about the 'process of design' than problem solving alone.

Back in 2000, Droog's *Do Create* collection included a metal armchair that owners bashed into shape with

Certeau's voyeur emerges, a pedestrian, on the street. The street becomes the opposing 'other' of the view atop the building. 'Escaping the imaginary totalizations produced by the eye' the walker experiences the city without preconceptions, which makes him receptive to chance and possibility. For this, the pedestrian (and our designer) needs a multitude of tactics as evinced from the details of everyday life. This experience of the street is analogous to the notion of process in design.

The ways in which these alternative images of 'the designer' translate into design thinking (and real people!) was teased out in replies to the article on the Limited Language website...

One reply quoted Matthias Hillner,[3] head of the Studio for Virtual Typography, commenting that: '[a] problem with design education...is that it ignores the accompanying questions...', and then continued: 'It's not the camera that determines the perspective, it's basically where you position yourself and where you are looking. If you have the capability to orientate yourself and determine your position you have a very good start.'[1]

And yet... James Souttar points out a tension between old Western ideals and design: 'Isn't the "problem with design"...that "designing" wasn't enough for designers. We had to be political activists, cultural commentators, conceptual artists... people with an intellectual agenda, not just an aesthetic one.'[11]

Whilst design can't be situated outside a larger network of visual discourses, what's instrumental is the way this is conceptualised. Social responsibility in modernist European/American design has coalesced around specific, morally neutral tags: design for charity, the environment and so on. (The if-you-do-a-film-about-the-Holocaust-you're-guaranteed-an-Oscar line of thought[4].)

But neutral design is an illusion. Even irresponsible, in that it can't be held to account. Anne Bush proposes 'social response-ability'. This would involve responding in dialogue with each project or scenario, rather than acting on pre-set ideas about socially responsible design.

'In the most fundamental sense, then, responsibility is the ability to respond. It is not just the willingness to act, but also the ability to understand one's actions.'[5]

This goes further than orientating oneself to ask: From where am I speaking? To whom? And with what bias? What can my tools do? And crucially, what can't they do? This is less about the abstract idea of social responsibility and more about an embedded practice that is ethical and accountable.[6]

And yet, again... for Souttar, the problem with postmodern Western design – exacerbated by its binge on French philosophy – is that its context might already be bankrupt. Instead he looks to a Latin Renaissance, specifically in typography. 'No philosophy, no cultural theory, no more fucking head-stuff, but just sheer passion and fascination for type, and a willingness to play and explore, without the constant fear of crossing the ill-defined boundary between layered irony and simple naivety. And really the Latins show us the simple answer to "the problem with design (in the Anglophone world)": it has no soul.'[III]

A reply to Souttar counters that this is 'a rather clichéd view that non-western (currently Latin) = soul = passionate'.[IV]

So, what is soul? It would seem to be a deep level of human engagement with the world around it: for instance, demanding not just instinctual answers, but real questions. We might find soul in graffiti on the streets of São Paulo[7]... But, can't it be found anywhere where need is spoken with an authentic voice?

Take just two examples... *Jugaad*, is a free-standing shade canopy, made out of discarded oil cans, in the Indian village of Rajokri on the outskirts of New Delhi. This was built over a period of three months by ninety members of the village, led by Sanjeev Shankar, whose interdisciplinary work draws on practices across art, craft, design research and architecture. *Jugaad* is a Hindi term for attaining any objective using available resources at hand and, in this project, both cooking oil and repurposing are central to Indian culture. Shankar

a sledgehammer and a rubber-lined (hence unbreakable) porcelain vase that gained character the more it was dropped or smashed against a wall. Here, Droog was investigating process, rather than commenting on a global condition of violence. But they are equally likely to engage in 'changing the world': *Urban Play*, implemented from 2007 and on, has been described as 'an international project... [that] believes that street-level inventiveness, energy and innovation is the future of creativity in the city... [c]reated as a catalyst to inspire creativity in the public domain...' Droog are interested in new materials and the cross-fertilisation of technologies and processes. For them, design is quintessentially a temporal phenomenon, a 'moving forward'.

FAT's architectural work such as *The Blue House*, a house/office/apartment finished in 2004, is always technologically precise and cognate, but the overall impression is filmic. It is a collage of the visual objet d'art of urban experience, remixed and presented back to us. The FAT methodology is the antithesis of the New Urbanism movement, which uses the paucity of ideas in much contemporary architecture to validate old thinking, old architectural forms and class divisions. New Urbanists say their gated communities are in response to the needs of occupants, unlike the top-down ideologies of the 1950s and 1960s modernist building programmes. FAT and muf respond differently to the same criticism. Their work is designed to grow from the middle; it's about communication and engages in participatory workshops with the local community. muf's small-scale urban design projects are another example of this working ethic. Design needs to reflect the mores of its times rather than produce a banal B-movie of an imagined community.

Networking and a cross-fertilisation in methodology between the digital and analogue worlds (different to inter-disciplinary practice) will become increasingly important to design thinking, be it MySpace or the more tangible network of projects in inner city areas across the world. Good design develops incrementally and, in a

Jugaad, a public art project with Sanjeev Shankar (2008).
Photograph by Sundeep Bal.

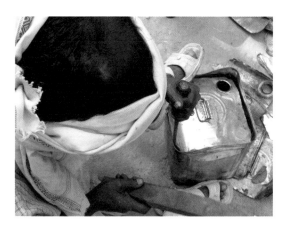

A can lid being cut off.
Photograph by Sanjeev Shankar.

Cans being cleaned in big communal vessels.
Photograph by Sanjeev Shankar.

The Fantastic Norway caravan.

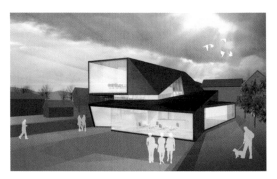

Brønnøy Kunstbase, Norway. An arena for contemporary art for the last public space in the village of Brønnøysund, proposed following workshops with the local community by Fantastic Norway (ongoing).

globalised community, good design projects bounce off other ones. In these small explosions of technical nous and creative spirit we see the materialisation of social concerns; environmental issues, globalisation, consumerism, ethics etc. But, not as doctrinaire monoliths, rather as small-scale, individual investigations into contemporary culture.

What if a designer's social responsibility (should they feel the need) was to ask questions rather than emphasise problem solving... What if designers were to stop making simplistic overtures to saving the world... What if they were to stop the mantra for socially-responsible design that ignores the issues of religion, politics and personal taste... What if they were to stop telling consumers that the choice of one design over another equates to sound ethical/political judgement...

If only designers could stop measuring the impact of design solely on how big the problem is. Instead, wouldn't it be better if they focused on how important the question is?

See further images here
www.limitedlanguage.org/images

References
1   Arjun Appadurai, *Fear of Small Numbers: An Essay on the Geography of Anger* (Durham, NC: Duke University Press, 2006).
2   Robert Levit & Ellen Levy, 'Design will save the world!' in *Harvard Design Magazine*, Spring/Summer 2006.
3   Or, in Britain, perhaps even going back to the first design schools founded in the 1830s.
4   The Alessi design collection gave us the iconic designs of the 'Juicy Salif Citrus Squeezer' by Philippe Starck and the Bird Whistle Kettle by Michael Graves amongst others.
5   *Wallpaper** 103, guest-edited by Dieter Rams, September 2007.

reflects: 'Initial resistance in the village to work with an outsider and explore the discarded oil can, a common symbol of "waste", was an important challenge... Global issues of environment, sustainability and recycling can inspire [people] only if they are linked to their daily lifestyle. Through deep human level engagement, there was a gradual change in perception and...gradually, the entire community was inspired... The fabrication process and vision of *Jugaad* became an integral part of village life and its people.'[8]

Fantastic Norway is a group of architects whose red caravan – which travels around from town to town as an open-door, working office – embodies the idea of the socially responsive, 'public architect'. In each scenario, they find out through a 'mapping process' what projects are needed and how they might come about; in interaction with local residents, traditions, media-outlets, politicians and planning processes (all facilitated by serving waffles!). Erlend Blakstad Haffner suggests that 'People don't necessarily know what they need. But this process helps them find the right arenas and forms, through architecture, to politically anchor them.'[9]

This isn't instrumental (top-down) but 'dialogical' design. More colloquially, we might call it reciprocal: where there is genuine dialogue and people's particularities and feedback are looped into the process. No 'Big Idea', no one-size-fits-all and no designer as author. Instead design in this mode is project-specific, experimental, open and value comes at any point. It takes its thrust from collective wisdom,[10] which isn't solely attainable from 'expert' knowledge. This is a recognition that the world is complex and that no one person or discipline can solve its problems.

Mikhail Bakhtin in *The Dialogic Imagination*,[11] suggests that the dialogic work is in a reciprocal relationship with other work, informing and continually informed by it. Dialogically, you can never have closure. The act of appropriation cannot be complete. This transcends any idea of design being evaluated in terms of impact or contextualised in terms of movements. Instead, it's to continually trace and re-trace design shifts as increments.

For Bakhtin, the dialogic has an imagination. As does the term project, as verb, where the etymology of ject is the act of throwing forwards.[12] Design's voice projects into a continuum of critique, consumption, and contribution. What can design's voice contribute to the social imagination?

See full responses + carry on the conversation here
http://tiny.cc/chapter1_1

Reader credits
I   and another 17/03/2008
II   James Souttar 20/03/2008
III   James Souttar 20/03/2008
IV   and another 20/03/2008

References
1   Nigel Cross, *Designerly Ways of Knowing* (Basel: Birkhäuser, 2007).
2   Michel de Certeau, *The Practice of Everyday Life* (Berkeley: University of California Press, 1984), 153.
3   Matthias Hillner as quoted on www.knowyourvalues. com, 2008. See: Matthias Hillner, *Basics Type: Virtual Typography* (AVA Publishing, 2009).
4   Kate Winslet parodied herself by saying this in *Extras* (dir. Ricky Gervais & Stephen Merchant, 2005) and later won the 2009 Oscar for Best Actress for, *The Reader*.
5   Anne Bush, 'Beyond Pro Bono Work' in Steven Heller and Veronique Vienne, *Citizen Designer* (New York: Allworth, 2003), 30.
6   See Donna Haraway, 'Situated Knowledges' in *Simians, Cyborgs and Women* (London: Free Association Books, 1991).
7   See, for instance, François Chastanet, 'Pichação' in *Eye* 56, Vol. 14, Summer 2005, 40-47. This is an account of the blackletter forms of the São Paulo 'pichação' graffiti movement, through which the dispossessed differentiate themselves from political anti-dictatorship slogans and integrate their own identity into the Brazilian urban fabric.
8   http://sanjeevshankar.com
9   Email exchange (2009), http://fantasticnorway.no
10 See Charles Leadbetter, *We Think* (London: Profile, 2008).
11 Mikhail Bakhtin, *The Dialogic Imagination: Four Essays* (Austin; London: University of Texas Press, 1981).
12 See also Wolfgang Jones, 'Design, Ethics and Systems-thinking' in Paivi Tahkokalli and Susann Vihma (eds.), *Design: Pleasure or Responsibility* (Helsinki: UIAH 1994), 42-53.

Ezri Tarazi

Design in crisis

At first sight, all branches of design seem to be prospering. Design activities all over the world are increasing exponentially, filling the sky with bright new stars. Design reacts to technology faster than art, and this is very conspicuous as regards to the digital developments that have been taking place ever since the mid-1970s.

Designers have been involved in this digital revolution from its very beginning and actively influenced its development. This was not a fringe culture, but an integral part of the digital revolution. They created the mouse, the window, the button and the Web's visual experience. Whereas art is still trying to comprehend the video innovation, design determined the way in which people work and act in the cybernetic world. But at the same time design is going through a crisis. Grey clouds gather beneath its wings – ethical issues related to consumerism, pollution and the exhaustion of raw materials as opposed to temptation, the creation of endless collections and the sterility of renovation. Design finds itself coveted by new disciplines that boast of dealing with 'aesthetics'. The weak flutter which began with plastic surgery to correct damages after accidents or war, gradually becomes 'redesigning the human body' for capricious aesthetic reasons. Standard operations, such as nose jobs or skin grafts are replaced by new interventions that include 'overhauling' the body and cosmetic surgery. The physician no longer heals. (S)he 'creates'. The intention is more to design than to cure. 'Body designer' or 'appearance designer' are more correct terms to define these professionals, and they are closer in their intention to fashion designers and hair stylists than they care to believe.

See further images here
www.limitedlanguage.org/images

Too much history

Design and history are shackled, if not synonymous: design suffers from either too much history or too little. Design is (often) subordinate to art, in part because of a lack of sanctioned history, but equally is kept in its place by a connection to the historical passage of Consumerism and Capitalism.

Design has historians but, it could be argued, lacks a Giorgio Vasari or a Clement Greenberg[1] – critics whom act as ensigns – or, even, a distinct avant-gardism to forge an intellectual separation from capitalism: without this, design is marooned.

Ezri Tarazi, an Israeli industrial designer, in his article, spies a crisis in design because of its unanchored nature. Its very popularity in recent times has refloated it upon the public consciousness but without the proper coordinates to whence it came, it will remain a ghost ship. Design, for Tarazi, is becoming splintered. It is creating a collection of surface incisions where the intention is more to design than to cure.

As we write, the notion of a crisis is becoming increasingly frequent fodder in contemporary design – for instance, [Design] Crisis at the 2009 Milan Furniture Fair which explored the relationship between creativity and crisis. One exhibit was *Spamghetto*,[2] a visually baroque wall covering which recycles junk-email, 'in order to turn the ugly spam into a beautiful wallpaper…'. *Spamghetto* makes visible a contemporary problem and repurposes it to another end. But it also brings a broader question to mind: can we design ourselves out of a crisis beyond simply making the ugly beautiful?[3]

In responding to Tarazi's dilemma – to design or to cure? – replies to the post addressed design's heritage as part of the problem. As James Souttar suggests, certainly the 1960s inherited a design culture moulded as a 'product of modernism – [in] an era when there was a popular appetite for grandiose personal visions, and for being led'.[1] A modernism of Taylorism and Ford Motor Company, '[o]bsessed with utility, efficiency and rationality',[II] inspired production lines as much as it inspired the Bauhaus or Le Corbusier. It was also a modernism bloated by the victors of World War Two: the USA.

It is the diaspora of European thinkers and practitioners who went to America during and after the war, many staying on long after appeasement, who, to this day, influence how design is critically assessed and, in many cases, the creative process itself. Theodor Adorno, Herbert Marcuse, Erich Fromm – under the leadership of Max Horkheimer – arrived at Columbia University, finding themselves in the eye of the approaching pop-culture storm. The Frankfurt School, as they were collectively known (referring to their original academic institution), began to assess the cultures of Europe from the vantage point of the USA. They provided the cross-disciplinarity in critical investigation which informs liberal arts education today: a mix of sociology; philosophy; psychoanalysis and anthropology. Commodity became the new enemy.

Ever since this period, in the cross hairs of much critical thinking is the predatory role of commodity. Design is the most visible foot soldier in the advancement of a modern material culture. Design, technically and aesthetically, develops for the most part unimpeded by the counter flows of avant-garde movements. Avant-gardism periodically self-audited its advances during the same period; a check and balance of politics and aesthetics.

The consumer culture born in the 1960s (reaching its nadir in the 1990s) amplified the voice of disciplines from photography to graphic arts, product design to architecture.

But today, there is an irony in design activities increasing exponentially because, by and large, it is driven by the postmodern

Spamghetto: junk wallpaper covering by
To Do. Technical Partner: Jannelli & Volpi (2009).
If consumers provide the dimensions of their room,
To Do's software can produce a wallpaper design
that 'wraps' around objects, such as windows or
pictures.

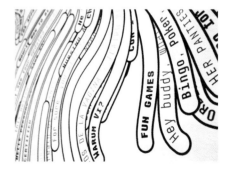

Moving by Ezri Tarazi (2005).
Photograph by Studio Warhaftig Venezian.

rupture of high and low culture (if indeed this split ever really occurred outside of certain philosophical discourse). Essentially, this link to consumerism negated the cognitive thrust of design and designers which underpins Tarazi's original post.

An important conceptual framework, first taken up by the Frankfurt School, and since used in sociology and cultural studies, is that of kitsch. Kitsch is an important conduit between the worlds of art and design. When Tarazi suggests that 'design finds itself coveted by new disciplines that boast of dealing with "aesthetics", kitsch is influential. Here, we are arguing kitsch on an economic level not a postmodern 'Oh that's so kitsch' level!

Design, historically, is written up as part of the mechanics of modern taste formation. It is a component of a fashion industry of surface and simulacra. Sewn into the very sinews of this relationship is the notion of kitsch. The intellectual and cultural formations (and interactions) with kitsch act as a catalyst in how design is understood, consumed and to some extent, created. As one commentator observes by the late 19th century: 'Kitsch was the only art of the period which involved unconditionally almost the whole of society.'[4]

It's the very reproducibility of design which both provided an everyday language of visual form whilst equally acting as an opiate to dull the senses, attaching it to the dangers of kitsch (...picture Philippe Starck's gold-plated machine gun lamps?...). You can see how design fits the bill when Clement Greenberg explains that: 'Kitsch is mechanical and operates by formulas. Kitsch is vicarious experience and faked sensations. Kitsch changes according to style, but remains always the same. Kitsch is the epitome of all that is spurious in the life of our times. Kitsch pretends to demand nothing of its customers except their money – not even their time.'[5]

But what is embedded within this notion of the commercial and the kitsch is the intrinsic power of popularity; pop culture. Design provides a readily available, literally off the shelf, construction of identity. It is this very popularity, and by extension voice, of design culture which makes it attractive to cultural studies in the latter half of the 20th century.

Commercial design provided the building blocks between high and low culture. Kitsch could be seen as an authentic voice of the disenfranchised – those who did not frequent art galleries or read more than pulp fiction. The hierarchy of high and low was substituted by 'taste cultures'.

Andrew Ross, in his book *No Respect: Intellectuals and Popular Culture*, articulated the relationship between taste and identity thus: '...an unstable political definition, variably fixed from moment to moment by intellectuals and tastemakers, and in this respect, is often seen as constituting, if not representing, a political identity for the "popular classes."'[6]

So kitsch can be seen as both [a]political, as instrumental for identity in a fragmented world of consumption (which brand best reflects the true me?) or, equally, instrumental in providing a clear dividing line between high and low in the visual arts. The point where our examples do coalesce is in the relationship between material culture/design/kitsch and the popular. All sides see kitsch as an active agent. Either this is positive, as in identity politics; camp aesthetics for instance with an element of Lyotard's *Postmodern Condition*[7] (where 'anything goes'). Or, in its negative incarnation, it becomes an aesthetic corruption.

Finally, we need to place this analysis in an ethical context, as both Tarazi's original essay and its responses on the Limited Language website raise ethical issues. As James Souttar suggests these are issues '[of] communication on a human scale...which really means not one person telling everyone else how it is, but an opportunity for a community and diversity of voices to be expressed, and for dialogue to take place'.[III]

Design is part of the cycle of consumption and identity. You consume to declare your subjective place in an increasingly unstable world. Identity cannot be fixed or essentialised in anyway, as complete. My identity evolves – it is a process.

If identity is in a constant state of becoming, it is also in a constant flow of consuming. This is an ethical dilemma for design today.

This dilemma is addressed by the philosopher Rosi Braidotti in *Transpositions: On Nomadic Ethics*, where she looks to define a sustainable ethics. In her concluding chapter she posits, 'How do you make people want to be free, generous, decent and caring?'[8] This is the perennial question at the core of both ethics and politics. Braidotti takes the notion of the Nomad as emblematic of the nature of modern identity, of non-fixed abode. She argues that the fear or reactionary stance against political change means the agency of desire (a desire for the new) is reduced to the 'docile and compulsive forms of consumerism'.[9] In this sense desire, in the absence of politics and because of its consumptive nature, becomes unsustainable.

Braidotti calls for new forms of cross-disciplinary cooperation. She is addressing philosophy and the social sciences, but is the same not needed in design practice?

Replies to the post called for 'a paradigm shift of an unprecedented kind'[IV]; one 'driven to disrupt the dreams of the comfortable'.[V] Here we might need to look at the role of processes rather than the mechanics of material outcomes. As Adriana Eysler puts it: 'designing no longer necessarily means producing something visual/concrete/lasting/consumeable'.[VI]

How can we use a notion of design thinking – process – to overcome the contradictory practices of 'development', where any 'new' in design means further consumption: an unsustainable paradigm?

See full responses + carry on the conversation here
http://tiny.cc/chapter1_2

Reader credits
I   James Souttar 29/05/06
II   The Swarm 17/05/2006

III James Souttar 29/05/06 – Souttar qualifies this:
    'The really exciting mavericks of the life sciences –
    Lovelock, Margulis, Goodwin, Sahtouris, Maturana
    et al. – have been suggesting for some time that life
    is not a "top-down" creation, but a complex self-
    organising and "emergent" phenomenon. When this
    understanding eventually filters into our conceptions
    of communication, we will undoubtedly see a
    paradigm shift of an unprecedented kind…'
IV James Souttar 29/05/06
V   The Swarm 17/05/2006
VI Adriana Eysler 03/06/2006 – She follows this with;
    '…The times are changing and so are the ways in
    which design manifests itself. I can only refer to
    Cedric Price who demanded there to be enough
    space accommodated in the design (process/object)
    for doubt, delight and change.'

References

1 Giorgio Vasari is credited to be the first art historian
   who wrote about key Renaissance painters, Clement
   Greenburg is an American art critic who championed
   the Abstract Expressionists. He wrote a key essay
   called 'Avant-Garde and the Kitsch'.

2 http://infosthetics.com/archives/2009/05/spamghetto_
   junk_mail_wall_covering.html

3 This theme particularly responded to the global
   economic crisis. See 'Milan Furniture Fair 2009: Soft
   Options for Hard Times' in *Building Design Online*,
   1 May 2009, where Caroline Roux asks, can we really
   design our way out of a recession?
   www.bdonline.co.uk/story.asp?storycode=3139446. In
   particular here, the show [Design] Crisis explored the
   relationship between creativity and crisis.

4 G.T. Noszlopy, 'The Embourgeoisement of Avant-
   Garde Art' in *Diogenes*, Vol. 17, No. 67 (1969), 83-109.

5 In Charles Harrison & Paul Wood, *Art in Theory
   1900-1990: An Anthology of Changing Ideas* (Oxford:
   Blackwell, 1999).

6 Andrew Ross, *No respect : Intellectuals and Popular
   Culture* (London: Routledge, 1989).

7 Jean-François Lyotard, 'The Postmodern Condition:
   A Report on Knowledge' in *Theory and History of
   Literature*, Vol 10 (1979).

8 Rosi Braidotti, *Transpositions: On Nomadic Ethics*
   (Cambridge, UK; Malden, MA: Polity Press, 2006), 205.

9 Ibid.

Nicky Ryan

Patronising Prada

'When I buy art, I want to keep it separate. You don't want people to think you are doing what you are doing because you want to make your company better.' (Miuccia Prada)[1]

In 2002 a sculpture by artist Tom Sachs entitled *Prada Death Camp* caused outrage when shown in the exhibition *Mirroring Evil: Nazi Imagery/Recent Art* at the Jewish Museum in New York. *The New York Times* critic Michael Kimmelman[2] reported how he had received 'anguished emails' from Holocaust survivors stunned at the inclusion of the model of a concentration camp made from a Prada hatbox. The controversy generated by the exhibition inevitably drew attention to the fashion brand and speculation about its response to an artist who had also created the *Prada Toilet* in 1997. Well the critics needn't have worried, 'We really like his work,' said Pandora Asbaghi from the Fondazione Prada (a contemporary arts foundation owned and managed by Prada), who also confirmed that Prada had given Sachs an unlimited supply of shoeboxes.

Indeed Prada liked Sachs' work so much that he was commissioned to produce a site-specific installation for his very own exhibition at the Fondazione Prada in 2006. In the accompanying press release[3] we are informed that the artist's work mixes status symbols of mass culture with 'the symbols of American wealth that sees in luxury, conformism, and designer labels a reinforcement of their elite social status'. So here we have a luxury brand commissioning art that critiques its own institutional working practices. Of course this is nothing new for Prada (or many other brands) who have extended patronage to a range of 'cutting edge' practitioners including photographer Andreas Gursky and architect Rem Koolhaas.

What is at stake in the corporate appropriation of 'avant-garde' positions within the parameters of the

Critical effects

What's at stake when avant-garde critique of consumerism transfers 'edgy' prestige to a brand? How might this appeal to or patronise an 'art savvy taste community'? Although these were the questions posed in the original article, replies focused less on stakes and more on a complex range of effects; from simple, 'good conversation'[I] to consumers re-affirming 'a sense of themselves as culturally sophisticated, clever decoders'.[II]

But appealing to an audience's knowingness isn't the same as appealing to their awareness, an aim of critical practice. And when the critical distance it depends on has collapsed, it's criticality itself which is at stake. This response asks; where might criticality be found today?

It's worth taking Miuccia Prada at face value when she says, 'When I buy art, I want to keep it separate.' Her comment acknowledges, by implication, that the conflation of art and commerce destroys the very conditions of distance needed for the critical autonomy of practice; an 'outsider' position that attracts the Fondazione Prada in the first place. As Jade Adams-Wood's comment on the Limited Language website reminds us, it's only when 'Art and fashion continue to work within different value systems...' that their collaborations can resonate 'beyond the synthetic surface of fashion'.[III]

Back in 2001, in SoHo, New York, a notice appeared in the window of a small gallery: 'Opening Soon Prada'.[I] That year, the Prada Flagship store did open on a site once part of the Guggenheim Museum. However, it was by architect Rem Koolhaas, not Michael Elmgreen and Ingar Dragset, artists of the original note. Their promised 'store' materialised in 2005, as *Prada Marfa*, in the Texas Desert near to the town synonymous since the 1970s with the minimalist artist Donald Judd.

The rub: the door of the full-scale construction, complete with retail fittings supplied by Prada, was never meant to open. A permanent public sculpture and critique of gentrification via consumerism, it seeks to address its context, one gentrified by art tourism.

In this installation (Readymade?), and Tom Sachs' *Prada Toilet* (1997), we have a link back to the historical avant-garde. When, in 1917, Dada – and Marcel Duchamp's urinal/fountain – aimed to negate and re-energise art with everyday life, the critical effect relied on distance between autonomous art and the mass-produced everyday. This autonomy hides the way that both art and the everyday operate one within the other. But, if this distance was once nominally upheld, it is unsupportable today.

So, what happens when artists appear to transplant this critical tactic, ready made, into contemporary culture? This is a culture, for Jean Baudrillard, in which we live in a 'desert of the real'.[2] Here the referent of the 'real', critical to Duchamp's critique, has abdicated. *Prada Marfa*, for instance, is made surreal by the desert; both as a backdrop recalling the sublime register of nature and also the sublime register of recent advertising. In addition, the Prada brand is already a quasi-autonomous entity which, as Nicky Ryan puts it in the original post, 'obfuscates commercial operations'.

Today, if there is still a sense that abounds that art and commerce work in different value systems, then it's either a construction or an intellectual difference. Rem Koolhaas, a leading architect for Prada, employs both techniques. Koolhaas, is known for his rethinking of the relationship between retail and urban space in writing[3] and in practice. The *Prada Transformer* event structure (a pavilion of sorts) in Seoul, South Korea makes this literal. Based on a tetrahedron, it rotates to foreground different programmes: art, cinema as well as style events for the brand. Within the more 'traditional' private space of commerce – the flagship stores – it is murals, installations and digital interfaces that interrupt the usual

market has been a hot topic of debate for some time. From the perspective of the brand, Prada is able to construct an artistic identity for the business that obfuscates commercial operations. For artists, who are generally canny and knowing in relation to corporate culture, there is the possibility of subversion from within – a tactic used by the historical avant-garde to facilitate critical distance. However the patronage of artists like Sachs and the public endorsement of Michael Elmgreen and Ingar Dragset's permanent *Prada Marfa* installation in Texas, inevitably endows Prada with an edgy appeal and gives the company an opportunity to neutralise the critique of its 'other'.

So is the nurturing of cultural cachet through an association with the arts an effective strategy for a luxury brand like Prada? Armani, Louis Vuitton, Cartier and numerous other brands also engage with the arts through patronage and sponsorship. Do consumers really conflate Prada's image with the innovative, critical and liberal values associated with 'avant-garde' art? The identity of Prada may be constructed to appeal to an art-savvy taste community who get the irony and complex codings of contemporary art, but aren't they also just a little bit too cynical and worldly-wise to enjoy being patronised in this way?

See further images here
www.limitedlanguage.org/images

References
1   Quoted in Michael Specter, 'The Designer' in *The New Yorker*, 15 March 2004,
     www.michaelspecter.com/ny/2004/2004_03_15_prada.html
2   Michael Kimmelman, 'Art Review: Evil, the Nazis and Shock Value' in *The New York Times*, 15 March 2002, www.nytimes.com/2002/03/15/arts/art-review-evil-the-nazis-and-shock-value.html
3   Fondazione Prada press release on Tom Sachs, 2 March 2006, www.fondazioneprada.org/en/comunicati/TS.ENG.pdf

Prada Toilet by Tom Sachs (1997). Cardboard, ink, thermal adhesive, 28 x 29 x 22 inches.

Michael Elmgreen and Ingar Dragset's *Prada Marfa* (2005).
'It's not really a Prada store, and it's not quite in Marfa, so it must be art.'
Photograph by Marshall Astor, http://bit.ly/2u6TSe

'Repairs are under way at the burglarized
Prada "store" outside Valentine' as reported
in the *Houston Press*, 27 October 2005.
Photograph by A.C. Conrad.

'Cowboy hat interrupts the fantasy of luxury
as the installation is restocked' as reported
in the *Houston Press*, 27 October 2005.
Photograph by A.C. Conrad.

homogenous retail experience with external factors; from the Fondazione Prada's art through factory footage from Italy to sales of Prada fakes across the world. If we follow Koolhaas, 'difference' manifests itself in the subjective unpredictability of the interventions, providing 'rough luxury' in contrast to the smooth marble minimalism of the store.[4]

Invariably, with habitual use, rough art (and economoic reality!) become the decorative interface in the commercial realm. And, it's criticality itself which is in danger of becoming decorative. Hal Foster comments: 'In a wry move Koolhaas now copyrights his catchy phrases, as if to acknowledge this commercial curdling of critical concepts on the page.'[5]

A more nuanced lineage from Duchamp to today can be traced via the neo-avant-garde of the late 1960s. As Foster argues, the latter had also looped back to the historical avant-garde, but in doing so shifted practice. They were to 'develop the critique of the conventions of the traditional mediums, as performed by dada... [etc.]..., into an investigation of the institution of art, its perceptual and cognitive, structural and discursive parameters'.[6]

Institutional Critique sought to expose the relations between art and everyday life that, in earlier work, had remained hidden. Hans Haacke juxtaposed the corporate logos of museum sponsors with photographs of associated (and often exploitative) activities, both set against the 'autonomous' backdrop of the gallery itself.[7] The gallery aesthetised these documents, but it also brought these exchanges into the realm of everyday awareness.[8]

Institutional Critique, which is always site-specific, provides an alternative engagement because it can't be read semiotically as signs and icons. Instead, it concerns itself with art's processes and their effects. As comments on the website revealed, semiotics has informed a generation of designers[IV] who, in turn, 'use those tools to create "clever" and "radical" layered messages for commerce – ready-to-decode in two minutes like so many microwave meals'.[V]

But, design is lived and not (just) read. An alternative spatial engagement with design would transfer emphasis from its meaning to its effects. For instance, a semiotic reading of *Prada Marfa* might throw up echoes of Duchamp, whilst a spatial/temporal reading can tease out the ways it addresses urban issues. Thus, if you trace the effect of the sculpture on locals through the *Houston Press* (replete with break-ins) it becomes evident this is a continual process...

As Jeffrey Kipnis argues, 'lived space' is already a political space.[9] However, homogenised retail malls and gallery spaces erase the spontaneity and heterogeneity needed to enfranchise political space. Koolhaas' store – both cause and effect of what he calls the 'commercialised desert of SoHo'[10] with its echo of Baudrillard's commodity rhetoric – proposes design as an opportunity to reinject the heterogeneity of political space into New York. So, hosting external cultural events, or being open to art that criticises the brand, allows for the kind of unpredictability that brings life to space.

Crucially, this practice is not social, political or critical in itself. However in its effects it could be. It's the design of possibility.

Of the controversial art – and label – Prada pursues, James Souttar comments on how '...it's hard to imagine that any of these items – or the conversations they initiate – make any real difference to the issues they are supposed to be about'.[VI] Although we'd agree, following the idea that political space is lived and not read, any blanket critique that commerce neuters art is meaningless – as are sweeping calls for critical practice.[11]

A design of possibility would be assessed on a case-by-case basis. To locate criticality, if we follow Haacke, we will have to look at a work's residual effects. We may see them: in the audience response; in the way design frames events and space and, in turn, gets reframed[12] by them; and as these effects re-insinuate themselves in the networks of art, commerce and daily life. Critical effect can be seen at the level of atmospherics.

Exterior of *Prada Transformer*, on
the site of Kyunghee Palace, Seoul.
Photograph by Hyun-Joo Chun.

Waist Down exhibition at the *Prada
Transformer*, AMO's Asian Pavilion
for Prada, Seoul, South Korea
(concept design 2008, opened 2009).

See full responses + carry on the conversation here
http://tiny.cc/chapter1_3

Reader credits

I   Hayley Solomon 12/06/2006 – 'I do not think their
consumers are being patronised at all. I think they are
very aware of what they are being confronted with and
probably enjoy wearing a brand that can provide good
conversational pieces.'

II   Anonymous 13/06/2006 – 'It's about a group of elite
people re-affirming a sense of themselves as culturally
sophisticated, clever decoders. The Death Camp piece
isn't meant to be ironic I imagine, but in this particular
milieu, it's hard to "read" it in any other way.'

III Jade Adams-Wood 14/06/2006 – 'Art and fashion continue to work within different value systems and this
may be the only reason why art-fashion is so fashionable…Glen Luchford's famous campaign for Prada
(1998)…[is] noted for the tongue in cheek sexuality and
violence that was inspired by French photographer Guy
Bourdin…The published images were imbued with the
mystery of film noir and addressed concerns beyond
the synthetic surface of fashion.'

IV Anonymous 13/06/2006 – note above how Tom Sachs'
Prada Death Camp is 'read'…

V   Anonymous 03/07/2006

VI James Souttar 14/06/2006

References

1   Michael Elmgreen and Ingar Dragset's first solo
show at Tanya Bonakdar Gallery, New York 2001.

2   Jean Baudrillard, *Simulacra and Simulations* (Ann
Arbor: University of Michigan Press, 1985).

3   See Rem Koolhaas, *Harvard Design School Guide to
Shopping* (Cologne; New York; London: Taschen, 2001)
and 'Junkspace' in *Content* (Cologne: Taschen. 2004).

4   Nicky Ryan, 'Prada and the Art of Patronage' in
Fashion Theory, Vol 10, Issue 3 (2007), 10.

5   Hal Foster, 'Design and Crime' in Alex Coles,
(ed.) *Design and Art* (London; Cambridge, MA.:
Whitechapel/MIT, 2007), 72.

6   Hal Foster, *The Return of the Real* (Cambridge, MA.;
London: MIT, 1996), 20.

7   See Hans Haacke, *Framing and Being Framed*
(Halifax: The Press of Nova Scotia College, 1975) and
Hans Haacke and Pierre Bourdieu, *Free Exchange*
(Stanford: Stanford University Press, 1995).

8   Travis English, 'Hans Haacke, or the Museum as
Degenerate Utopia' in *Kritikos*, Vol. 4 (March 2007):
http://intertheory.org/english.htm

9   See Jeffrey Kipnis, 'Political Space: Moonmark'
in Richard Roth and Susan King Roth (eds.),
Beauty is Nowhere: Ethical Issues in Art and Design
(Amsterdam : Gordon & Breach, 1998), 79.

10 Rem Koolhaas quoted in Nicky Ryan, Op cit., 11.

11 Janet Wolff, *The Social Production of Art* (New York:
NYU Press, 1993), 85.

12 'Framing' and 'reframing'; it's the instability of
political space that undermines the stability of
semiotics. This effect is called reframing, as used by
Haacke, Foster and Kipnis (Op cit.).

Johnny Hardstaff
Love/hate

Base and superstructure

The purpose of graphic design is shifting towards a future defined as a vocal medium of personal expression and authorship. The designer as master of his or her content has become a sustainable economic model, working for those wanting to work free from commercial restraint. Seemingly, graphic design has the capacity to say anything it chooses to an audience educated in all its nuances and references and who are willing to play its visual games.

Why then, within this work, do designers consistently invoke the visual systems of their former oppressors? In the retention of their image, language and techniques, have designers learnt to love their metaphorical captors, these political and industrial kidnappers of creativity?

Stockholm Syndrome is a psychological response found in hostages whereby they begin to exhibit loyalty to their captors.[1] Is this in effect in graphic design authorship? Industry has never been smoothly serviced by the creative arts. There have always been rebellious attempts at rejecting the status quo, both formally (graphic designer Ken Garland's *First Things First Manifesto*, 1964 and 2000[2]) and informally, with militancy being the daily agenda for countless commercially successful designers. Has the shared experience of this continual conflict manifested itself in a mutual dependency?

It's easy to see how the Canadian anti-advertising magazine, *Adbusters*[3] or artist Barbara Kruger[4] knowingly invoke the sophisticated language of advertising to further their cause and art. But does this employment of developed media languages betray a designer's innate attraction to their efficacy and emotional gravitas? Or, is this about the thrills of conjuring the aesthetics of 'the enemy' with the forbidden and the taboo? Deep down, do we really love the enemy, or do we just love to make enemies?

Why are the infamous punk designer Jamie Reid,[5] contemporary graphic designer Aleksandar Maćašev[6] and

At the time of writing, President Obama has announced the imminent closure of the Guantánamo Bay Detention Camp. The first British prisoners have been released and returned to Britain. At the same moment we have a global economic 'meltdown'. This response will try to tease out the ideas in the original essay by Johnny Hardstaff in a post-Obama, post-Guantánamo era – a context that influences any response to the original.

The original article embodies that rare thing in design: a polemic. Johnny Hardstaff is angry because, as he sees it, in a time of relative economic boom there are not many in the design community entering into a political/ethical affray with the corporate establishment – unlike the avant-gardist movements between the two World Wars that took issue with the bourgeois status quo, both in visual culture and politics more generally. Today, individually or collectively, this lack of gusto is especially noticeable in visual communication.

A call like this tries to galvanise the somnolent beast of ideology and is firmly established in the Humanist/Modernist tradition of the individual – the authorial voice – against both the plebeian and the ruling (corporate) class. It is this question: 'How much do we want change?' Which is prescient and foretells the campaign for change in us politics. However, now, there is an understanding that binary sloganeering needs to be replaced by a more plural engagement with change. Of course, how much will change in the world-order is still to be seen... What can be observed in the election of President Obama is a re-engagement of graphic design and the political; the political poster has risen from the ashes and holds currency once again. The most visible example is perhaps the

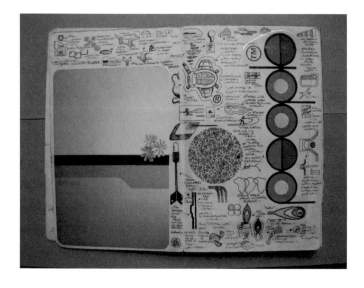

1992 / 97 – Johnny Hardstaff – 3 spreads
from Sketchbook 1.

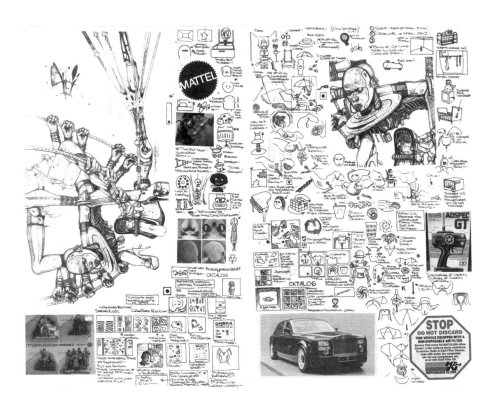

2002 / 04 – Johnny Hardstaff – Sketchbook 3.

Obama *Hope* poster by street artist Shepard Fairey which has become synonymous with the 2008 US election campaign, even iconic.

This is an example of the contingency of visual form: how graphic design can monitor the changing political/ethical/cultural visual pulse. In the constant flow of images, you can see a developing economy of visual culture – one as paradoxical and as unpredictable as any monetary economy. Metaphorically, the visual economy has its own stock exchange – where the present and the past are bartered; rising and falling in value, generation to generation. When the African-American middle classes collect slavery memorabilia or when there is a preoccupation with swastikas and artifacts of the Holocaust, it is, in part, 'conjuring the aesthetics of "the enemy" with the forbidden and the taboo' as the original article proposes and it is an 'example of professional admiration' too. In a reply to the article on the Limited Language website, graphic design historian Steven Heller, who has written widely on symbols of hate, provides an example of this when he comments, 'It's not that I want to be the enemy – or love thy enemy – but rather I have seemingly endless fascination with systems of power (and oppression) and how they are made manifest through our design profession.'[1] These examples are the actions of a dynamic economy: an 'image economy'.

In *Vision, Race, and Modernity*, Deborah Poole defines the three principle elements needed for a robust image economy. Firstly, an organisation of production [the designer or image maker]. Secondly, the circulation of goods [images/artefacts] including the technology of dissemination. Thirdly, and this overlaps with the second, 'the cultural and discursive systems through which graphic images are appraised, interpreted and assigned historical, scientific and aesthetic worth'.[1] She points out it's important 'to ask not what specific images mean but, rather, how images accrue value'. Images can gain and lose value due to market fetishisation, becoming memorabilia or more directly ideological reasons

writer and art director Steven Heller[7] (to name three diverse examples) attracted to the swastika and/or other fascist imagery? Is this paradoxical given design's initiatives for social progress? Or, given that Hitler is said to have 'personally' designed the NSDAP swastika 'logo', is their interest simply professional admiration?

Why, as Steven Heller asks in his *Graphic Design Reader*,[8] do some African-Americans collect racist memorabilia? The emotive reasons for doing so are complex. But within graphic design, which pales in comparison, has the victim come to love the abuser in some way, having perversely thrived under the tough love of their industrial masters? Do designers now seek to perpetuate this oppressive presence? Has counter-culture's dependence upon mainstream commerce bred an intimacy which has now, inevitably, become an attraction?

If so, is this attraction beyond the designer's control? Are there certain graphic qualities, colour combinations and iconographic forms, that are psychologically resonant for mankind? Is there a hierarchy or taxonomy of efficacy and power within graphic attributes themselves...the raw materials naturally loaded, if you like? Certainly, the term 'graphic' is imbued with preternatural appeal. This is a vivid, lurid, shocking and desirable quality. But is this innate or is it that the industrial origins of graphic design have shaped the language of political manipulation and extremism?

If we are indeed seduced by the potency of hate-based visual systems, does this mean that our attempts at social reform and responsibility are 'designed' to fail? So far, social reform through design must surely be, globally, the most pitiful and unsuccessful of graphic projects.

Is our collective heart not in it? Secretly, do we love to hate?

See further images here
www.limitedlanguage.org/images

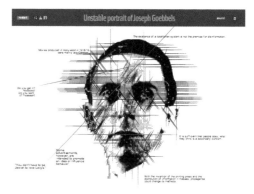
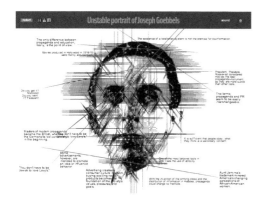

Unstable portrait of Joseph Goebbels by Aleksandar
Maćašev (2004).
www.goebbels.info/goebbels-campaign.htm

'[the] Joseph Goebbels project was about media culture
executed through the very means of mass communication.
[Steven] Heller once asked why didn't I use [Edward

Louis] Bernays for instance. Well, because outside
of professional circles no one has heard of him. So
I used the Nazi propaganda mastermind and yet
another play on the swastika to convey a message
about...well, conveying messages.'
From an email exchange, 16 June 2009.

which allow a re-articulation of meaning and even use. Think of the culture jamming and ethical stance of, say, *Adbusters* magazine, mentioned by Johnny Hardstaff. The value (meaning) of images, graphic or pictorial, can gain and lose value both culturally and economically. It could be argued that the swastika of today is not the irrational symbol of the 1930s. Its value has accrued since, and in a more rational, market-driven manner of collectables and historiographies.

A more contemporary example of the image economy, and an example of the direct action in visual communication advocated in the original essay, is the political poster. Fawwaz Traboulsi, in his foreword to *Off the Wall: Political Posters of the Lebanese Civil War*, comments: 'Every day, posters are torn in the streets of the cities of the world at the hands of persons who object to their messages. But you might not be content with wounding a poster with a knife or a lance; you might attempt to kill a poster.'[2]

The power of the graphic image is seen in the proliferation of posters of political leaders. Many British newspapers carried editorial images during the Iraq War of posters and murals of President Hussein, his image punctured by a volley of bullets, for instance. This is a brutal reminder of the contingency of graphic imagery and also how 'the efficacy of representation relies on a ceaseless exchange with other representations'.[3] But, it is also a positive example of the power of design.

So often, calls for change in design in the polemic mode focus on the artefact (and material production) as the site of change. Political and ideological agency is identified in the visual outcome as a possible new language; as Hardstaff puts it, a vocal medium of expression and authorship. An example of this can be seen in a comment by Sim Downs: 'Let [the client/boss] pay us for producing candy-coated symbols of need, fear and belonging all morning, so that we can speak with our own voice in the afternoon.'[1] And a counterpoint in a comment from James

References

1 Stockholm Syndrome was a term coined by criminologist and psychiatrist, Nils Bejerot, after hostages in the Norrmalmstorg robbery in Sweden in 1973 defended their captors on release.
2 The *First Things First* manifestos called for a 'mind shift' in design practice away from purely commercial ends.
3 *Adbusters* magazine is a 'Journal of the Mental Environment'. Editor Kalle Lasn and the magazine's spoof adverts became a visible force in the anti-consumerist 'culture jamming' movement in the late 20th century.
4 Arguably, Barbara Kruger's most iconic work is *I Shop Therefore I Am* (1987), a parody of René Descartes' philosophical observation, 'I Think Therefore I am'. This later served as advertising for London's Selfridges department store.
5 Jamie Reid is best known for his 1960s connections to the Situationists, 1970s graphics for punk band the Sex Pistols. In the 1990s, he designed club flyers which incorporated his infamous punk ransom note typographic style and the swastika with contemporary corporate logos.
6 This references Maćašev's *Unstable Portrait of Joseph Goebbels* in particular.
7 See the covers of both; Steven Heller and Jeff Roth, *The Swastika: Symbol Beyond Redemption* (New York: Allworth, 2000) and *Iron Fists: Branding the 20th Century Totalitarian State* (London; New York: Phaidon Press, 2008).
8 Steven Heller, *Graphic Design Reader* (New York: Allworth, 2002).

Souttar: [these] 'designers...don't seem to want to be part of a self-organising community of voices, celebrating a diversity of points of view and encouraging participation and sharing. They want to tell it how they see it – to be "brands", celebrities, stars – and to get people to pay attention to them...but who actually cares?'[III]

An alternative approach in today's climate is to look beyond the material outcome of political posters or environmental campaigns and look, instead, at process as a possible site of agency. Agency, here, still fulfils the aim of creating a dynamic, politically astute, visual communication, however a difference is that process-oriented design is the antithesis of the BIG BANG, revolutionary design that, since the 1960s, informs much polemical discussion in visual communication practise. And yet, both want the same outcomes.

Process is a mixture of the 'ceaseless exchange with other representations', the mundane how-to-do-it-in-time for the deadline and also the more cognitive discussions, usually shared, which inform the project. It's not only the creative arts, but the hard sciences through figures like Bruno Latour, that are looking at this: for instance the history of scientific fact, where discovery is 'a process rather than a point of occurrence' ...a process of 'making sense together'.[4]

As John Forester observes, 'By recognizing design practices as conversational processes of making sense together, designers can become alert to the social dimensions of design processes, including the organisational, institutional, and political-economic influences that they will face – necessarily, if also unhappily at times – in everyday practice.'[5] As Fell on the website puts it: 'A designer is essentially a part of a larger social machine.'[IV]

See full responses + carry on the conversation here
http://tiny.cc/chapter1_4

Reader credits

I   Steve Heller 28/04/2006 – 'I've written on lots of
     design themes, but I always come back to this theme.
     And these issues contributed to writing extensively
     about the Swastika in the past and...my book for
     Phaidon, *Iron Fists: Branding the Totalitarian State*.
     [The] book covers key totalitarian regimes of the
     20th century, attempting to address the mechanisms
     for propagating faith (as well as loyalty and
     submission)... It talks about what seem like innocent
     "mascots" and "tokens" graphically designed as
     constant reminders of the respective ideological
     creed.
     I must admit to a certain fetishism here. Over time
     I've obtained a lot of very rare material, which, as
     someone writing history I treasure because they are
     original documents that shed light on a dim past. But
     I also find them appealing because they are so damn
     charged. It's not that I relish engaging with demonic
     artifacts, but holding them in my hands forces me to
     experience what others might have experienced...'
II   Sim Downs 02/05/2006
III James Souttar 31/05/2006
IV   Fell 29/05/2006

References

1   Deborah Poole, *Vision, Race, and Modernity : Visual
     Economy of the Andean Image World* (Princeton:
     Princeton University Press, 1997), 263.
2   Fawwaz Traboulsi, *Off the Wall: Political Posters of
     the Lebanese Civil War* (London; New York: I. B. Tauris,
     2009).
3   Norman Bryson et al., *Visual Culture: Images and
     Interpretations* (Hanover, NH: Wesleyan University
     Press, 1994), 429.
4   Bruno Latour, *Icon Clash: Beyond Image Wars in
     Science, Religion and Art* (MA: MIT Press, 2002).
5   John Forester, *Planning in the Face of Power*
     (Berkeley: University of California Press, 1989), 283.

Shock and awe: the politics of production

The 1996 right-wing thesis *Shock and Awe: Achieving Rapid Dominance*[1] is the book that acted as a conceptual sound bite for framing the technique and technology for bombing people (a lot). In the aftermath of 9/11, the off-the-peg response in design consumption was a proliferation of Khaki and camouflage, and an upturn in the sale of Humvees and suv vehicles. Now, the shock and awe mantra has fed into an 'age of anxiety' and a 'culture of fear' in the Western psyche.

Design's response has been an aesthetic of shock and awe. This can be seen in the Audi ad[2] from 2005, in which a car explodes in a Western financial district. As the blast fragments land, their letters reform as 'Vorsprung durch technik' (progress through technology): a tagline as relevant to the ad's creation by CGI (Computer Generated Imagery) as the zeitgeist of shock and awe. And, it can be seen in the advert's darker doppelgänger the same year in a viral depicting a terrorist, sitting inside a vw Polo, detonating a bomb: 'Small but tough'.[3]

CGI, rapid prototyping and ingenuity allow designers to quickly respond to any cultural situation. The original *Shock and Awe* essay states four characteristics are needed for its application: total knowledge, control of the environment, rapidity, and brilliance in execution. An example, in its most corporate form, was the MP3 phenomenon and design's response – an invasion spearheaded by the hardware of the iPod but backed up by an infantry of advertising, graphic design and moving image whilst coordinated with iTunes software. It was a classic shock and awe scenario.

Other examples might sit more comfortably with a traditional leftist critique. For instance, Philippe Starck's *Gun Collection* of lighting for the Italian lighting company Flos is based around 18 carat gold plated guns – one with a Kalashnikov AK-47 as its up-stand, a Beretta bedside lamp and a M16 table lamp. This can be

The process of consumption

'If one can design a vase that can serve as a catalyst for world peace,' says New York-based designer Ron Gilad, 'I will get re-circumcised.' His own vase, *Run Over by Car*, describes its production methods. Run over by different cars, each vase is unique (with the results from a Mercedes sedan the best...). Gilad is interested in process rather than politics: 'I am only a designer, but the impact of politics is inevitable, and a reaction in 3-D is one result. The observer decides its connotation, be it political or aesthetic.'[1]

As the original article showed, the violence of our times is reflected back to us through the prism of the commodified object. The everyday commodity invariably makes the poignant and the political – even as kitsch – banal. And yet, the day-to-day is a live environment. In this sense, it's no less politically charged – although certainly less well theorised – and provides something different to the usual discourse at the interface of art/design, politics/commodity and the public sphere. It's here this response takes its departure.

Change comes through action. If we look to visual culture then it is posters and placards which give visual presence to protesting voices in the public domain (even if they can't change things in themselves). Art, like film, mediates the (violent) world, extracting its fragments and splicing them back together as meta-comment; reflection, for the long run. We can see this quite well in *Collision*, a short animation by Max Hattler. Here, Islamic patterns and American quilts, the vernacular of two different cultures, kaleidoscope into the geometry of flags to the rhythm of artillery fire, fireworks and the muezzin's call to prayer. Although the film draws on the everyday, and is downloaded back into it via

Collision, an animation by Max Hattler (2005).
Distributed by Autour de Minuit.
www.maxhattler.com/collision

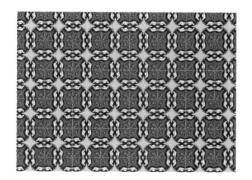

Violence is a Motif by
Remco Swart (2004).

3Guns Table Vase by Suck UK (2003).

seen as a bizarre Starck media event until you understand the inspiration for his idea: a cache of gold plated arms found in one of Saddam Hussein's Palaces. With black lampshades representing death, they reflect the world back to us. Remco Swart has designed ceramic tiles which perform a simple decorative function whilst their kaleidoscopic motif is made up of war imagery: men in gas masks and a woman leaving hospital with a baby after a gas attack in Palestine. Viktor & Rolf have, in conjunction with l'Oréal, produced the perfume *Flowerbomb* which is presented in a bottle shaped like a hand grenade, replete with safety pin. Their intention: a scent both 'romantic and aggressive' whilst remaining 'explosive but also kind of innocent'.[4]

Suck UK have made a white vase where the barrels of three guns converge to become the flute, the packaging displays photos complete with red rose. However irreverent, this can't be separated from the anti-war photograph of a young demonstrator confronting the Military Police during 1967 Vietnam protests by inserting a flower into the barrel of his gun. The original image, now on museum walls and in coffee-table books, has arguably lost its critical power. What the gun vase might do is reinvigorate some of the issues the gun/flower image raises, but in a personal context. In contrast to the more didactic dialogues of, say, a political poster that simplifies things to right and wrong, Suck UK's design leaves the emphasis on the individual's interpretation. Suck UK say that, in America, parents are buying it for children who are rediscovering Guns N' Roses music. This illustrates how prescriptive readings of the vase's 'meaning' are of limited use for understanding design in a live environment. So, shock and awe can manifest itself in the pimped Humvee and in designer eulogies to the 1960s. These may be consumed politically or not.

Design inspired by shock and awe may appear to reinforce the message of irreverent, sanitised, glamorised violence or muscular right-wing thinking. It's often

the personal desktop, it doesn't become dissipated by 'use'. W.J.T. Mitchell suggests that a condition of mediations of art is that they appear to speak from a mythic field of reflection 'beyond capitalism and outside history.'[2] Even when they operate through commodity channels, art appears to be unaffected.

In response to the original article, Nicky has observed: 'Art has a tradition of avant-gardism (the politics of which is usually inconsequential) – it is its oppositional stance which is most important. A tradition, which is less easily definable in a wider design/craft/applied-arts context… Opposition, from this perspective, is created via a mirroring of the day-to-day of our lives…'[1]

When product design mirrors the violent world, it is held to account – although usually by others! – for the contradictions encoded in its own situation. That is, how it oscillates between the pull of the global market and the way it is consumed in a more personal, local way. Hence, a critical framework has been slower to emerge. This is, perhaps, the knowing wink in the double meaning of *Fully Loaded Chair* by Alexander Reh which is made up of over 450 used 12 gauge shotgun shells. Their red hulls flare out of the back of the chair, whilst the brass tips push through the seat like studs, where another might have cushions. On the Web, it is sold through Yanko Design, with its tagline: form beyond function.

'Form beyond function' knowingly locates it in a historical dis/continuum of product semantics (what does it mean?) and everyday living (what's it for?). The design adage 'form follows function' might more comfortably locate its history in an *Eames Chair*[3] but, as Alan Beardmore reminds us: 'Aircraft, or for that matter guns, are a good example of form following function and always example elegance if you view it from a non-political stand-point'.[II] But, if the modernist chair – or gun – added functionality (with beauty…) and the postmodern chair[4] added poetic narrative and play, then both were constructive. That is, the design-in-use gaining from attached meanings – and aiming to transcend the everyday via efficiency, luxury or fantasy.[5]

With the more literal *Fully Loaded Chair* the detritus of another more violent everyday is bolted onto our own. Reh, coming from an American hunting community, doesn't seek to translate it into something else. His chair aesthetisises of course but, for a while at least, he hopes to offer a 'dichotomy of comfort and demise'.[6] One Web-blogger, in possession of a similar shell, converted into a wall-mounted vase, muses 'I wonder what it shot...'[7]

Without a definitive explanation, people tend to draw on memory. This detachment of meaning as a work passes from designer to user(s) can be seen when Dominic Wilcox melts down plastic toy soldiers to make his *War Bowl*. He literally and metaphorically recycles childhood memories and war imagery. 'On the one hand they were a fun childhood toy that brought back happy memories and on the other, they were a representation of war with its associated horrors. This is a contrast that I find slightly uneasy.' However, even in this more troubling piece, his own memories aren't accessible to others and design becomes 'material for projecting their own social or political critiques'.[8]

In contrast to the sequential revealing of information of, say, an animation or poster, design works as gesture: it gives its meaning all at once. So, even if a design's political intentions are emphatic, comparatively the effects only last a short time.

This takes a temporal approach to design – inspired by Adam Richardson's essay *A Design's Work is Never Done*,[9] which takes into account the effects of (and on) design over time. A semiotic reading (which sits more comfortably with the postmodern view), for instance from Grant McCracken, argues that whilst product design can recombine meaning (bowls with soldiers/guns with chairs), it can't provoke new meaning.[10]

A temporal approach to design can account for new behaviour. In just one example, the *Design Noir*[11] of UK interaction

assumed that this 'criticality' would need to come from a position outside (and a bit to the left) of consumer culture. But when designers reflect our culture back to us like this, the visual reinterpretation allows discussion; not in the Oval office, but in the consumer's living room.

See further images here
www.limitedlanguage.org/images

References
1   Harlan Ullman, James Wade and L.A. Edney, *Shock and Awe: Achieving Rapid Dominance* (National Defense University Institute for National Strategic Studies 1996).
2   Audi advert (dir. Pleix, 2005).
3   VW Polo viral advert (2005).
4   Polly Vernon, 'We Are One Brain, One Person, One Designer' in *The Observer*, 13 November 2005.

Fully Loaded Chair by Alexander Reh (2005).

War Bowl by Dominic Wilcox (2002).

designers Dunne and Raby focuses on the psychological dimensions of experiences offered by products. As part of a series of objects treating phobias as though they were perfectly reasonable, they designed *Huggable Atomic Mushrooms* for people afraid of nuclear annihilation. In a pattern of treatment, different sizes allow for gradual exposure.

Design either needs you to see it in a different way or use it in a different way to draw attention to, or subvert, use. Dunne and Raby argue that there are already so many objects consumed uncritically that we need this kind of critical mediation which questions and challenges industrial agendas more than we need more objects. Mindful of the way that any replacement will soon become the 'new normal', they propose their objects as research prototypes or for rent.

Within the global domestic market, designer Ettore Sottsass suggests we aim for 'Objects that won't yield too quickly to pleasure or to the rhythm of consumerism.'[12] Here he is talking about meaning again, but the time gap is important for therein lies the potential, however fleeting, for poetry.

Drawing on the rhetoric of change through action, Victor Margolin[13] suggests we ask the same question of objects: Are they active? Active, here, isn't in the literal doing/shouting/marching sense that the essay started with, but in the discursive sense... the act of asking questions. For him, these kinds of objects are 'active' if the verdict is still out on what they can achieve (as an active and ongoing discursive space). Once the interpretation is 'decided' (even 'yes, this is political') the object ceases to be necessarily active. Here, criticality is located not in the object itself, but in its temporal process.

Nicky provides a reminder that, 'I think you could argue the authors provide a pretty idealistic snapshot of the reality of contemporary product design.'[III] It's right to question what mute objects can tell us about the world and what they ask of us. And yet, when design finds a political dimension, it's interesting because it locates itself not within 'big P' politics per se, but the 'small p' politics of its own production; challenging its conditions and contradictions. Along the way, teasing out some of the tensions and possibilities in the relationship between the industrial design of use and a world of events.

See full responses + carry on the conversation here
http://tiny.cc/chapter1_5

Reader credits
I   Nicky 29/09/07
II Alan Beardmore 24/09/2007 – We have somewhat taken this out of its context and his full gist reads thus: 'What has all this got to do with design?...There have been some very good 'right-wing' artists and designers even if you do not like their politics.' And on 06/10/2007 he continued: '...Aircraft, or for that matter guns, are a good example of form following function and always example elegance if you view it from a non-political standpoint. This is one area where the ultra-left were able to continue a dynamic aesthetic. Don't forget that we all owe our jobs (and standard of living) to "consumerist" activities. Art and design cannot flourish in totalitarian regimes.'
III Nicky 29/09/07

References
1   Ron Gilad in conversation with Limited Language, 2005.
2   W.T.J. Mitchell, 'The Violence of Public Art' in Richard Roth and Susan King Roth (eds.) Beauty is Nowhere: Ethical Issues in Art and Design (Amsterdam: Gordon & Breach, 1998), 207.
3   Charles and Ray Eames are considered paradigmatic modern designers, known for their innovations in designing comfortable, mass produced furniture for a more democratic (affordable) market.
4   Alberto Alessi, 'Design and Poetry' in Design Issues, Vol. 5, No. 2 (1989).
5   Klaus Kippendorff, 'Redesigning Design' in Paivi Tahkokallio and Susann Vihma, Design: Pleasure and Responsibility (Helsinki: UIAH, 1994), 151.
6   Alexander Reh, in conversation with Limited Language, 2005.
7   http://blog.makezine.com/archive/2005/08/shotgun_ shell_f.html
8   Dominic Wilcox, in conversation with Limited Language, 2005.
9   Adam Richardson, 'A Design's Work is Never Done' in Design: Pleasure and Responsibility, Op cit., 116-17
10 Grant McCracken, Culture and Consumption (Bloomington, IN: Indiana University Press, 1990), 62.
11 Anthony Dunne and Fiona Raby, Design Noir: The Secret Life of Electronic Objects (Basel: Birkhauser, 2001), 58-9.

12 Quoted in Peter Dormer 'The Salon de Refusé' in *The Culture of Craft* (Manchester: MUP, 1997), 13.
13 Victor Margolin, 'Politics of the Artificial' in *Beauty is Nowhere*, Op cit., 171.

Multiverso

Embodied information

The multiverse (or meta-universe) is a state of parallel realities.[1] Once confined to the realms of science fiction, as the digital-information world overlays the physical world, the multiverse has become an everyday fact.

The globalisation of markets has been inseparable from rapid and complex developments in virtual technology. And yet how this affects our everyday world has often been hard to grasp. It was only the speedy collapse of the markets and banking system in September 2008, which brought home how everything (including the wo/man on the street) is drawn into this process. What became clear in the fallout was that, philosophically speaking, any old ideas we may have had about singular experiences are untenable, be they individuals, single markets, protected rates of exchange or safe pots of cash. All are interlinked. A change in one effects dramatic shifts in all the others.

Design developments are impossible to separate from changes in technology and global markets. This critical period in the 'global collapse' collided with *Multiverso: Nodes, Connections and Currents in Contemporary Communication Design*, the Icograda conference held in Torino, Italy in October 2008. Planned in the heady days before the crisis, the conference's aim struck a more optimistic note: to explore ways design can 'record and give exposure to a complex and flowing, imperfect world that is prone to error but that is nonetheless alive for those very reasons'.[2] This is a departure from a Modernist tradition of information design, which sought to rationalise and simplify the chaotic world in order to 'explain it'. Nor does it ask us to submit to a kind of data sublime. Instead, design index links people

The original piece was the starting premise of a Limited Language lecture at the Icograda *Multiverso* conference which took as its theme, 'nodes, connections and currents'.[1] For us, this represents a dominant cultural condition in which people collaborate; meanings proliferate; information changes; images mutate and media 'fold' into one another. This response looks at contemporary practice which seeks to re-emphasise human experience at the centre of this world. And, as a rewriting, it incorporates some of the projects and comments that emerged as pertinent during and after the conference.

Any old idea of a singular experience is now untenable. How can we engage with this complex world without destroying our own temporal rhythms?

Firstly, the didactic, one-way, top-down model of information is being stripped away. Instead, what is increasingly being written into design briefs is how to harness a new understanding of information as collaborative. This shift is clearly visible in the website for the American design consultancy Modernista![2] This curates an encounter with the living, breathing, and collaborative, social Web.[3] Modernista!'s only design element is the navigation menu, which takes you to various sites on the Internet where their work can be found and edited or commented on (e.g. Flickr, Wikipedia etc.). Here, the enjoyment of information comes out of its live and collaborative status.

Secondly, as the media theorist Lev Manovich suggests: 'The cultural unit is no longer the single image but a large scale structured or unstructured (such as the Web) image database.' These are the 'billions and billions of images being stored on our laptops, network drives, memory cards and so on'.[4] The question for him is this: How can all that information out there be translated back to the scale of human perception?

Manovich's new media examples include the zoom function which allows you to engage with the micro and macro view at once, to see how things relate. In his view, the most era-defining tools are the search engine and tagging functions which do more than give us new ways to look at information: they give us a way to sift through it. But, can this help us make sense of the information? That's a moot point... however, for Manovich and for the immediate purposes here, the significance is that there is no truth in a single image. Instead, significance comes from the relationship between images.

Thirdly then, this reminds us that any ideas of singular or universal meaning have long since imploded.[5] Meaning is multiplicitous and relative to situations and context. It's constantly shifting.

One artist's response comes from Peter Luining: Click Club[6] was an art project/website without content except link buttons. Like channel surfing, the link has become the fetish itself. Constantly zapping to chase the new – to capture what we might be missing? At the Icograda conference, the artist/designer Paul Elliman suggested this example served as a metaphor for how we consume the visual image today. And this calls for a far more critical engagement with Multiverso culture.

If Click Club highlights the extreme of the postmodern abyss where everything is relative and ultimately elusive, then a more pragmatic design approach seeks to make sense of the mass of information from the human/subjective perspective. Donna Haraway, a historian of techno-science, argues that, 'We need to learn in our bodies... In this way we might become answerable for what we learn how to see.[7]

(not figures!) to the global flux.

And so we can say that any old idea of a singular experience of design is increasingly untenable. This includes: ideas of a singular author; finite images or texts; self-contained media or stand-alone contexts. Instead: people collaborate; meanings proliferate; information changes; images mutate and media 'fold' into one another.

The question of agency (or how little of it we have) becomes renewed. Back in 2002, the music promo Remind Me by Röyksopp[3] showed how the minutiae of a city worker's day is connected to the global flows of capitalism. It is reminiscent of just how un-reciprocal this relationship can be. Set to the beat of pop and cued into the media image-circus (then MTV, at the time of writing YouTube), any critical comment intended by the musicians/designers (appropriately!) becomes suckered up too.

Design changes come quite simply because the technology allows it. However, as relationships between people, technology and contexts evolve, new ways of thinking philosophically about design start to take shape.

One strand of practice that has emerged aims to bring people into a more reciprocal relationship with this world. In this process, the manifold ways in which agency can be enabled (and disabled) by design are thrown into relief.

One example of this practice is Christian Nold's Bio Mapping project.[4] This involves asking local community members to walk around their area wired up to a GPS (Global Positioning System) device which records emotional arousal in conjunction with their geographical location. This data is annotated onto maps, which can be used in discussion with councils, to make meaningful changes to the local area in response. Here, there are no 'end users' any more. People are mapped into the world from the start and, also, all the way through. If Röyksopp presented a world that is alienating because it is disembodied, then this project might provide a kind of 're-embodiment'. Nold's project was part of his research for the Royal College of Art's Design

Interactions programme where 'people are [the] primary subject matter, and people cannot be neatly defined and labelled. We are contradictory, volatile, always surprising.'[5]

We can't escape exposure to the erroneous dataverse. New approaches to design will have to respond to (or depart from) the way people are complex, imperfect and alive (!) too. The question now is this: How we can engage with a global, technological world without destroying our own temporal rhythms of living? Or to turn it around: How can design engage with the world through our bodies?

See further images here
www.limitedlanguage.org/images

References
1   The idea of the Multiverse has been much discussed in science fiction and fantasy; but also in cosmology, physics, astronomy, philosophy, and transpersonal psychology. Here the term refers to the realm of virtual worlds and the digital information sphere which overlays our physical world.
2   *Multiverso* Conference, Icograda Design Week Torino, Italy, 2008 http://icogradadesignweektorino.aiap.it/section/111
3   www.royksopp.com/videos/remind-me
4   www.biomapping.net
5   www.interaction.rca.ac.uk (accessed 7/7/08).

Haraway, like Manovich, takes a postmodern view but in a feminist framework. Like the *Multiverso* premise, Haraway finds enjoyment in the world's independent sense of humour. In the same way that people's contradictory behaviour becomes difficult for traditional market analysis, 'Such a sense of humour is not comfortable for humanists and others committed to the world as resource.'[8] In any of these encounters, the only possibility for human agency comes if we also acknowledge the world as a witty agent. She reminds us (them) that: '...we are not in charge of the world. We just live here and try to strike up non-innocent conversations by means of our prosthetic devices – including visualisation technologies.'[9] As with the world and as with people, these non-innocent conversations remind us that technology is not neutral.

Visualisation practice is an important new way for designers to capture a complex and flowing, world. This is what interdisciplinary designer Laura Kurgan calls the 'confusing nowhere-anywhere-somewhere'.[10] One example of her work is *Million Dollar Blocks*, which maps relationships between us state expenditure on prisoners, the locations of their homes and investment on regeneration in those same blocks (i.e. the areas where they live). She provides valuable tools for revealing previously unseen dimensions of criminal justice and social policy. In part, this is because the information had previously existed in separate spheres. In part, it's because visualisation technology can reveal dimensions previously hidden by their old representational technologies; info charts and data spreadsheets.

In his conference paper, *Towards Relational Design*, designer and curator Andrew Blauvelt pointed out that these older 'technologies' of modernist information design are rhetorical.[11] That is, they reflect back on themselves, reconfirming what's already there. 'Visualisations capture the unexpected to tell a new story. This information isn't fetishised but embodied.' This would resonate with Haraway.

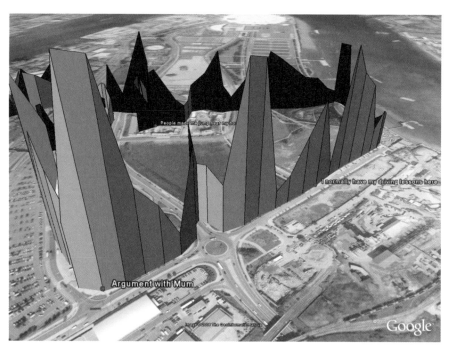

Bio Mapping, Greenwich: Emotion mapping
hardware by Christian Nold (2004-8).

If modern information graphics are like the photographic snap-shot (which isolates and fragments the world for contemplation, denying inter-connectedness) then contemporary visualisations are more like the screen-grab, impressions of a discursive space.

Finally, then, the unique forms of singular media have been eroded in the switch from analogue to digital. From print, through photography, film to music and so on, media fold into one another. Common terms are blended, merged or hybrid media, where one media becomes the content of another. A more useful term in this context might be articulated media,[12] where the tempo and nature of each media is distinct – even when networked. Visualisations end up as objects in the world. However rather than think of them as finite objects, we would do better to compare them to the A4 paper that usually spews from the printer on 'Send to Print' during the on-going design stage of any job. Like rapid-response printing and rapid prototyping they are both finite 'analogue' objects and a 'discursive' part of an ongoing digital process.

And yet, how can we avoid fetishising this technology? Rapid response technology comes from war: like the global economy, war is not reciprocal but disembodied, with people reconfigured as 'collateral damage'. Designers can hi-jack these technologies but – hopefully – to a different and more reciprocal end. That is, engaging with the nature and tempo of technology – and markets – but with our own nature and tempo also articulated. But even here, technology and design experimentation will so often just become the next consumable. This demands more than a simple 'humanising'. As Haraway encourages us to ask, How can we learn in our bodies? And, in doing so, question our technologies?

The critical effects, as discussed elsewhere in this chapter and in the rest of this book, will only be seen in the process of engagement with the world...

Percent Persons of Color, 2000.

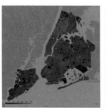
Percent Persons Below Poverty Level, 2000.

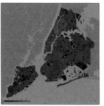
Percent Adults Admitted to Prison, 2003.

BROOKLYN COMMUNITY DISTRICTS	% POPULATION	% POVERTY	% ADMISSIONS
BROOKLYN CD 1	6.51 %	9.08 %	5.37 %
BROOKLYN CD 2	4.03 %	3.58 %	4.64 %
BROOKLYN CD 3	5.83 %	9.10 %	16.51 %
BROOKLYN CD 4	4.74 %	6.34 %	9.34 %
BROOKLYN CD 5	7.04 %	9.30 %	14.45 %
BROOKLYN CD 6	4.33 %	2.60 %	3.06 %
BROOKLYN CD 7	5.02 %	5.03 %	3.82 %
BROOKLYN CD 8	3.78 %	4.15 %	9.46 %
BROOKLYN CD 9	4.26 %	4.14 %	4.43 %
BROOKLYN CD 10	4.96 %	2.79 %	0.91 %
BROOKLYN CD 11	7.05 %	5.54 %	1.35 %
BROOKLYN CD 12	7.39 %	8.54 %	1.32 %
BROOKLYN CD 13	4.23 %	4.94 %	3.41 %
BROOKLYN CD 14	6.76 %	6.22 %	3.79 %
BROOKLYN CD 15	6.48 %	4.42 %	1.20 %
BROOKLYN CD 16	3.48 %	5.92 %	8.43 %
BROOKLYN CD 17	6.75 %	5.40 %	5.29 %
BROOKLYN CD 18	7.96 %	3.91 %	3.30 %
BOROUGH TOTAL	100.00 %	100.00 %	100.00 %

Comparisons Expressed as Percent of Borough Total.

Prisoner Migration with Expenditures by Block, 2003.

BROOKLYN,
NEW YORK CITY

ADDED UP BLOCK BY BLOCK, IT COST $359 MILLION DOLLARS TO IMPRISON PEOPLE FROM BROOKLYN IN 2003, FACILITATING A MASS MIGRATION TO PRISONS IN UPSTATE NEW YORK. 95% EVENTUALLY RETURN HOME.

Prisoner Migration Patterns, Brooklyn, New York (2003). Architecture and Justice 2006, Spatial Information Design Lab, GSAPP. Columbia University. Project Team: Laura Kurgan (project director), Eric Cadora, David Reinfurt, Sarah Williams.

See full responses + carry on the conversation here
http://tiny.cc/chapter1_6

References

1   *Multiverso* Conference, Icograda Design Week Torino,
    Italy, 2008.
2   www.modernista.com/7/
3   This sense is taken from Patrick Burgoyne, Web
    2.Oh! in *Creative Review*, May (2008), 68.
4   Lev Manovich in 'Metadata, Mon Amour', 2002
    www.manovich.net/DOCS/metadata.doc
5   This has been discussed in a body of postmodern
    literature including Frederic Jameson, Roland
    Barthes, Jean Baudrillard, Jacques Derrida etc.
    who introduced a de-centred universe made up of
    multiple meanings and manipulations.
6   Peter Luining's *PC Click Club* (1995-2000). See also
    www.luining.com
7   Donna Haraway, *Simians, Cyborgs and Women: The
    Reinvention of Nature* (London: Free Association
    Books, 1991), 190.
8   Ibid, 199.
9   Ibid.
10 Laura Kurgan, 'You Are Here' in
    www.thephotographyinstitute.org/journals/1998/
    laura_kurgan.html
11 Andrew Blauvelt, in his paper *Towards Relational
    Design*, which later fed into a blog post on
    www.designobserver.com/archives/entry.html?id=38845
12 Michele Jannuzzi and Richard Smith, *Dotlinepixel:
    Thoughts on Cross-Media Design* (GCE, 2000), 37.

Agency

Modernism 2.0 / Designers of possibility
Design politics / Design and the good cop/bad cop scenario
Ben Wilson / Notions of visibility
Work ethics / How much of this can we take?
Escape from the tyranny of things / Sustainable design
State Britain / Rebuilding protest

SPECIAL REVIEW

This chapter explores how design interacts with politics and ideology: from ethics to green politics; art to modernism.

OFFICE OF INSPECTOR GENERAL

QUAERE VERITATEM UBICUMQUE DUCAT

CENTRAL INTELLIGENCE AGENCY

(TS COUNTERTERRORISM DETENTION AND
INTERROGATION ACTIVITIES
(SEPTEMBER 2001 – OCTOBER 2003)

7 May 2004

Keywords
Dissemination (8,840,000)
Graphic design (32,700,000)
Space and theory (4,900,000)
Sustainability (12,800,000)

Keywords and their Google hit rate in conjunction with the word design.

Modernism 2.0

If you've ever been troubled by what they call a 'postmodern moment' – disorientated, disconnected and detached – worry no more. Postmodernism is over, according to Nicolas Bourriaud the French writer and curator behind the *Tate Triennial* in Britain, held in 2009.[1]

Instead, the altermodern is emerging. This rejection of postmodernism (after modernism) is a rejection of 'history as an arrow'. Alter proposes multiplicity and otherness. It's the 'reloading' of modernism for today's (digital) context; global, nomadic, creolised but – crucially – connected. 'Today we are living in a maze and we have to get meaning out of this maze and these are the big stakes around the altermodern,'[2] Bourriaud claims. Meaning is back in fashion!

Altermodern at Tate Britain was based on four themes – Alter, Exile, Travelling and Borders – which provided cluster points for Bourriaud's manifesto of the same name. Here, his interest is in how artists can meaningfully connect across moments. One example is Walead Beshty's *FedEx Sculptures* where a series of glass cubes which had been 'FedEx-ed' were displayed, all cracked and chipped on top of their packing cartons. The damage, as well as making the cubes visibly unique, stands testimony to their different journeys and different handlings. In a world where the sheer number of daily transactions and their global traverse is unintelligible (and invisible) then, for Beshty, it's only in 'palpable moments of error, when... the distance an object travels results in damage'[3] that we get a glimpse of other (alter) realities.

Places of Rebirth by Navin Rawanchaikul, is a tableaux which is made up of a composite of different Bollywood posters and, in Tate Britain, stretched the length of a wall within the theme of 'borders'. Rawanchaikul uses this to talk about immigration. Signs, like people, become displaced. One effect, as Bourriaud suggests, is 'to illuminate their history. [Artists working

Designers of possibility

In the original article we asked, via the thinking of the French curator Nicolas Bourriaud, 'How do we make sense of the cultural chaos?' This 'chaos' is a (digital) cultural condition which is global and nomadic, where information, images and identities have become creolised; extricated from their origins and transformed. This is the postmodern malaise.

A better question might be: 'Who will make sense of it for us?' In his earlier work, Bourriaud had coined the term 'semionaut'.[1] This term takes its departure from semiotics/semiosis,[2] which describes the process by which meaning is constructed and understood (through signs). For Bourriaud, the semionaut is the figure who, visually and politically, best 'imagines the links, the likely relations between disparate sites'.[3] As an example, Bourriaud refers to the rise of the DJ and the Web surfer as ones who connect new spaces and new narratives.

The idea that a New Man, with a new mind-set would emerge in the transition from analogue to digital technology had already been foreseen by media theorist Marshall McLuhan in *The Gutenberg Galaxy*[4] in 1962. These two terms, new man and semionaut, of course aren't important to fixate on as they are of their own moment (male-dominated 1960s/French 1990s theory). However, we need language to help us think about these things and so, as metaphors to capture an alternative way of operating, they are useful.[1]

This alternative way of thinking can, unsurprisingly, be seen all the way back to the predecessor of the computer, the *Analytical Engine*, dated 1871. Charles Babbage had been working on this from 1834 with Ada Lovelace (the daughter of a mathematician and Lord Byron, the poet). This historical

Altermodern World Map, Where Are We Going? (2009) by M/M (Paris). Poster/Wall label for the exhibition *Altermodern* at Tate Britain. 120 x 176cm approx, 4 colours silkscreen.

'Altermodern', 'Wandering' and 'Viatorised' chapter dividers from the publication *Altermodern* by M/M (Paris), © Tate Publishing (2009).

in this vein] could be said to "viatorise" them (from the Latin viator, "traveller"). For them, historical memory, like the topography of the contemporary world, exists only in the form of a network. Signs are displaced, "viatorised" in circuits, and the work of art presents itself in the form of this dynamic system.'[4]

A significance for designers is that this matrix of relationships – between people, signs and moments – is one in which design is already embedded, long before the Bourriaud sound bite machine came along. We can see this in the way that the work above speaks through the global service brand and the film poster. However, a difference is that design usually seeks to erase error, minimise cognitive disruption and (re)establish meaning.

What, then, can design gain by 'reloading' the latest art criticism? A link here is M/M (Paris), the show's designers who have worked with Bourriaud since he was a director of the Palais de Tokyo in Paris, where he developed the curatorial practices that, by the end of the 1990s, had informed his first book *Relational Aesthetics*.[5] This book explored art which creates 'scenarios' and generates relationships between people. It was followed by *Postproduction*[6] in 2002 which relocated and reconnected the relational into the Internet age.

Paul Elliman, a practitioner who works across both art and design, has noted that if art adds or emphasises the relational, then 'design, which is always already relational by definition, is a kind of super-relational [. . .] in terms of its production, not just its use or reception'.[7] M/M (Paris), for instance, join in the same debates as Bourriaud's artists, but using real networks of communication.

In these networks, M/M (Paris)'s design often functions as co-ordinates; points at which the art, design and fashion communities meet. If that sounds like the way a multitude of other designers work, then an interest here is the way they bring these ideas into conscious practice. For instance, the *Altermodern* logo and typeface is a confect of ornamental letter designs with different images inside. This looks like a familiar postmodern eclectic

encounter marks a key moment of transition because, whereas Babbage's previous invention the *Difference Engine*[5] could do no more than add, the *Analytical Engine* could predict the outcome of calculations not yet made. In this sense, it embodied almost all the conceptual elements of the computer. But when thinking about this Babbage, with what McLuhan would call a linear Typographic mind (a logic of which women were not in possession), felt his 'intellect was beginning to become deranged'.[6] It was Lovelace who had the capacity for lateral and predictive thinking; the 'power of seeing all possible contingencies (probable and improbable, just alike)'.[7]

This is the design of possibility. It resonated well with the operationality of the new Engine. In her footnotes to a memoir on the machine, Lovelace outlined her own invention; what we now call software, two hundred years before the hardware was available to run it on. The footnotes themselves – marginalia – have proved more seminal than the text they were attached to, and in the structure of this writing is a precursor to hypertext. One note read, 'It must be evident how multifarious and how mutually complicated are the considerations', adding, 'All, and everything is naturally related and interconnected...'[8]

In a parallel story, whilst Steve Jobs worked on the Apple Macintosh from 1981-4, it was two women who were given the task of developing the Graphical User Interface – the connector between human and software. Joanna Hoffman devised the operating system conventions and Susan Kare the desktop icons and visual system.[9] Of all the Mac's innovations, it's these that have had the most impact in the long run; 'user-friendliness' and interface design.

It is this function of women as infrastructure (of being 'the very "possibility of mediation, transaction, transition, transference – between man and his fellow creatures..."'[10]) which might usefully connect us back to the function of designers writ-large, beyond gender. Could we say that designers, too, function as infrastructure?

They mediate between clients, audiences and signs (meaning) and work across areas of knowledge, bringing them together and translating them for alternative engagement.

And yet, if designers have always fostered the links and likely relations, what makes it different now? Over the years, suggestions have emerged on the Limited Language website in response to a series of articles addressing the question of the semionaut. In response to *Who are the semionauts?* Stephen argues: 'I am not sure if designers really ever capture – or point towards – something completely new...they are making, or mapping, links which already exist; but has design not always done this?'[II] To which Joseph replies: 'I do believe, as artists or designers we unearth new material – experience – in our work. The debate might be to the consciousness of the act? What the artist creates with conscious intent, the designer might produce as a simple rhetorical sermon of belief?'[III]

A key figure in the design of possibility of conscious intent might be Muriel Cooper who set up the *Visible Language Workshop*, an interdisciplinary graphics laboratory founded in 1975, and part of MIT's Media Lab. The designer/researcher David Reinfurt has commented on how, through experiments at the VLW, they had noticed that, with electronic communications, information and images don't just stay within the computer, but operate through networks of readers, writers and users. The group began to design interfaces offering 'routes, pathways or even self-guided tours through this soft architecture.'[11] In *Information Landscapes* (1994) Cooper pioneered a new space for this information. What she had already understood was that information transmitted, accessed and transformed in this way, could be open to an unlimited set of connections, meanings; new narratives.

Does this bring us back to Bourriaud's DJ and Web surfer? James Souttar suggests that an alternative conscious practice marks a shift from the: '...traditional sense of the artist [designer] as someone with something to say,

aesthetic and yet the postmodern emphasised difference of origin (this is Victorian, this is Cyrillic or this is white man in Native American Indian head-dress...) and, then, the way all were made relative – what Ted Polhemus called going shopping in the 'supermarket of style'.[8] M/M (Paris) enjoy what happens when images come together at this new moment of intersection, not to relativise, but to produce new meanings. This is the same 'scenario' building found in relational thinking, but going deeper into language; to build up stories with images. For them, it's like a conversation which becomes the 'engine' to produce new images. In another example, their visual identity for the Palais de Tokyo was later released on their website for re-use; allowing it to become something else. This is design that *sets up possibilities*. It's only a modest example of this thinking, but we can see the bigger potential.

In 2006, M/M (Paris) had a solo show in London at the Haunch of Venison gallery. This was an installation-collage of much of their preceding work. Uprooted from its original context, some of their visually baroque, story-building work lost its original meaning. However, in a parallel talk at the Tate Modern gallery,[9] they explained that to re-edit old images to 'create a new history' was a deliberate process. This is the sense of creole that affiliates them to altermodern – where the connecting of signs is time-, not site-specific. Modernism 2.0?

By the time art-cultural ideas such as Bourriaud's begin to resonate in design, their moments have usually passed in the art world. And yet, the underlying premise of all of Bourriaud's work – How do we make sense of the cultural chaos? – remains valid. The art world looks to the way artists answer his questions. What happens when the design world asks the same of designers too?

Modernism 2.0 was published simultaneously on Limited Language and the *Eye Blog*, on 6 February 2009 as a (p)review of *Altermodern*. A review of the show was posted by Paul Matosic – 07/04/2009 on the *Eye Blog*, http://bit.ly/24dKll. Following this, and a visit to the exhibition, we've taken the liberty of including some descriptions of

FedEx Sculptures by Walead Beshty (2009).

Left : FedEx® Large Kraft Box ©2005 FEDEX 330508, International Priority, Los Angeles-Tijuana trk# 865282057997 28 October-3 November 2008, International Priority, Tijuana-Los Angeles trk# 867279774918 2-6 January 2009, International Priority, Los Angeles-London trk# 867279774870 14-16 January 2009.

Middle: Fedex® Large Kraft Box ©2005 FEDEX 330508, International Priority, Los Angeles-Tijuana trk# 865282058022 28 October-3 November 2008, International Priority, Tijuana-Los Angeles trk# 867279774892 2-6 January 2009, International Priority, Los Angeles-London trk# 867279774860 14-16 January 2009.

Right: FedEx® Large Kraft Box ©2005 FEDEX 330508, International Priority, Los Angeles-Tijuana trk# 865282058000 28-30 October 2008, International Priority, Tijuana-Los Angeles trk# 867279774907 2-6 January 2009, International Priority, Los Angeles-London trk# 867279774859 14-16 January 2009.

Places of Rebirth by Navin Rawanchaikul (2009).
Acrylic on Canvas, 220 x 720 cm.
Image courtesy of Navin Production Co., Ltd.

and the emerging role of the designer as someone who enables something – as yet unknown – to come to be.'[IV] Nicky calls this first type: 'the designer as sledgehammer'[V]; Jess: 'Semionaut and semionaught then?'[VI]

Rather than focusing on visual or graphic expression, designers like Cooper look at the structures of information. Laurie Haycock Makela and Ellen Lupton comment on how 'Cooper worked to build an electronic language that will support the work of future designers, helping them to make complex, malleable documents in real-time and three-dimensional space.'[12] More recently we can look to visualisation technology which helps envision previously hidden or unanticipated information. In contrast to the spaces of modernist information (bar charts etc.), which are rhetorical and reconfirm what's already there, 'Visualisations capture the unexpected to tell a new story.'[13] Modernism 2.0; designs of possibility?

The designer of possibility sets up – supports – a possibility of infinite connections. Communication, here, is understood as a process with the designer, the semionaut, initiating a point or trajectory and creating work which is not, ideally, snared by its own finitude. The beauty of this process is that it can have no starting or end point and, as reloaded into each new moment, there needs to be a reassessment of what makes sense and for whom.[VII]

Carry on the conversation here
http://tiny.cc/chapter2_1

Reader credits
I Stephen 03/07/2007 – This is a response to his point about language; 'What we see is an increasingly sophisticated language…to discuss communication design BUT…the language needs to be fixed to something otherwise you reduce it to simple floating naut in space!'
II Stephen 03/07/2007
III Joseph 21/08/2007
IV James Souttar 18/05/2007
V Nicky 20/06/2007
VI Jess 25/06/2007
VII The Swarm 30/08/2007 – This post raised the question of who has the cultural authority to enable new meanings and to whom they might make sense.

the works on show in this reprint.

See further images here
www.limitedlanguage.org/images

References
1 Nicolas Bourriaud, 'Altermodern: A New Kind of Modern', Interview with Kirstie Beaven for Tate Online 17 October 2008. blog.tate.org.uk/turnerprize2008/?p=74 (accessed 05/02/09).
2 Ibid.
3 Walead Beshty in Nicolas Bourriaud, Altermodern (London: Tate Publishing, 2009), 54.
4 Nicolas Bourriaud in ibid., 22. See also http://www.tate.org.uk/britain/exhibitions/altermodern/explore.shtm (accessed 5/6/09).
5 Nicolas Bourriaud, Relational Aesthetics (Paris: Presses du Réel, 1998).
6 Nicolas Bourriaud, Postproduction (New York: Lukas & Sternberg, 2002).
7 Email correspondence following the Multiverso Conference, Icograda Design Week Torino, Italy, 2008.
8 Ted Polhemus, Streetstyle: From Sidewalk to Catwalk (London: Thames & Hudson, 1994).
9 M/M (Paris) Artists' Talk at the Tate Modern, 14 September 2006 www.tate.org.uk/modern/eventseducation/talksdiscussions/5958.htm (accessed 05/02/09).

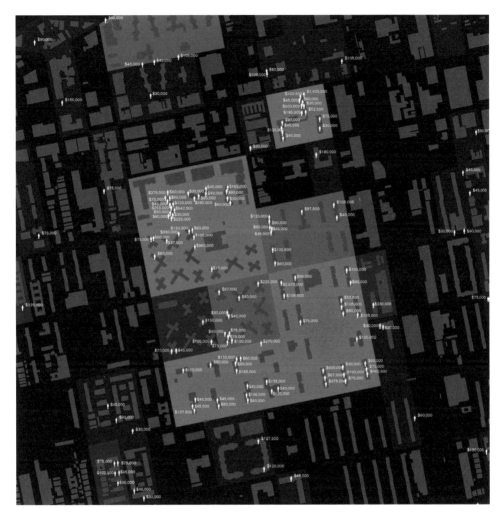

BROWNSVILLE, BROOKLYN

IT COST 17 MILLION DOLLARS TO IMPRISON 109 PEOPLE FROM THESE 17 BLOCKS IN 2003. WE CALL THESE MILLION DOLLAR BLOCKS. ON A FINANCIAL SCALE PRISONS ARE BECOMING THE PREDOMINANT GOVERNING INSTITUTION IN THE NEIGHBORHOOD.

Million Dollar Blocks, Brownsville, Brooklyn, New York (2003). These maps depict relationships between US state expenditure on prisoners, the locations of their homes and investment on regeneration in those same blocks (i.e, the areas where they live). This reveals previously unseen dimensions of criminal justice and social policy. See also pp. 61 and 64.

Architecture and Justice 2006, Spatial Information Design Lab, GSAPP. Columbia University. Project Team: Laura Kurgan (project director), Eric Cadora, David Reinfurt, Sarah Williams.

However, fittingly, he, The Swarm offered only the question; 'semionaughty?' and added the link: http://bit.ly/1qC5ko (posted 20/08/07, accessed 30/08/2007).

References

1   The term 'semionaut' was introduced in Nicolas Bourriaud, *Relational Aesthetics* (Paris: Presses du Réel, 1998) as one who facilitated human, convivial relations. In his follow-up publication, *Postproduction* (New York: Lukas & Sternberg, 2002), which shifted its focus to the matrix of relationships between cultural products in the Internet Age, the semionaut became pivotal. In the Altermodern Manifesto he doesn't use the term semionaut, but the sense he invokes is the same.

2   See for instance, Umberto Eco, *A Theory of Semiotics* (London: Macmillan, 1976) or, for a graphic/design focus, David Crow, *Visible Signs: An Introduction to Semiotics* (Lausanne: AVA Publishing, 2003).

3   Nicolas Bourriaud, Op cit., 12.

4   Marshall McLuhan, *The Gutenberg Galaxy: The Making of Typographic Man* (New York: Mentor, 1962).

5   Charles Babbage's *Difference Engine* 1 (1832), designed to perform fixed operations automatically, was one of the earliest automatic calculators. Sections of Babbage's *Analytical Engine and Difference Engine* 2 (1847-9) have been built for the Science Museum in London.

6   Charles Babbage quoted in Sadie Plant, *Zeros+ Ones: Digital Women + the New Technoculture* (London: 4th Estate, 1997), 20.

7   Ada Lovelace quoted in ibid.

8   Ada Lovelace's Translation of, and Notes to, Luigi F. Menabrea's Sketch of the *Analytical Engine* Invented by Charles Babbage, Esq. (1842/1843).

9   Ruth Levy, 'GUI & WYSIWIG: A History of Graphic Design Software' in *Things*, No. 6 (Summer 1997), 48.

10 Sadie Plant, Op cit., 36.

11 David Reinfurt, 'This Stands as a Sketch for the Future: Muriel Cooper and the Visible Language Workshop' in *Dot Dot Dot 15*, 24 October – 7 November (2007), 46. Also available online: www.o-r-g.com/view.html?project=117 (accessed 04/05/09).

12 Laurie Haycock Makela and Ellen Lupton, 'Underground Matriarchy' in Michael Beirut et al. (ed.), *Looking Closer: Critical Writings on Graphic Design* (New York: Allworth, 1997), 138.

13 Andrew Blauvelt, in his paper 'Towards Relational Design' at the *Multiverso* Conference, Icograda Design Week Torino, Italy, 2008. See also Peter Hall, 'Critical Visualization' in Hugh Aldersey-Williams, Peter Hall, Ted Sargent and Paola Antonelli, *Design and the Elastic Mind* (New York: Museum of Modern Art, 2008), 120-31.

John Russell
Design politics

It could be argued that the progressive depoliticisation of politics has been mirrored in recent times by a superficial pseudo repoliticisation of art and design – in other words, the transformation of political action into merely symbolic action or pseudo-activity. The art critic J.J. Charlesworth describes this tendency when he criticises this new politicised art as 'an excess of representation of the political' which he claims is 'an effect of the disarticulation of political agency within western democracies after the end of the Cold War'.[1] In this respect, Jeremy Deller's *Battle of Orgreave* (2001), where a key moment in the 1984 British Miners' Strike was re-enacted by many of the original miners, could be seen as the equivalent of *Adbusters* magazine's anti-corporate gestures.

Designers are very good at saying what they could or should do. For example, from the graphic design realm, *The First Things First Manifesto* (2000), which in itself was an up-date of a 1964 manifesto calling for designer consciousness, said this: 'We propose a reversal of priorities in favour of more useful, lasting and democratic forms of communication – a mind shift away from product marketing and toward the exploration and production of a new kind of meaning. The scope of debate is shrinking; it must expand. Consumerism is running uncontested; it must be challenged by other perspectives expressed, in part, through the visual languages and resources of design.'[2]

These types of call-to-arms seem to be based upon the generally held belief that, because design is in the business of communication, it is in a privileged position to manipulate this communication to political effect. But, does this ever happen? For instance, on a previous blog on this site Paul Bowman calls for '... all visual communicators to address the world', and goes on to urge: 'SREBRENICA: EUROPE, 1995, DECLARED un SAFE HAVEN, 7-8000 MEN AND BOYS MASSACRED. What

Design and the good cop/bad cop scenario

The original post by John Russell and its ensuing responses capture a critical problem in all visual culture and, specifically, graphic communication: the possibility of political reflection/action. The post and responses can be seen to create a *good cop/bad cop* narrative through which it tries to interrogate the possibilities of political affect on visual culture as a whole, and graphic design in particular.

The critical debates regarding the political effectiveness of art are complex and multifarious but their very existence exposes the soft underbelly of design to attacks on its political fortitude. For, art has long entangled itself with representation. In the 1920s George Lukács, in his essay *Critical Realism and Socialist Realism*, proffered art a political role: vis-à-vis to provide a critical reflection of society. Or later, the eventual rupture from realism with Marcel Duchamp and the Ready-made: the urinal, or a mustachioed *Mona Lisa*, all acting as cognitive attacks on a bourgeois assimilation of aesthetics.

In Design, the trajectory of aesthetic and intellectual inquiry is less clear.

The questions asked in the original post are made with a Nietzschian delight (as bad cop) where the slippage in political realities is exposed by providing a modern day context for the observation of Nietzsche that it is a 'utilitarian fact that only when we see things coarsely and made equal do they become calculable and usable to us'.[1] This coarseness and, in modern parlance, *dumbing down* of political life is illustrated by John Russell's reference to the American animated TV show *The Simpsons* which he comments, provides a 'corrective moral function'.

To provide an interpretation of this phenomenon: at its narrative centre *The

Kopf an Kopf – Politikerporträts (Head to Head – Political Portraits) exhibition poster by Emanuel Tschumi (2008). Museum für Gestaltung, Zürich.

can we do people?'[3] This seems to be asking for something like politics, but designers/artists seem singularly unqualified to communicate political ideas. (Because they haven't got any?)

What is political design? Does it exist? What does it do? And what does it look like? Or, is it all pseudo-activity?

John Miller makes this last point about pseudo-activity in a 2002 roundtable discussion in the magazine *October*, with reference to art criticism/critical theory: 'John Miller: And of course art writers don't mostly write for cash (for there is none), it's more for the position in academia that's secured by publishing. So the payoff isn't the writer's fee, it's mostly the prestige that comes from first establishing an apparently negative relationship to the market per se. As it accumulates, that symbolic capital can always be converted to real capital.'[4]

See further images here
www.limitedlanguage.org/images

References

1   J.J. Charlesworth, 'Twin Towers: The Spectacular Disappearance Of Art And Politics.' *Third Text*, Vol. 16, Issue 4 (2002), 357-66.
2   *The First Things First Manifesto* was written by Ken Garland in 1964 and republished in 2000 in conjunction with *Adbusters* and a few other key international design magazines. With the exception of a few minor word and product changes, it remained the same in text and spirit.
3   Paul Bowman in a reply (26/05/2005) to his own post *Illustrators, rather like women in the Bible...*, Limited Language, May 2005. http://bit.ly/paul_bowman
4   John Miller, 'Round Table: The Present Conditions of Art Criticism', in *October*, No. 100 (Spring 2002), 205.

Simpsons provides a conflation of *moral* and *liberal* thinking in contemporary society. In the show the bad character, Mr. Burns (owner of the local nuclear power plant), is confounded by the *good* blue-collar *naif* of Homer Simpson (employee of said nuclear facility). The storylines often allow a simple moral tale of good and bad. The use of irony (a nuclear spill due to Homer's incompetence, exposes the dangers of laissez-faire economics, but will always end happily for instance), compounds the liberal viewers notion of right and wrong: without any recourse to critical, cognitive expenditure.

The narrative structure of *The Simpsons* provides a false consciousness: a belief that through the assimilation of radicalism (watching the Simpsons as apposed to a Walt Disney-esque animation, for instance) we achieve an equivalence of being radical.

We can equally see the same action with *Adbusters*, the Canadian 'subvertising' magazine, where the words and images of big brand adverts are reworked to overturn their meaning (utilising the same language of promotion and consumption as the advertising it denounces).

In both examples, we see a shift from a material to a symbolic politic. That is, we watch and consume our politics, rather than have a material engagement with them: strikes, bombs and collective revolution.

By extension, this leads to an avant-garde, as ultimate bad cop, whose response to the cognitive, ethical and aesthetic is quite unequivocal. 'Truth is a lie; morality stinks; beauty is shit.'[2]

If the bad cop advocates an impossibility of politics or any cognitive, aesthetic, visual language, the good cop uses a soothing rhetoric of collective consciousness. In Britain, this is seen to be played out through issues of class and unionisation against the idyll backdrop of village greens and industrial landscapes. For instance, *Orgreave* in northern England; the site in 1984, of one of the most strident clashes between striking miners and the British Police during the reign of Margaret Thatcher. Here, the Trade Unions acted as the superego of capitalism – filtering out the more carnal, base elements of the capitalist psyche.

This event is recast in the work of artist Jeremy Deller's *The Battle of Orgreave* for instance, where the 1984 Miners' Strike was restaged by many of those originally involved. This artwork assimilates a collective consciousness; where men fight on the frontline and 'her in doors' patiently paints placards and fights the bailiff at the front door...

The *non-art form* of Graphic Design, with its long history of political communication, is the hostage between the two dialogues of avant-gardism and commercial opportunism: it wants to be part of the discourse as both insider and outsider; producer and consumer. This is part of the treacherous ground that J.J. Charlesworth[1] and others, in their replies to the post, have mined.

But can political design exist? For many it is unequivocal: like Kourosh Shishehgaran, who comments: 'My first graphic designs with political subjects date back to 1975. I designed a poster for peace in Lebanon that was then involved with the civil war. As an Iranian artist I intended to be present in important world issues so in that poster I had a symbolic look at peace that was emerging in Lebanon back then. I regarded that peace with skepticism and the future proved that I was right in my perception. The SAVAK (Iranian intelligence service) interrogated me that year on my intention and purposes.'[3]

Now compare this with Shepard Fairey's 'iconic' Barack Obama *Hope* poster, for instance.

Part of the reason why graphic communicators feel as if they have a legitimate position in contemporary politics is due to an interpretation of the history of the discipline. Dada, Constructivism and De Stijl have a tradition in the (political) poster. Indeed contemporary designer, Hamish Muir, a founder of 8vo, describes the poster as the graphic designer's version of an artist's canvas. (Although, it is

An Obama poster by the artist Shepard Fairey (2009). He is most well known for his *Obey Giant* street poster series. The Obey campaign has been described by Fairey as an 'experiment in Phenomenology' which attempts to 'reawaken a sense of wonder about one's environment'. http://obeygiant.com/about

Design for Obama. This is a website which collates Obama posters and rates them. The founders write; 'Many artists including Shepard Fairey have already proven that poster art is not a dead medium in the United States and have also shown how much of an impact a single poster can have... At such a turbulent (yet exciting) time in our nation's history, collaboration has never been more important.' http://designforobama.org/

also worth noting that 8vo depoliticised their work by using the term 'visual engineering' when describing their later work at the end of the 1980s.)

But today, the connection to these early 20th century art/design movements is appropriated as a visual surface alone. It becomes *disarticulated* from the material reality of its context – of construction or creation. A prime example of this appropriation is the Constructivist aesthetic which has long influenced the work of graphic designers Neville Brody and Jonathan Barnbrook.

A visual language thus appropriated, provides a politics of symbolism rather than an embodied – from cradle to grave – political sphere of 1920s Russia. Constructivism was a movement which aimed at 'the creative processing of practical materials'.[4] Here, the 'political' is evidenced within all disciplines of the time: graphic design, art and architecture; not in and of themselves but as agents in the external material world of housing and literacy for example – constructing a new era! '[B]y means of intellectual-material production, the constructivist joins the proletarian order for the struggle with the past, for the conquest of the future.'[5]

Of course, any visual style is historically contingent and to contemporary eyes at least, can be little more than symbolic at best, and ironic at worse. But, the processes of politics are still available to us – although they might be increasingly found in a convergence of media. Where a 'convergence is characterized by the flow of content across multiple media platforms, the cooperation between multiple media industries, and the migratory behavior of media audiences'.[6]

Design as a political act is difficult to define, but as part of the process of enlightenment – leading to political awareness – it can be an active participant. Graphic design is in the process of redefining itself in digital culture – and the possibilities of convergence – and it will need more than manifestos to re-establish its centre-of-gravity. But it is worth remembering, the Graphical User Interface

JOHN RUSSELL

Was a popular and charming jokester.

312/953

Not Just a Statistic

Not Just a Statistic campaign (2004), New York City.

Poster by Bijan Sayfouri.
Mahriz Publishers (2009).

Saadi (Persian: سعدی), was one of the major Persian poets of the medieval
period. One of his famous quotes is from the poem that focuses on the
oneness of mankind. The same poem is used to grace the entrance to the Hall
of Nations of the UN building in New York with this call for breaking all barriers:

بنی آدم اعضای یک پیکرند   Human beings are members of a whole,
که در آفرینش ز یک گوهرند   In creation of one essence and soul.
چو عضوی به درد آورد روزگار   If one member is afflicted with pain,
دگر عضوها را نماند قرار   Other members uneasy will remain.
تو کز محنت دیگران بی غمی   If you have no sympathy for human pain,
نشاید که نامت نهند آدمی   The name of human you cannot retain.

makes the World Wide Web visible. Literally and metaphorically this interface, might be a lifeline for graphic design as a political agent.

Reader credits
I   J.J. Charlesworth 28/06/2005

References
1   Friedrich Nietzsche, *The Will to Power* (London:
     Weidenfeld & Nicolson, 1968), 576.
2   Quoted in Terry Eagleton, *The Ideology of the
     Aesthetic* (Oxford: Blackwell, 1990), 426.
3   Quoted in Saed Meshki, 'Political Graphic Design of
     Kourosh Shishehgaran' in *Neshan Magazine*, No. 18 ,
     www.neshanmagazine.com/articles.asp?id=110
     (accessed 12/07/09).
4   Stephen Bann, *The Tradition of Constructivism*
     (London: Thames and Hudson, 1974), 44.
5   Ibid, xxxv.
6   Henry Jenkins, *Convergence Culture: Where Old and
     New Media Collide* (New York; London: New York
     University Press, 2008), 353.

Esther Leslie
Ben Wilson

Ben Wilson paints little acrylic paintings on discarded chewing gum that has been stamped into the pavement. His pictures are emblems of contemporary social life. Some are declarations of love, some commemorate the absent or dead, some celebrate a gang or the bonds of friendship, while others record memories or tokens of identity.

Over a number of days or weeks passers-by, from alcoholics to housewives to community police officers, are held up for a while in order to involve themselves in discussions and affective relations with the artist who appears as a mad drunk, prostrate on the ground for hours on end, painting his miniatures as city life rumbles around him. Passers-by propose their own images or have their images' contours drawn out of them through long processes of conversation and enquiry. They contribute sketches, suggest colours, tussle with the artist over what could and should appear. They give their consent to be photographed which produces, alongside the colourful micro-paintings, an archive of the London public in the first years of the 21st century.

Through this activity, which he has done nearly every day for over three years along the roads from Barnet (North London) to Central London, Wilson has challenged the seemingly exclusive rights of the commercial imagescape to decorate our environment. The images and their commissioning generate, in micro-form, a redistribution of the ability to participate in the system of patronage. Wilson has also contributed to a mapping of urban relations, as they exist on the ground. He has brought people and their affections to expression. And he has stepped over lines of property and perceived property. He has been assaulted once by young men, arrested twice and beaten seriously by City of London police as they forcibly extracted DNA from him though he had, in painting a discarded item raised a few millimetres from the ground, not committed the

Notions of visibility

In 1852, Charles William Day wrote, in *The Art of Miniature Painting*, 'There are three kinds of materials on which miniatures are painted, namely: ivory, paper and vellum; but as the first two are the most usual in England, I shall confine my remarks to them...'[1] Over 150 years later Ben Wilson added a further material: chewing gum. Wilson's paintings, which use discarded chewing gum as their canvas, carry on today the tradition of the miniature which, historically at least, is perceived as a legitimate English art form: 'To the English people, the art of portrait miniature is a national asset of exceptional worth, and it is rightly considered in some ways exclusively an English art.'[2]

The miniature style was exported to the colonies. It is still a popular art form in India, for instance, where it has materially utilised the trafficked booty of colonialism, namely ivory. In a parallel drawn from Michael Redclift in *Chewing Gum: The Fortunes of Taste*, the modern day canvas of spat-out gum has a link to North America's colonial past where gum 'came to represent pre-modernity and resource extraction for tens of thousands of families in the Yucatan'.[3] The branded names of this gum, *Chiclets* and *Black Jack*, signify their own racial overtones of Mexican and African cultures. It is in this sense that one can agree with Redclift's comment that chewing gum is an 'icon of modernity'.

So, why this particular historical context for a bloke who paints on discarded chewing gum?

As discussed elsewhere in this book, art and politics are problematic and this is further borne out by the responses to the article on the Web as it was originally written by Esther Leslie. Comments from readers make their own links from Ben Wilson to the politics of

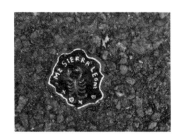

Chewing gum paintings by Ben Wilson, London. http://bit.ly/bubblegum_art

crime of which he was accused; criminal damage. His is politics already instituted and already probed by an art practice that tests its own possibility of being in the most exposed way. At the time of writing in 2007, Wilson was involved in a court case brought by the Crown Prosecution Service. He was charged with obstruction for he dallied in handing over his camera when asked by a policeman. His argument was that he had not completed and documented his commission and would be breaking the terms of the relationship with his patron. As the case continued, the City of London magistrates' court was treated to expositions on environmental art and the socially curative powers of public acts of creativity!

This little incident is part of a shift of power relations on London streets. It is significant that it happened in the City of London, where paranoia about terrorism is at its highest. But it is also a reflection of an attitude, reinforced by the police, that unlicensed, or unprofitable activities, in socially shared spaces are illegitimate or 'mad'. What might be the possibilities of reclaiming public space as a place of non-commodified expression? Do you have to become like a 'street person' or 'marginal' to exist as a human in the streets?

See further images here
www.limitedlanguage.org/images

the slow movement[i-ii] or, in another example, to a Marxist call regarding the 'abstraction of social relations?'[iii] and even de-couple him from the political, as a non-event.[iv] The historical context above situates Wilson's work in a timeline of artistic practice, whilst bringing into focus the contingency of production. Wilson is clear about his social (political) role: 'Our environment is very controlled and what we need so very strongly is diversity. Even galleries, museums, publishing companies are all very controlled. I want to be able to do my work and bypass bureaucracy.'[4] Here he is articulating his practice as a political one.

The rationale for his work is intrinsic to its production: 'I know a lot of the shopkeepers, road sweepers and local police. As I walk down the street, every few steps I think of a picture I have to do for someone...which makes me feel closer to the place and the people.'[5] But how the work is disseminated – social distribution – is extrinsic and provides a disarticulation from the artist's social aims. It is the World Wide Web which drives a network of distribution.

Wilson is aware of this other audience when he comments, 'The pictures [of his work] have their own life...we live in a digital world. The pictures move around. People take pictures on their mobile phones, send them to their friends.'[6]

This process of dissemination is also part of the contemporary notion of visibility – a visibility which the miniature format gently transgresses. Google Maps, Genome Mapping, Digital imaging, CCTV are all elements of this need to see – even the enforced DNA test that Wilson suffered at the hands of the police is part of this need to record – make visible. The World Wide Web (as database) is a natural progression in visualising the world as carrying on from the 19th century anthropological preoccupation of classification. Both phenomena prove a way of narrating the world.

The database and narrative have been central to many of the debates on the role of digital culture: the digital theorist Lev

Manovich was a major instigator of the debate. And latterly he asks, in the context of globalisation: 'How...to represent the typical modern experience of living "between layers" – between the past and the present, between East and West, between there and here?'[7]

It is the between layers that is the best way to conceptualise the reception of Wilson's work. The initial responses to Leslie's original essay, each take a different political, methodological or banal slice in how to understand the work.

Manovich sees the database as a cultural form which is anti-narrative: 'the database represents the world as a list of items, and it refuses to order this list. In contrast, a narrative creates a cause and effect trajectory of seemingly unordered items (events). Therefore, database and narrative are cultural enemies. Competing for the same territory of human culture, each claims an exclusive right to make meaning out of the world.'[8]

But in the dissemination of Wilson's artworks the reverse is true. It is the database of the World Wide Web which provides the narrative. This is a narrative curated on social networking sites such as Flickr where an interest group has specifically been created which is dedicated to photographing and showcasing Wilson's work. It is the accompanying image tags which create the narrative structure. Socially generated tags (often referred to as folksonomies) have become useful in social networking sites where social collaborations are being constructed. Networks of different interest groups such as art, writing, fascism etc., can live independent 'virtual lives', but share commonalties in their tagging infrastructure. This possibility of database and narrative structure is supported by Marsha Kinder who sees narrative as having a more ideological imperative, which is missing from Manovich:

'By database narratives, I am referring to narratives whose structure exposes or thematizes the dual processes of selection and combination that lie at the heart of all stories...the selection of particular data (characters, objects, settings, sounds, events) from a series of databases or paradigms, which are then combined to generate specific tales. Such narratives reveal the possibility of making other combinations, which would create alternative stories, and they encourage us to question the choice of categories and of what is included and omitted.'[9]

This more 'open' interpretation of the possibilities of narrative within the framework of World Wide Web/Database cultures is evidenced in the digital community which is attached to Ben Wilson, either tangentially or by notions of taste, geography and general interests etc.

Googling *chewing gum art Ben Wilson* at the time of writing gets 18,200[10] hits ranging from www.thisislocallondon.co.uk to the BBC World Service; Yahoo groups to Flickr and, of course, Limited Language.

When you leave the locale of the pavement where Wilson is working and interacting with his immediate community, what you find is an atomisation of audiences which does not necessarily mean an overarching democracy of taste, or even an appreciation of Wilson's political stance, but that of a Community and alternative spaces for interaction. What you find is a mapping of alternative cultures, from the banal to the transgressive.

Just as Wilson's artwork can be mapped onto its antecedents, so too can the technologies that provide its dissemination, especially the World Wide Web. The Web might provide a digital weave of new narratives but, it's worth noting Dorothy Kidd's concern about issues of 'sustainability; labour and power divisions...by gender. Some of these questions, of who gets supported, to say what, through which medium, are achingly familiar.'[11]

See full responses + carry on the conversation here
http://tiny.cc/chapter2_3

Reader credits
l   Rob Best 12/10/2007 – on slowness: 'Not only an
       obvious inversion of the big, brash, fast-changing

commercial image scape, but operating in inverse proportion to the amount of controversy it has caused at the level of those who regulate the streets.'

II   Michael Newman 30/10/2007 – on slowness: 'Making your self an obstruction, literally by moving at a different pace, is an act of emasculation in the contemporary urban environs of cities. Think of the 'work to rule protests' in the 70s – not withdrawing your labour but working on a different temporal terrain. Ben works in the same interstice – it is not the artwork of protest but rather a critique of the flow of capitalism, which our city streets are a synecdoche for.'

III John Russell 07/11/2007 – on the abstraction of social relations: 'I thought this was meant to NOT be about simple binary oppositions – so how come you're talking about SLOWNESS/immovability as a critique of the FLOW of capital; or relationality as opposed to the abstraction of social relations?'

IV   Alan Beardmore 21/11/2007 – on the non-political: 'Has Ben Wilson got nothing better to do with his time? Why try to intellectualise what is, er, a non event?'

References

1   Charles William Day, *The Art of Miniature Painting* (London: Winsor and Newton, 1852), 11-12.

2   Dudley Heath, *Miniatures*, The Connoisseur's Library (New York; London: G.P. Putnam's: Methuen and Co., 1905), 319.

3   Michael Redclift, *Chewing Gum: The Fortunes of Taste* (New York; London: Routledge, 2004), 197.

4   Julia Elmore, 'Art on Chewing Gum: Ben Wilson' in *Raw Vision*, No. 55 (Summer 2006), 32-6.

5   Ibid.

6   Ibid.

7   Lev Manovich quoted in Peter Brunette, 'Book Review: Soft Cinema: Navigating the Database', *Journal of Visual Culture*, Vol. 5, No. 3 (2006), 411-14.

8   Lev Manovich, 'Database as Symbolic Form' in *Convergence*, Vol. 5, No. 2 (1999): 80-99.

9   Marsha Kinder, 'Honoring the Past and Creating the Future in Cyberspace: New Technologies and Cultural Specificity' in *The Contemporary Pacific* 15 (Spring 2003), 113.

10 Google search (18 March 2009)

11 Dorothy Kidd quoted in Chris Atton, *An Alternative Internet* (Edinburgh: Edinburgh University Press, 2004), 6.

Mario Moura
Work ethics

How much of this can we take?

When we leaf through design directories, we seldom wonder whether the work we see was paid or credited or whether the designer was ethically, politically or religiously coerced in any way. Designers somehow manage to keep themselves above the harsher realities of their own society in a plane of abstract, neutral mediation. The very presence of design, and graphic design in particular, in any given society may be presented as an index of freedom of expression. And yet, few people look into the subtle modes of restraint and control that permeate the magazine-lined white cubes of the design studios.

Designers so often see their job as value-free or ethically neutral. All they have to do to keep it that way is follow the rules and do the best job possible, regardless of beliefs and values (their own and their clients') and the possible effects of their work. When designers want ethics, they generally turn to 'outside' sources. In other words, design is ethical when it works for ethical clients (NGOS) or uses ethical materials (recycled paper) or encompasses ethical subjects (peace demonstrations), whilst remaining neutral on all other occasions. These causes are undoubtedly worthy but are we, in fact, objectifying ethics? Are we limiting them to certain accepted practices, while forgetting that design itself is an industrial activity with specific internal ethics and politics that remain largely unobserved?

Websites, corporate identities or magazines are, more often than not, designed by surprisingly large groups of people structured in hierarchies. The fact that the task itself is creative only makes these hierarchies more tense and difficult to manage. As the work of Italian philosopher Antonio Negri[1] demonstrates, there is an ongoing evolution from industries based on the mass production of commodities (material labour) to modes of production based on intellectual, creative work (immaterial labour). This change requires the

The environment, sexism, racism, ageism... Why should people care and what do we do with those who don't? Rosi Braidotti, in her book *Transpositions: On Nomadic Ethics* suggests these are the questions we need to face. A dilemma then, for all ethics and politics is this: 'How do you make people want to be free, generous, decent and caring?'[1]

A satisfying definition of ethics is hard to find. Generally it can be understood to be about a moral responsibility to others.[2] However, this invokes universal, timeless ideals and whilst we might abstractly agree with them, the question is whether we act on them. For Braidotti, to be ethical is to be accountable. Her interest is discovering the conditions most conducive to cultivating and sustaining change. So, whilst you can tell people to be green (or whatever else) all you like, it won't necessarily affect their behaviour. Braidotti argues that, 'Not rationality, but rather affectivity counts here; it is a question of "wanting to", of desire.'[3] In one instance, this wanting becomes central to the dilemma of *Green. Who cares?* a report on consumer behaviour and green branding by Composite Projects.[4]

This desire to care is also a perennial problem for Mario Moura's original blog, which called for a work ethics for design. Here he lamented that when design invokes ethics, it usually locates them externally within particular, well-established areas for concern: design for the environment, housing etc. This allows the operations of design, as an industrial practice, to remain unobserved. It is one of the key obstacles to ethical design practice. For Moura, ethics needs to start at home. In replies to the article on the Limited Language website, a series of ethical issues for the work place came forth.[I-VII] But, beyond focus on

Knit Chair, Designed by Emiliano Godoy. The strong, flexible rope connections allow the chair to adapt to the user's body and movements. All materials, glues and coatings are natural and biodegradable. www.godoylab.com

development of new ways to control a workforce that is radically different from the traditional factory worker. Some of these techniques of control are examined in the works of Edward Said[2] and Noam Chomsky.[3]

Obviously these techniques of control have to be embedded in the discourse and methods of every practitioner at every stage of their career. During their formative years, designers undergo a behavioural conditioning of sorts that effectively blinds them to the industrial nature of their own profession. While at school, designers are trained to be creative loners who sporadically work as part of a group, whereas out in industry they are frequently small cogs in complex corporate machines consisting almost entirely of designers employed in different capacities. Designers are trained to deal with clients who know nothing about design and who only want their problems solved. As it turns out, in the 'real world', designers deal primarily with other designers. Their employers are often designers and their co-workers are often designers. The myth of the designer as a creative loner is an effective way of diverting attention away from the middleman and, in fact, from the entire labour structure of the design profession. This labour structure, far from being an abstraction, reproduces local and global social dynamics and restraints.

A valuable way of connecting design to local realities and problems would be to see it as a concrete job, produced by people who are part of their own society and vulnerable to its pressures and shortcomings. A better knowledge of how design's inner workings and tensions operate locally would undoubtedly contribute to deepen the range of its overall ethical concerns. While it is comfortable to keep ethical, political and social concerns restricted to conveniently external goals, we tend to forget that design has internal ethics and politics. I'm not saying that we should forget the larger picture. My point is that the politics and ethics of the design workspace are part of that larger picture.

particular problems and the individuals involved, it was Joseph who addressed how work ethics connect to world ethics and, as importantly, why designers might care: 'How can design be taken seriously as a voice, or visual platform, against say, female body/ objectification, if the internal politics of most studios, client relationships etc are ingrained, both linguistically and structurally, on gender lines...? Posters decorate the world not change it.'[VIII]

The bottom line here is that we can't talk of ethics when the fundamental other – gender for instance – has not been addressed. A Body Shop poster bearing the graffiti 'less packaging, more beautiful' reminds (perhaps inadvertently) that it's not recycling that's the issue, but the promotion of beauty.

Communication design forms part of the decorative surfaces of the world, but it can also be a powerful device for mediating care. One strength is the way it connects the personal to the global, the micro to the macro. We see this in advertising, but we can also see it in the device of the carbon footprint. This simple bodily metaphor of human act-and-effect gave people, from individuals to governments and from corporations to countries, the same scale to check their own emissions against global ones. Whatever the criticisms of the science, it's hard to deny this communication device captured the popular environmental imagination in a way successive campaigners and their actions, designers and their posters have so often failed to do.

The issues may belong to the global or collective imagination, but the channels through which we can meaningfully act are located in the micro-politics of the everyday. This lends itself well to Moura's call for ethics to start in the work place. And yet a problem of 'personalisation', especially in a consumer capitalist framework, is that it too often puts the onus on individual (consumer) change. Whereas, in reality, this means nothing without support from the top: company, government etc. In the UK, the not-for-profit consultancy *Three Trees Don't Make a Forest*[5] and the related website *Lovely as a Tree*[6] offer environmental support for design consultancies between the two spheres.[7]

In *Cradle to Cradle*, Michael Braungart and William McDonough remind us: 'More control (being "less bad") is not the same as being good.'[8] The planet still gets depleted, it just takes longer. The overarching aim of their thesis is change at all levels, which involves questioning self-interest, not just extending it. For instance, adding an environmentally-friendly paper option or 'ethical strata' to a company or design course can often be no more than just good business sense. The term 'cradle to cradle' is about waste no longer being an afterthought (cradle to grave) but considered as a design problem. A design's next life has to be imagined from the start. For instance, the first edition of the *Cradle to Cradle* book was made out of polymer, a plastic where the ink can be washed off and the sheets re-used. The authors admit this isn't much use for a book to be kept forever but, the idea was soon taken up by a newspaper. The, idea, here is to design a future for products.

Cradle to Cradle is coy about the question of ethics: 'Don't make it an ethical question,' they tell us, 'make it a quality-of-life problem.'[9] But do these have to be mutually exclusive? Returning to Braidotti, she argues for a kind of pragmatics too but through the concept of sustainability. Sustainability attempts to come to terms with processes and interrelations across areas not usually connected. Sustainability can simply be assessed by asking the question: 'How much of this can we take?' This question goes beyond environmentalism and is able to connect across all ethical issues (racism, sexism, ageism etc.), all working practices, inside and outside of industry and at all levels; by clients, designers, ordinary people, government and so on. It goes beyond left or right, social constructivism or hippy idealism. It's about accountability.

Nor does sustainability discount pleasure – for either Braidotti or the *Cradle to*

See further images here
www.limitedlanguage.org/images

References

1   For instance see Michael Hardt and Antonio Negro, *Empire* (Cambridge, MA: Harvard University Press, 2000).
2   Particularly in Edward Said, *Representations of the Intellectual: The 1993 Reith Lectures*.
3   Noam Chomsky, *Necessary Illusions* (Cambridge, MA: South End Press, 1989).

Cradle ethos. If the answer is yes, we can take it, then fine. If the answer is that we, or the environment or our colleagues or what and whoever else, can't take much more, then it is unsustainable.

As a work ethics, sustainability is about accepting the limits of what designers can (or ought to) engage in and what they can endure.[10]

Allan Chochinov, teacher of industrial and product design, provides a good example of getting his students to question nearly every stage of their design process, including why they might be designing a product at all. He gives an example which is inspired by Ezio Manzini's *Sustainable Everyday Project*[11] where, in addressing the separate 'problems' of care for ill children and lonely elderly in the US, one outcome was neighbourhood-based childcare facilities staffed by the elderly. This resonates with an initiative in the UK, where housing young single people and support for old people did not result in new designs for single-unit flats or buzzer devices connected to the local doctor. Instead, they were brought together so elders with a room to spare rented it for free to the young in return for a small exchange of help. This way of thinking dovetails with service design which, from context to context, looks at 'modifying behavior, redistributing assets, goods, activities, talent, and seeks to improve the situation or contribute something new into the world'.[12]

It's this issue of addressing behaviour which links back to Braidotti. Braidotti suggests that in practice, ethics has two phases: a critical or reactive phase and an affirmative and active phase. The first is critical of the inert repetition of habit, as discussed in the examples above.[13] The other is the issue that this piece started with: how we cultivate and sustain the desire for change. Had we taken them in order, the first question ought not to have been, 'How much of this can we take?' but 'Do we need design at all?'

See full responses + carry on the conversation here
http://tiny.cc/chapter2_4

Reader credits

I   Joe D 18/11/2005 – on gender and race.
II   Gary Johansen 04/12/2005 – on crèche facilities, racism, transport, dentists etc.
III Arberor Hadri 06/12/2005 – on the ethics of charging charities for work.
IV   Anon 07/12/2005 – on double standards and 'lump it or leave'.
V   Rachel M 14/12/2005 – on standing up for what they think.
VI   Dhruv Kalan 15/12/2005 – on selling alcohol or not.
VII Zoe Collington 16/12/2005 – on style (and good pay) over substance.
VIII Joe D 18/11/2005.

References

1   Rosi Braidotti, *Transpositions: On Nomadic Ethics* (Cambridge, UK; Malden, MA: Polity Press, 2006), 205.
2   See for instance Paul Nini, 'In Search of Ethics in Graphic Design' in *Voice: AIGA Journal of Design*, 16 August (2004) www.aiga.org/content.cfm/in-search-of-ethics-in-graphic-design (accessed 14/05/09).
3   Rosi Braidotti, Op cit., 205.
4   www.composite-projects.com/content/recent_projects/rp_green.htm
5   www.threetreesdontmakeaforest.org
6   www.lovelyasatree.com (at the time of writing, soon to be amalgamated with the above).
7   See also Anna Gerber 'Design and Sustainability 1, 2 & 3' in *Creative Review*, November 2008 – January 2009.
8   Michael Braungart and William McDonough, *Cradle to Cradle: Re-making the Way We Make Things* (London: Vintage Books, 2009), 4.
9   Ibid., 12.
10   Rosi Braidotti, Op cit., 206-9.
11   www.sustainable-everyday.net/manzini/
12   Chochinov quoted in Steven Heller, 'To Design or Not to Design: A Conversation with Allan Chochinov' in *Voice: AIGA Journal of Design*, 17 February (2009), www.aiga.org/content.cfm/to-design-or-not-to-design-a-conversation-with-allan-chochinov (accessed 03/05/09).
13   These are of course only two; see also John Thackara, *In the Bubble: Designing for a Complex World* (Cambridge, MA: MIT, 2005).

Aaris Sherin
Escape from the tyranny of things

Several months ago, I was asked by a journalist to comment on the excessive consumption of technology by designers. She wanted to know if there ought to be rules dictating how long a person should be required to keep electronics and computer equipment. It occurred to me then that even though Americans consider themselves to be fiercely independent, most of us love to be told what to do. It's easy to think that we are one certification or set of regulations away from reversing the negative impact that humans are having on the environment. The reality is both more complicated and nuanced. If a designer needs new equipment to complete a motion graphics piece about the destruction of natural habitat, and the piece results in large tracts of land being set aside for sustainable agriculture, then who would argue that the replacement of the computer hardware was unwarranted? The right balance of consumption and use of resources is more the stuff of personal responsibility and individual circumstance than it is appropriate fodder for regulatory authorities. That being said, there is no doubt that those of us residing in the developed world are consuming more than our fair share of resources, largely at the cost of those living in the developing world. The question remains, what to do about it?

In *Toothpicks and Logos: Design in Everyday Life*,[1] John Heskett argues that a postmodern interest in ideas and meaning has been covertly appropriated as a means of creating and selling consumers useless, expensive and exclusive goods that rarely fulfil an actual need. Luxury and our desire for it is nothing new, but what luxury means has been redefined and is now primarily about name-association and branding as opposed to fine materials and higher quality construction. After World War II, a burgeoning middle class meant not only more disposable income but also an explosion of aspirational consumption. Products became badges of social status and economic

Sustainable design

Aaris Sherin's essay opens up many of the concerns and debates about the role of design/designers in a sustainable economy – it was an essay that addressed consciousnesses (as opposed to material things) and this was reflected in the replies it drew from the Limited Language readership.

'...we don't have a mission as designers and we only have the power to do something if we act as individuals'.[1]

The above comment captures the paradigm shift needed in obtaining any sense of a sustainable world: it is through a process of thinking – personal agency – rather than instrumental problem solving alone. Designers cannot choose the problem to solve but rather, through the correct questioning, they can make the problem apparent. These thinking/psychological processes have been called 'metadesign'.[1]

Put simply, what we mean by this is, for example, introducing recycled materials into the production/design of a disposable coffee cup might solve the problem of saving a few trees (or the ozone) but it erases (or at least masks) the real question of: why coffee? Why take-away? Why disposable etc., etc.?

To expand this premise we need to look to the reasoning of inventor Saul Griffith. Griffith is quoted in Sherin's original article due to his interest in the relationship between energy/consumption and design. His reasoning might lead us to ask: how many joules of energy are needed to make a disposable coffee cup compared to a ceramic mug, a glass or a flask? And, crucially, what is the energy expenditure over the life of the object? Furthermore, do we covet the design of a paper cup like we might a hand-made ceramic mug, or the sculptural form of a Marcello Morandini cup and saucer

Advert by Enoch Bolles (1937). The Zippo Manufacturing Company was founded by George G. Blaisdell who chose the word 'Zippo' in 1932. He liked the sound of the word 'zipper' so he formed different variations on the word and settled on Zippo, deciding that it had a 'modern' sound.

The first Zippo lighters sold for $1.95 each. And, from the very beginning, they were backed by Mr. Blaisdell's unconditional lifetime guarantee – 'It works or we fix it free.', http://tinyurl.com/ldudyf

achievement regardless of how well they were produced. In her 2005 book, *The Uncommon Life of Common Objects*,[2] Akiko Busch writes about seemingly ordinary products including cereal boxes, a snowboard, a desk and an Adirondack chair all of which carry cultural significance. Busch's objects take on a dreamy, reverent place in our psyches and this gives them value and in some cases staying power.

That objects are richly embedded with meaning is certain. What is less sure is whether greater acknowledgement of this relationship might help us to become better owners and, therefore, better consumers. This is not a small point because objects have, for decades, been made to have finite lives. Manufacturers are terrified of what might happen if products were so ecologically and functionally well made that consumers wouldn't need to replace them. The question of how to keep a viable economy going while using less weighs heavily on the mind of inventor and renewable energy innovator Saul Griffith.

Griffith, from whom the term heirloom consumption was borrowed, is an energy junky. He states the job of the designer simply: 'It is to make us use less, allow the developing world to use more, while increasing everyone's quality of life.'[3] Griffith believes that it will be necessary to reduce the embodied energy in objects if we want to keep the earth at a temperature that can sustain human life. In practical terms this will require designers to be more efficient, and to make things either very lightweight or last ten times as long. Certainly our conception of products will have to change if we are expected to spend decades with them. Some companies and designers have already begun to explore what a new terrain for objects might look like. Inax Corporation, a manufacturer of tiling, building materials and sanitary fixtures based in Japan, uses the technique of backcasting to imagine future products that have a subtly different relationship to their owners. A bath that fills with warm foam bubbles gives comfort without wasting precious water

for instance: which do we hand on to our family or friends; as a heirloom and a representation of our good taste?

A coveted, or loved object, can be its link to sustainability – we want to keep it rather than replace with a newer model! Of course the flipside of this thinking is the peril of consumer fetishism – where we only buy the product in the first place when we are told it is to be coveted.

So much greenery in design (graphic communication is especially at fault here) has played a peek-a-boo game with questions on sustainability and use: the first question should always be why does it need to be designed? For every design is a culturally active agent, or put another way: 'Design is a political act. Every time we design a product, we are making a statement about the direction the world will move in.'[2]

This reflects in one sense, the networked world we have alluded to elsewhere in this book – the fluid nature, and the fluidity, of contemporary visual culture and its relationship to community: part of the cosmopolitan vision.[3] This allows for, not top-down relations, or even, Eurocentric, but the possibilities of a 'cultural mixture' in how design thinks and engages with the world.

For the sociologist Ulrich Beck, we all have a cosmopolitan outlook, whether it's the war on terror, or the Iraq anti-war protests, we can no longer perceive the world within the confines of our own back yards – the world intrudes and permeates our experience or as Beck himself evangelically espouses:

'For in the cosmopolitan outlook...there resides the latent potential to break out of the self-centered narcissism of the national outlook and the dull incomprehension with which it infects thought and action, and thereby enlighten human beings concerning the real, internal cosmopolitanization of their lifeworlds and institutions'.[4]

Sustainability will only work if it breaks out of the confines of green problem-solving and focuses on the holistic, process led re-engagement with the material world of design. Sustainability – as a methodology – is a collective of many initiatives made under the banner of green and environmental art and design, but places them within a broader matrix of aims and processes – what Bruce Mau named *Massive Change*.[5]

The top-down – non-relational – design practice is nowhere more damaging than in sustainable design and the need for new relational thinking, with its focus on process and community, is paramount:

'... rather than believing that we can design universally applicable blueprints to bring about sustainability by prediction and control-based, top-down engineering, it may be more useful and appropriate to think of the outcome(s) as an emergent property of the complex dynamic system in which we all participate, co-create, and adapt to interdependent biophysical and psycho-social processes'.[6]

Design not only has to see itself in the wider world of things but needs to develop relationships with consumers. As Sherin asks, what 'might help us to become better owners?'

This can be brought about by a process of education with designers becoming more explicit in the processes of their work: for how do we know design? And how can we grow to covet an object beyond simple monetary value?

Design practice, it can be argued, suffers from its accessibility and reproducibility – printed, digitised, scanned and photocopied – it literally wraps our lived experience; whilst equally, mass produced, self assembled, flat packed and rapid prototyping provide many – if not all – of the material artefacts which inform our lives. As John Heskett in his book: *Toothpicks and Logos* observes: 'design has splintered into ever-greater subdivisions of practice without any overarching concept or organization and so can be appropriated by anyone',[7] this ubiquity is compounded by its utility.

Utility itself can lead to a sense of invisibility and impermanence – more knowledge of the design process would provide a provenance that might help anchor its ephemeral

and the company's concept kitchen provides not only the usual surfaces and fixtures but also includes built-in waste disposal and recycling systems and an area for growing fresh produce.

Work shown as part of the exhibit *Design and the Elastic Mind*[4] at the Museum of Modern Art in New York skirted the edge of what might be considered marketable products. Noam Toran, a Professor in the Interactions Department at the Royal College of Art, created products to alleviate men's loneliness by providing traces of their missing companions. *Accessories for Lonely Men* (2001), a collection of eight objects, including a *Sheet Thief*, a pair of *Cold Feet*, and a *Heavy Breather*. Toran's models suggest that designers can be tasked with providing comfort and by doing so may help to alleviate our compulsion to constantly acquire more stuff. Michiko Nitta, a student in the same department, explored both our obsession with objects and our desire for physical closeness with loved ones by creating wearable products made using vitro-cultured meat production technologies (see page 219). Her concept would allow consumers to grow selected parts of their partners on their own bodies. The replica of an original nipple or patch of living hair is designed to foster memory and human connection and provides psychological rather than physical sustenance.

The Danish poet, designer and mathematician Pet Hein writes of being possessed by objects in his poem *The Tyranny of Things*. Hein suggests that if one has more than eight objects, one ends up being owned by rather than owning the things in one's life. The interchangeable use of the terms want and need has led people to think that it is their god-given right to buy the products that they desire. In the US we work harder and longer than many of our neighbours in other industrialised countries and yet we are no happier with the life that our riches have afforded.

After visiting the homes of several European designers I began to wonder whether they were on to something that the rest of us had missed. First I will say that these people are connected by the fact that they work in design and little else. They come from different countries, speak different languages, are from different generations and yet they obviously had something in common. First, they didn't have very many things; and second, the objects that they did own were well designed, usually beautiful, and almost always supremely functional. My hosts all had a near obsession with the possessions that they lived with. They knew the story of the designer, they could tell you why one teakettle was functionally superior to its competitors and they unabashedly revelled in the beauty of objects. And I began to think, 'This is what I want' ...an escape from the tyranny of things. All of which was convenient since I live in New York City, a place where having less is often dictated more by the skimpy size of apartments than by any concern over excessive consumption. I have found that the best objects are not necessarily the most expensive, and that knowing you will keep what you have purchased tends to mean that you will buy less. I thought that sustainable consumption would primarily be achieved by denying oneself the pleasure of having things. Instead, I have found that smarter choices and a greater appreciation for real rather than perceived value can make me a happier consumer and also a less wasteful one.

See further images here
www.limitedlanguage.org/images

References
1   John Heskett, *Toothpicks and Logos: Design in Everyday Life* (Oxford University Press, 2002).
2   Akiko Busch, *The Uncommon Life of Common Objects: Essays on Design and the Everyday* (New York: Metropolis Books, 2005).
3   Saul Griffith, *Compostmodern 09*, hosted by AIGA, the professional association for design in America.
4   Hugh Aldersey-Williams, Peter Hall, Ted Sargent and Paola Antonelli, *Design and the Elastic Mind* (New York: Museum of Modern Art, 2008).

nature – the Zippo lighter is a simple example of this: 'Application for the original Zippo patent was filed on May 17, 1934.... The design of the Zippo lighter basically remains the same to this day, with minor improvements'.[8] The company promotes its design credentials as part of its marketing strategy. It is the 'windproof' lighter 'that looked good and was easy to operate'.[9]

Education, especially museumology, can also help to develop better owners: so often museums focus upon, and thereby increase, the fetish value of design rather than enlightening the processes – ergonomic and production – as part of its semantic make-up. A positive example is the role of exhibitions; *Beyond Green: Toward a Sustainable Art*, curated by Stephanie Smith helps to bring design thinking and art together to look at sustainability – in this sense it can be seen to, 'respond to the zeitgeist'.[11]

To close with Stephanie Smith's opening essay in the exhibition catalogue, which begins:

'Sustainable design has the potential to transform our everyday lives through an approach that balances environmental, social, economic, and aesthetic concerns. This emerging strategy emphasizes the responsible and equitable use of resources and links environmental and social justice. By doing so, it moves past a prior generation of more narrowly eco-centered or "green" approaches.'[10]

See full responses + carry on the conversation here
http://tiny.cc/chapter2_5

Reader credits
I   helder 21/07/2009
II   Sarah 20/07/2009

References
1   '...the term "metadesign" refers to the concepts and onto-epistemological assumptions we employ to define ourselves, and to make sense of experiencing our participatory involvement in complex ecological, cultural, and social processes'. Wahl and Baxter. 'The Designer's Role in Facilitating Sustainable Solutions, *Design Issues* (2008), 73.

2   Stefano Marzano quoted in: Loe Feijs and Seaton
    Meinel, 'A Formal Approach to Product Semantics
    with an Application to Sustainable Design,' *Design
    Issues* (2005) Vol. 21, 73.

3   '…the cosmopolitan outlook is both the
    presupposition and the result of a conceptual
    reconfiguration of our modes of perception' from the
    Introduction: Ulrich Beck, *The Cosmopolitan Vision*
    (Cambridge: Polity, 2006).

4   Ibid. 2.

5   Bruce Mau and Jennifer Leonard, *Massive Change*
    (London; New York: Phaidon, 2004).

6   Daniel Christian Wahl and Seaton Baxter, 'The
    Designer's Role in Facilitating Sustainable
    Solutions,' *Design Issues* (2008), 73.

7   John Heskett, *Toothpicks and Logos: Design in
    Everyday Life* (Oxford: Oxford University Press, 2002), 7.

8   www.zippo.com/corporateInfo/index.aspx (accessed
    26/07/09). It is worth mentioning, since its inception,
    the lighter has been marketed with a whole series of
    graphic surface designs to increase its individuality
    and uses for corporate marketing.

9   Ibid.

10 Stephanie Smith, *Beyond Green: Toward a Sustainable
    Art* (Chicago, IL.: Smart Museum of Art; Bristol:
    University Presses Marketing [distributor], 2005),
    12-13.

State Britain

Rebuilding protest

In the closing years of the 1960s, the Vietnam war and sexual liberation made protest popular; a time of sit-ins, love-ins and *Woodstock*. In this milieu the young architectural group Archigram[1] created the concept of the *Instant City*, a mobile habitat that could arrive and be bolted together overnight. This provided the architectural landscape for an instant community. In 2007, walking into the Duveen Galleries situated at the heart of London's Tate Britain gallery and stumbling upon *State Britain*, an installation by artist Mark Wallinger, this somehow recalled the Archigram dream that architecture could bring change. And yet, it wasn't an instant community but instant protest that spread out before the eye.

Mark Wallinger's installation created a facsimile of the 'peace camp' that, since the early days of the Iraqi conflict, has become a popular tourist attraction in London. Brian Haw, architect of the original site, has protested outside the Houses of Parliament, day and night, since June 2001 and at the time of writing is still there. His camp is made up of the usual detritus of protest: banners; daubed white bed sheets; plastic sheeting and posters of the key protagonists, George Bush and Tony Blair. The site grew as visitors have collaged their own rudimentary additions to the portable structure of the protestor's stakeout. It's a coalition made up of religious groups, anti-war protesters and general well wishers. All have added to Brian's 'home'. From the humble beginnings of a banner or two, sleeping bag, cooker and chair, the protest crept along the pavement until it reached fifty metres or more. Like a favela, it grew imperceptibly in the shadow of Big Ben until, under a newly constituted law (the 'Serious Organised Crime and Police Act', 2005, which prohibited unauthorised demonstrations within a one kilometre radius of Parliament Square), Brian Haw's protest was raided by the police and reduced to a mere fraction of its original size.

Wallinger's *State Britain* was both artwork and

Looking back at the original article which reviewed the Mark Wallinger installation *State Britain* at the Tate Britain in 2007 (a facsimile of Brian Haw's anti-war peace camp), what captures the imagination now is not the role of art, but how the article and the comments it inspired focus on the construction of space in its material and imaginative presence.

From the late 1950s onwards, following on from Martin Heidegger's essay *Building, Dwelling, Thinking*,[1] the political/imaginative role of space was brought into focus in the writings of Gaston Bachelard, Henri Lefebvre and Michel de Certeau. All provided methodological frameworks to interrogate space emotionally, as part of the everyday and politically, as a cultural phenomenon in Europe and the USA.

Much of this thinking is captured in Bachelard's comment from his book *Poetics of Space*: 'A house that has been experienced is not an inert box. Inhabited space transcends geometrical space.'[2] The Home, for Bachelard, becomes a repository of memories, from basement to loft, where, meaning comes through occupation; a moving through space. This phenomenological perspective is counterintuitive to modernist rationalised architectural space. However, it allows an emotional depth, a psychic three-dimensionality to the modern experience.

Lefebvre endeavours to provide a conceptual framework which provides a 'unitary theory'. That is, space as physical, nature and the organic; the mental, abstract and architectonic and finally, the social, how we are actors in space. These combine to form space as social product.

It is social space/place which has preoccupied art and design, whereby they perceive space as more than a sequence of abstractions

Brian Haw's peace camp, Parliament Square (June 2001 and ongoing). 'I saw him get out of his tent a few minutes before I took this.' Brian Haw is in the middle, his tent on the right. Photograph by Jennifer Whitehead (2 February 2009).

Fabrication of *State Britain*, Mike Smith Studio (2006). Photography by Project Manager Michelle Sadgrove.

Mark Wallinger's facsimile at the Tate Britain Turner Prize (2007). Photograph by Chris John Beckett.

archive. Painstakingly recreated, Wallinger made the snaking tail of the original protest into another, equally venomous, statement on contemporary Britain. If the original protest was a place you eyed from a bus window or quickly walked past to a backdrop of traffic noise and police sirens, then the experience became completely reorientated in the context of an art gallery. It was a question of scale. For the slogans easily read at speed or distance (BEEP FOR BRIAN, CHRIST HAS RISEN INDEED!), seemed less interesting as you become aware of the minutiae of its bulk. Wallinger's installation allowed the viewer to study the sprawling encampment like an archaeological dig. One of the landmarks was a 'bloodied' T-shirt with the slogan BLIAR, which hung from a makeshift cross, forming the epicentre and one of the highest points of the piece. Overall the structure, along its length, was pockmarked with PhotoShopped images of faces (mainly of Blair and Bush) warped into nightmarish gargoyles. These fabricated images sat uncomfortably next to photographs of adults and children; dead, dying and dismembered in war zones across the world. Alongside these computer-generated images were the more traditional fare of a 1960s protest; sloganeering, transcribed Buddhist chants and peace flags. There was a large canvas by Banksy depicting heavily armed soldiers in the process of painting a peace sign; the Campaign for Nuclear Disarmament logo, blood red.

Wallinger's installation, the Tate website suggested, sits on the edge of the police exclusion zone which was enforced by the change in the law that led to the original dismantling of the site; 'Wallinger has marked a line on the floor of the galleries throughout the building, positioning State Britain half inside and half outside [of this zone]'.[2] Was this an imagined political frisson the exhibition did not need? The work was a success, or not, because it captured one man's uncynical, unmediated action: that protest can still change things. Even in the gallery, with a silent, deodorised facsimile of the original, the graphic language of protest still carried a faint clarion call to the conscience.

or texts. For Lefebvre an artwork which is simple mimesis, a facsimile of a historical event, would miss the complexities of spatial practices: 'space may be said to embrace a multitude of intersections, each with its assigned location'.[3]

Mark Wallinger has been reported as remarking that he prefers to deal with the world as it is, than with the question of what art is, so it might be unfair to scrutinise his work too harshly in relation to his spatial investigations but, that said, it is worth considering the *State Britain* installation as a statement on the importance of home in contemporary culture.

It has been said that 'Capitalism strives to distil its essence into buildings' and no more so than in the home. The home is at the centre of material culture: the family unit. Brian Haw's home is, in itself, transgressive. The capitalist notion of home is stable and fixed (mortgaged bricks and mortar), consumptive (products) and a nexus of familial codes (gender divisions, sexuality etc.).

As a home, Haw's snaking architecture of protest signs becomes a sacred place within the symbolic extents of the British Parliament. In reality, the area is one great big traffic island. It is a non-place on the edge of the River Thames, before you tumble into the residential sprawl of South London across Westminster Bridge. It is the very stillness of the original protest site which makes it stand out in the blur of traffic passing through Parliament Square.

The notion of sacred space is not fanciful in the case of Brian Haw's original protest – or in many other peace encampments: Greenham Common for instance which, during the 1980s, was a high-profile site for anti-nuclear protestors. In one sense Wallinger's fetishisation of the encampment through art is part of the process of sanctifying the place; its ritualisation.[1]

'Ritual is not an expression of or response to the "sacred"; rather, something or someone is made sacred by ritual...'[4]

Hackney Shelf 2005. Concept and design by Ryan Frank.

References
1   Archigram was a group dominating the architectural avant-garde
    in the 1960s and 1970s, see www.archigram.net/index.html
2   www.tate.org.uk/britain/exhibitions/wallinger/

Haw's protest also provides an example of the tensions between contested space: between individual and state. This, in turn, strengthens its sacredness, for: 'sacred space is inevitably contested space, a site of negotiated contests over the legitimate ownership of sacred symbols'.[5] When the site was eventually raided by police and torn-down[ll], it could be argued it was an example of defilement; desecration.

So, how can a contested notion of space, or the understanding of home, be utilised in everyday contemporary visual culture?

We only need to look at advertising to see the use of home and place in marketing. The Marlboro Man derives some of his product strength from being situated 'in place', the mythical 'Marlboro Country'. Likewise, countless products have the byline 'Homemade'.

The computer this is being typed on is branded with 'Designed by Apple in California'. Increasingly place – home, city or state – is used to differentiate the products we consume.

'In marketing, products must be denied both in terms of their similarity or difference from other objects that might occupy the same social space (in relation to competitors) and in terms of their integration in social life (in relation to consumers).'[6]

And finally, space is defined by a geography of barrier making: uptown/downtown; commercial/private. Graffiti and advertising hoardings unofficially zone our urban environs and, increasingly, we live in a digitally configured topography of wireless and Bluetooth communication. Digital technology reconfigures space and erases inside/outside in the process. These are opportunities still to be fully exploited by the design profession.

This notion of the inside/outside is exploited in the designs of Ryan Frank. His *Hackney Shelf* furniture conflates the urban outside/inside experience of public/private space. His process involves placing white boards at various points in East London and then waiting for the inevitable graffitiing of the boards. They are left for weeks until they have 'matured' to his liking. Then the boards are removed and transformed into designer furniture. This places the transgressive visual language of urban space into the interior of urban place; the home.

See full responses + carry on the conversation here
http://tiny.cc/chapter2_6

Reader credits
i   Gaby 28/02/2007 – '[Brian Haw] has been heard
    advertising the Wallinger exhibition through his
    megaphone in Parliament square...in this very
    simple gesture has turned the gallery into an
    extension of his protest ...re-asserting his voice
    into areas/institutions he could not reach. A form of
    re-orientation of the representation?'
ii Gregor 26/06/2007 – 'What the Tate tells us is this:
    On 23 May 2006, following the passing by Parliament
    of the 'Serious Organised Crime and Police Act' ·
    prohibiting hemithoraces demonstrations within
    a one kilometre radius of Parliament Square, the
    majority of Haw's protest was removed. Taken
    literally, the edge of this exclusion zone bisects Tate
    Britain. Wallinger has marked a line on the floor of
    the galleries throughout the building, positioning
    State Britain half inside and half outside the border.'

References
1   Martin Heidegger, 'Building, Dwelling, Thinking' in
    Martin Heidegger, *Poetry, Language, Thought* (New
    York: Harper & Row, 1971).
2   Gaston Bachelard and Maria Jolas, *The Poetics of
    Space* (Boston: Beacon Press, 1994).
3   Henri Lefebvre, *The Production of Space* (Oxford:
    Basil Blackwell, 1991).
4   J.Z. Smith, *To Take Place: Toward Theory in Ritual*
    (Chicago: University of Chicago Press, 1987), 183.
5   David Chidester and Edward T. Linenthal,
    American Sacred Space: Religion in North America
    (Bloomington: Indiana University Press, 1995).
6   Celia Lury, *Brands: The Logos of the Global Economy*
    (London; New York: Routledge, 2004), 198.

Tactics

Visual communication in 0.4 seconds / The buzzword and creativity
Rethinking tactile graphics: a propositional methodology / Rethinking craft
Boredom, b'dum, b'dum... / Boredom to freedom
Part of the process / Community service
Slow times... / The slow fast

This chapter explores tactics of practice; from a designer's inspiration through to making the relationship with the end user.

Keywords
Divergent thinking (87,500)
Haptic (623,000)
Process (243,000,000)
Relational (5,610,000)

Keywords and their Google hit rate in conjunction with the word design.

Visual communication in 0.4 seconds

The buzzword and creativity

'Beautiful as the chance encounter, on an operating table, of a sewing machine and an umbrella.'
(Comte de Lautreamont, *Songs of Maldoror*, 1869)[1]

For the Surrealists, the work of Lautreamont was an inspiration, and this line, taken from *Songs of Maldoror*, captures the essence of surrealist thinking, their search for the marvellous, the surreal, the eureka moment!

Some 140 years after a chance encounter between Alfred Nobel, nitroglycerine and silica created dynamite, a controlled explosion is detonated in secluded woodland in Stockholm in a deliberate attempt to capture, 'the creative moment'. At the detonator stand the Swedish design team, Front. In that moment of spark and ignition, the form of *Design in 0.4 Seconds* is created – a soft lounge chair made from the mould of the explosion.

Front's creation of 'design by explosion' can be seen as part of their broader rationale of creative thinking: 'Every product has a moment in which it is "made". Usually, though, this is implicit. We are interested in capturing – as if to freeze-frame – that very moment of making and make it explicit.' Front's real interest here is how its form is a product of randomness – a product of chance? A chance of sorts, but it's different to Lautreamont's idea, for while the form of the chair is different each time, you always know – by design – that you will get a chair (unlike René Magritte's famous pipe!). Front's experiments capture the tension between creativity and thinking, the rational and irrational. It is this tension between the two worlds of inspiration and materialism that seduced the Surrealists, who remain, as ever, relevant today. But how can their work be re-evaluated in relation to visual communication, not least for its endeavours to capture the creative impulse?

The geometric and rationalised typographic layout grid for instance, so often the basis of graphic design, would have been cheese wire around the throat of

Limited Language's original article looked at how design cultivates creativity. We looked at surrealism and contemporary practice and tried to examine, in part, a methodology for creativity – an impossible task?

Creativity itself has become a buzzword over the last ten years or so. At the beginning of the millennium *Business Week* magazine noted: 'Now the Industrial Economy is giving way to the Creative Economy' and 'the growing power of ideas'.[1]

In the 21st century, creativity has moved centre-stage; it has economic power, both materially and in its cultural capital and it has become an increasingly global language of creative enterprise!

Creativity was originally the preserve of the Genius, an intrinsic attribute of the maker that separated the creative from the mere artisan.[2] By the end of the 20th century the preserve of the genius has been overturned to a more egalitarian notion of high/low cultures – as Mike Featherstone comments, a perceived '...surface "depthlessness" of culture; the decline of the originality/genius of artistic producer'.[3] This democracy has allowed creativity to become omniscient across disciplinary traditions: creative cookery, accounting, or simply the creative.

As an element so essential to design practice, its mechanism is surprisingly underresearched. The perennial question; how do you maintain and foster creativity?

For the purpose of this essay the mechanics of creativity break down into two main productive spheres: the technical and the psychological.

Surrealism is a good example of the psychological investigation of creative output. Often simple games were used to fuel

Explosante Fixe by Man Ray (1934). © Man Ray
Trust/ADAGP, Paris and DACS, London 2009.

inspiration in surrealist thinking. André Breton wrote in his *Surrealist Manifesto* of 1924, 'We are still living under the reign of logic... But in this day and age logical methods are applicable only to solving problems of secondary interest.'[2]

Every idea has its moment of inspiration, the moment in which it takes shape, but that taking of shape isn't literal like Front's lounge chair design, where the shape captures what is already there. If design creativity is driven by intention, then the Surrealists wanted to shake up convention. André Breton said that 'beauty should be convulsive' – ideas and objects can be transformed into something else through representation. The Surrealists had many rationales for excavating such inspiration, capturing the moment that bridges thinking with the beautiful, the sublime. One that is relevant here is the explosante fixe, literally a fixed explosion: a camera can capture what the eye cannot see – creating a new reality out of the fabric of our day-to-day world. So, a photograph by Man Ray captures a whirling dancer whose seductive figure, at the split second of shutter release, is transformed into a sensuous lily.

...and strange objects come together in a poem, or elsewhere, and spark the imagination. Like an explosion in a moment of quiet repose...

In these 'illogical' methods, can we find new ways to make solving the problems of visual communication of primary interest?

See further images here
www.limitedlanguage.org/images

References
1   Comte de Lautreamont, *Songs of Maldoror* (1869).
2   André Breton, *First Manifesto of Surrealism* (1924).

the surrealist spirit, its ideological aim of overturning the expected and repeatable in creative production. In the Surrealist game *Exquisite Corpse*, one person sets down a line on a page, folds it over, and hands it to the next. Once the page has been fully circulated amongst those present, the resulting 'poem' is conceived without consciousness intervening. The name derives from the first line produced in this way: the exquisite/corpse/shall drink/ the new/wine.

Many contemporary designers like Swedish design group Front, and in Germany, Jerszy Seymour, use technology to catalyse the relationship between materials and creative processes. Both, as we will see, provide very different interpretations.

In a world of increasingly convergent media the need for divergence – divergent thinking – is required to stop the techno-homogenisation of the creative process. This fear is articulated by Jon Wozencroft in his response to our original essay – in the field of sonics he comments:

'As for sound, we pass through various versions of the photocopier – tape, minidisc, CDRS and downloads. Software programs like Pro Tools do give myriad options for abstraction but the impact on (sonic) culture is more determined by the mode of delivery, not origination any more. There is no more Frank Sinatra or Joy Division I do suspect. Tricky, where are you?'[1]

It is in the Frank Sinatra era of the 1950s, in psychology and education that we begin to see a methodical investigation of the role of creativity. The work of American Psychologist, J.P. Guilford, is important to our understanding of creativity as an everyday process, and his early studies introduce the importance of divergent thinking, commenting: 'Most of our problem solving in everyday life involves divergent thinking. Yet, in our educational practices, we tend to emphasise teaching students how to find conventional answers.'[4]

Later (in the era of Joy Division!) this notion of divergent/conventional is mirrored

Design by motion. Front Design.

'Vases in movies are doomed to break – it's a part of a vases function. [Front] made a vase with built in fall, where the motion is one with the object'.
http://bit.ly/front_motion

by another psychologist, Abraham Maslow,[5] who introduced the notion of a two-tiered conception of the creative impulse: primary and secondary. The primary urge to creativity is subconscious and strives for the new experience. The secondary is our logical understanding of the world where creativity is built on our life or learned experience. The latter equates to the 'problem solving' tasks often associated with design. Whilst the former is the surrealist endeavour, Jenny Wright has suggested a more contemporary example of 'The Beat Generation ... looking at ways to jolt inspiration into life: From drug taking to the "cut-up" method of writing.'[11]

More recently in an overview of the literature, Mumford et al. conclude that the commonality in defining creativity is that it represents 'the production of novel, socially valued products'.[6] This is a valuable definition in contemporary design; social value can be sustainability itself, and the novel is often driven by a quest for sustainable materials.

The relationship between materials and divergent thinking is dynamically evidenced in the work of Jerszy Seymour. Whereas Front's designs, as discussed in the original article, are looking at process as a thing of and in itself, for Seymour the process becomes synonymous with the collective: the connections. His work uses new materials as a catalyst, not for product invention alone, but for the possibilities of thinking, communication and social interaction. One such event is *First Supper*, where the designer provides a micro-environment for a social event including the facilities for cooking and the production of the furniture needed to seat and feed a large crowd. Part of the installation included an impromptu library of books that the designer had read in the run-up to the production. His work interlocks thinking with industrial processes – whether it is the use of new organic plastics produced as a by-product of potato cultivation (polylactic acid) or using wax as a metaphor for connecting materials and emotions.

His philosophy is, 'doing, being and

sharing' and much of his work looks at the possibilities of the collective and creativity. Whether it is stacking chairs for Magis or Molineux hairdryers, you cannot help but think of dinner parties or teenage sleep-overs: places of communication.

His use of open source technology to make designs freely available and his thought-mapping project *The Amateur Diagram* which is described as an open source pie, further emphasises the use of communication as a conduit to creativity.

His philosophy of the Amateur was first cited as a form of practice by Asger Jorn, the Situationist who 'idealised the "free artist" as a "professional amateur,"'[7] and actively campaigned against specialisms. This position allows the designer access (and possible re-evaluation) to the languages and processes of design; and its creative possibilities.

This philosophy is captured in Seymour's *New Order Chair*, the nucleus of which is the ever-present plastic garden chair. In the hands of the Amateur its structure is unsutured and then reconfigured to allow access to the dynamics of a chair. The physical mechanics of tension, balance, and material which are erased from modern day processes of production are made explicit, we can see how the chair works: it becomes a contemporary piece of constructivist furniture.

This exposure of the hidden, the invisible, is also reflected in his use of polyurethane foam. A material usually hidden – literally beneath the skin of designed objects – becomes amorphous and dangerous in his *Scum* works. The scum installations combine the modernist dream of quick and repeatable production, with a darker contemporary notion of violence and unpredictability.

Seymour's work represents the two loci of creativity: the psychological and the mechanical. He provides a seamless connection between the simple problem-solving design of the day-to-day with the 1920s magical realism of imagination and ideology.

In conclusion, creativity of the primary,

First Supper by Jerszy Seymour (2008).

First Supper is a nowhere place, an amateur
soup and an open ended utopian question
mark. it is cooked on a non commodity flame,
and made with ingredients of doing, sharing
and being. should it exist? could it exist? what
will we eat? what will we talk about? you are
invited to dinner by jerszy seymour and the
coalition with love. please enjoy and viva la
utopia!

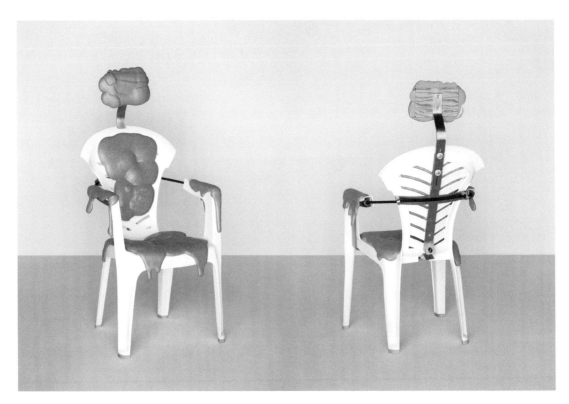

New Order Chair by Jerszy Seymour (2007).

Advertising and marketing are at the forefront in
the research and application of divergent thinking
strategies of creative thinking!
Ted Baker, London, Christmas 2007.

subconscious kind discussed will often come out of collisions between materials, processes and thinking. The eureka moment is a constellation rather than a strike out of the blue.

See full responses + carry on the conversation here
http://tiny.cc/chapter3_1

Reader credits
I   Jon Wozencroft 08/10/2006
II Jenny Wright 08/10/2006 – The Beat Generation
    were also looking at ways to jolt inspiration into life:
    From drug taking to the 'cut-up' method of writing.
    What would be interesting to look into would be how
    digital technology makes many of these avant-garde
    practices part of the day-to-day creation of visual
    work. Many of the practices that once hot wired
    our creative impulse are common and everyday in
    our visually mediated world. This is why the role of
    touch and sound are coming to the fore... How we
    bring these senses into our day-to-day practices is
    something both commercial practice and education
    need to address – interactivity is more than screen
    based interaction. We need to realise this otherwise
    we end up with a world that is out of balance –
    screen over touch!

References
1   Businessweek Online: 28 August 2000 issue.
    http://bit.ly/business_week
2   See for instance, Rozsika Parker and Griselda
    Pollock, Old Mistresses: Women, Art and Ideology
    (London: Routledge & Kegan Paul, 1981).
3   Mike Featherstone, Consumer Culture and
    Postmodernism (London; Newbury Park, CA: Sage
    Publications, 1991), 164.
4   J.P. Guilford, Intelligence, Creativity, and Their
    Educational Implications (San Diego, CA: R.R.
    Knapp, 1968), 8.
5   Abraham Maslow, American psychologist who
    described the concept of 'hierarchy of needs' which
    has been very influential in Management Psychology:
    http://bit.ly/psych_business
6   Lewis Mumford, Technics and Civilization [Electronic
    Resource]. (New York: ACLS History E-Book Project,
    2005).
7   Simon Sadler, The Situationist City (Cambridge, MA;
    London: MIT Press, 1998), 233.

Julia Moszkowicz

Rethinking tactile graphics:
a propositional methodology

There is a widely recognised tendency within contemporary graphic design towards the production of work
that intentionally asserts its off-screen condition, placing
itself in the context of a fully rounded three-dimensional
world of the maker and his or her creative process. From
the textile assemblages of Lizzie Finn to the embroi-
dered newspapers of Karen Reimer, graphic designers
and artists are actively generating artefacts that, initially
at least, resolutely occupy the time and space of hand-
rendered production. They emerge as objects of design,
which are then made ready for contemporary cultures
of consumption. As the work of Julien Vallée testifies,
they are invariably transposed into slick imagery, transformed from highly structured paper installations, in this
instance, into a book jacket design for *Tactile: High Touch
Visuals*[1] and a tele-visual sting for MTV.

Typically, designers and critics have discussed such
work in terms of their tactile attributes, describing
how off-screen artefacts bring a sense of touch and the
whole haptic sensorium (back) into play. In *Touch Graphics*,[2] for example, Rita Street proposes that 'handmade
work conveys a sense of personal contact between the
sender and the recipient because it's not something you
just look at but also have to handle. Even if it's printed
in some aspect, the tactile element makes the printing
seem more personal.' In this sense, 'tactile design' is
viewed in terms of a craft revival, inserting the hand-
rendered artefact into an oppositional relationship with
digital techniques, even though it frequently (and ironically) ends up being channelled through computer-based
systems of post-production and distribution. Indeed, it
is frequently signalled as the return of 'the hand'.[3]

Generally, these objects of design are interpreted as
creative and humane responses to digital imagery which
is eroding the heartfelt immediacy of handmade work. As
a result, many interpretations of tactile design are viewed

Rethinking craft

Tactile graphics ...characterised as a turn to
the hand-made (and away from digital)... If this
is a revival of sorts, what are we reviving?

In the original article Julia Moszkowicz
welcomes this momentary focus on production – the enjoyment in materials and making,
craft and skill – but argues, that as objects,
they invariably become (digitally) transposed
into the slick imagery of contemporary consumption. Instead, Moszkowicz locates the
tactile-turn within a broader interest in
design process. This return to a materiality
of things can be seen in the work of Karen
Reimer; her work is an attempt to isolate
handwork, or labour, and make it the central
process of her design by making 1:1 embroi-
dered copies of everyday mass-produced
'graphic' objects such as a gum wrapper. Here,
the value – or 'aura' – is the focus on making
and, by extension, the labour of production,
since the thing itself, is trash.

As a departure from this, Moszkowicz
proposes a revisiting of Gestalt psychology, as
a methodology which can possibly illuminate
design as process. This includes creativity and
intuition which are so often seen as ephemeral, and beyond the domain of criticism or
methodological scrutiny.

But what is missing from the original
article is an engagement with craft itself, as a
possible point of departure or re-evaluation
of contemporary (including digital) cultures.

In *The Culture of Craft*, Peter Dormer
comments on how: 'Craft relies on tacit
knowledge. Tacit knowledge is acquired
through experience and it is the knowledge
that enables you to do things as distinct
from talking or writing about them....'[1] This
provides an alternative methodology where
'making is thinking', as sociologist Richard

Sennett maps out in *The Craftsman*.[2]

Using Sennett's framework, Craft becomes an inter-disciplinary practice which can be found anywhere where an engagement with creativity, skills, tools and materials takes place: from computer programming to pencil sketches, through to the loop of the stitch.

This trajectory is also found in *Abstracting Craft: The Practiced Digital Hand*, where Malcolm McCullough reminds us we live at a time where 'designing' has so often become deskilled; abstracted to a series of pre-defined choices on drop-down menus.[3] Knowledge gained through making is open-ended and not discipline specific, equally able to foster old techniques through repetition or innovation of new ones – even with zeros and ones!

This openness of craft as a methodology dovetails well with Gestalt, where as Moszkowicz puts it, 'the Tacit encapsulate[s] that Gestalt principle of setting out with a sense of not-knowing (exactly) where things are going, being open to the possibility of taking practical steps and undertaking the "adequate" filling of gaps. It is only later, with a retrospective gaze, that one can conceptualize and systematize this experimental attitude'.[4]

A systematisation of the open-ended nature of material engagement, becomes literal in *Endless Set* by Karen Reimer where an endless set of pillowcases are decorated with prime numbers; each pillowcase is made of the same number of fabric scraps as the prime number decorating it. Prime number eleven, is eleven inches long and appliquéd onto a pillowcase made of eleven scraps of fabric. As the prime number values increase they obscure the pillowcases which are made of progressively smaller scraps. Reimer comments: 'Eventually the pillowcases will be very thick, useless as pillowcases, becoming sculptures instead. I plan to continue the series until I am no longer physically able to make the pillowcases according to this system. This series is a contest between the concept of infinity and the limitations of my body'.[5]

in the context of unholy and conflicting unions; man and machine, stitch and screen or 3D and 2D animation techniques. I would argue that this perceived dialectic or tension between a three-dimensional hand-rendered process and its 'new' technological context is conducive to rethinking the currency of dominant methodological schemes within graphic design criticism; in particular, the tendency to describe social and cultural changes in simplistic, historical and deterministic ways.

At least since the early 1990s, graphic design discourse has been dominated by language-based methodological schemes. In the dominant semiotic mode of analysis, for instance, the products of design have been predominantly viewed in terms of their overall visual appearance (or style), the honed decision-making skills of the designer and the semantic significance of individual formal elements.[4] In *Design Studies: Theory and Research in Graphic Design*, Audrey Bennett argues that Graphic Design theory needs to concern itself with 'rigorous' and highly 'structured' models of 'empirical' research, challenging those methods of analysis that merely seek to identify the individual genius of a practitioner.[5] In this way, semiotic modes of analysis are attributed with almost scientific qualifications.

Bennett argues that traditional theories about the 'creativity' of the designer and his or her 'intuition' are no longer 'adequate' to understandings of contemporary creative practice where a new technological, interdisciplinary and collaborative context of making has emerged. This effectively marginalises a discussion of process in any other terms than those relating to 'a new visual language ... that integrates both textual and visual objects'.[6] As the wording suggests, the focus of such critical analysis is resolutely located in the domain of products and outcomes rather than processes and nuanced practices of design. In this respect, social, technological and cultural contexts are reduced to historical inflections which merely contemporise otherwise continuous perceptions of the designer's role and the centrality of objects. Matt Cooke typically concludes, from a semiotic perspective, that: 'The thought of strictly following a process goes against our perception of design as an instinctive, intuitive and artistic practice. But the truth is, however informally, the majority of us follow a methodology when designing'.[7]

Semiotics, therefore, is generally offered an analytical model that simply formalises and structures the otherwise 'intuitive' approaches of everyday design. For this reason alone, I can see renewed value in traditional theories that have already investigated and framed these ongoing themes. Rather than marginalising creativity and intuition as beyond the domain of contemporary graphic design criticism, let's make them central to its discourse and available for scrutinising. Notions of creative intuition clearly constitute dominant concepts and concerns among practitioners and indicate, I would suggest, more than a nostalgic turn in this age of computing. Such a return to past values is to be interpreted, I would suggest, as a clear demonstration – not of a crafty yearning for the good ol' days of analogue design, but – of a continuing interest in discussing the vagaries and happenstance of design process.

I would advise a timely revisitation of a Gestalt methodology, one that focuses on the immediacy of the present moment (of making and viewing, for example), and respects the internal or subjective experiences of the maker as a relationship unfolds with the emerging object, through time. Its relevance is all the more pertinent because it aspires to analyse and understand the process of doing something in the present tense, placing the idea of real-time experimentation firmly on the methodological agenda. Contemporary psychotherapist Joseph Zinker argues: 'The experiment is the cornerstone of experiential learning. It transforms talking about into doing, stale reminiscing and theorizing into being fully here with one's imagination, energy and excitement.'[8]

A Gestalt approach to everyday practices, usually involves consideration of the body, voice and/or a capacity for imagination. The focus of Gestalt methodologies is clearly on experiential learning, placing value on the exploration of the human subject in terms of his/her

It's the transformation, or revelation, through making which represents the craft paradigm we are interested in identifying here. Work like this goes some way to overturning the mistaken belief, which so often abounds in the digital age, that any return to 'the hand', 'the trace of the human' or analogue processes is simply a romantic gesture. Material thinking is not a sealed 'dialogue' between man and his materials. It is – and has become – a process which is 'open to criticism and correction'.[6]

This undermines established thinking positing Craft as intrinsically linked to materials, as distinct from Design, where the act of thinking is instrumental and as such, independent from its materials. In this traditional dichotomy: the craftsman is said to ask 'How?' of his materials, whilst the designer would ask 'Why?'

Craft, as we have mapped it, provides a clear route from the world of making alone, to the cognitive world of 'problem solving'.

Problem solving becomes a tool with which to rethink the process of making where: 'The good craftsman...uses solutions to uncover new territory; problem solving and problem finding are intimately related in his or her mind. For this reason, curiosity can ask, "Why?"a[s] well as, "How?" about any project'.[7]

Sennett argues that this is not new to our age, but rather, has always been true of a certain level of practice whereby craft engagement with materials has been taken out of its comfort zone. He advances two propositions that illuminate this process of transformation, one developing from the other. Firstly, 'all skills, even the most abstract, begin as bodily practices' and following on from this: 'technical understanding develops through the powers of the imagination'.[8]

It's in this relationship where people perform with and between materials and the imagination that the potential of craft thinking enables the possibility to re-engage meaningfully in our future(s).

In part, the attraction of craft is the way that, in comparison to the perceived abso-

Event poster for the music festival *We Love Fantasy*. Art direction by Julien Vallée. Design by Julien Vallée, Guillaume Vallée and Eve Duhamel (2009). Photograph by Simon Duhame.

relationships (such as those with other people/audience and objects of design). The goal of a Gestalt framework is to support an individual in finding his/her own answers and to develop a heightened sense of self-awareness and increased self-understanding in the moment of making and doing. To my mind, this seems a valuable framework for analysing the three-dimensional, evolutionary worlds of 'tactile' design, as it pays attention to the experiential aspects of the production and consumption of artefacts, facilitating a fuller investigation of the immediate (and often physical) processes of design work.

As a type of therapy, Gestalt identifies three zones of awareness: inner, outer and middle. Within the course of a counselling session, the client is invited to put these zones into contact with one another; the body, the mind and the wider world are put into an active and conscious relation. Indeed, the aim of the Gestalt approach is to invite a shift from one state of awareness to another, always with the understanding that each zone exists in the context of a wider field of personal and social complexes. In this way, Gestalt offers a heightened sense of integration within and between these areas of everyday life or practice, with attention being paid to the ways in which the intimate and public aspects of one's 'self' and one's work are working together. It is simultaneously a macro and micro methodology, and one that is focused on feeling present.

One of the main aspirations of Gestalt experiments is 'to create conditions under which the person can see his life as his own creation'.[9] I believe it can assist designers in making decisions about how things are going to be (from now on); no longer acting as intuitively creative but as self-conscious agents of their own creative process. A Gestalt methodology can assist the designer in exploring the way in which aspects of his/her personal and social agency are integrated. Indeed, within a counselling situation, Gestalt techniques are adept at raising awareness of what 'figures' currently in a person's immediate field of operation, then encourages a stepping aside from this perspective to see what else exists in the field of his or her horizons.

lute nature of digital technology, it allows for 'happenstance'. This can include error and serendipitous mistakes materialising in the aesthetic: from wobbly 'hand-drawn' lines to the use of vernacular materials. Following Moszkowicz, happenstance can be 'the variety of human experience': 'Rather than symptomatic of a carefully formulated interpretation...what I say today might be different from tomorrow...my awareness keeps changing, with my everyday life and my environment...'[1]

The distorted but functional books created by Sofia Stevi are an example of what we would call craft orientated design. She writes: 'They say that a finished book is a corpse and the observer can only see the remains of all the possibilities the bookmaker got to know in the process... Bookbinding as every other craft depends on practice and perfectionism. I chose to use this vehicle to express the metaphor of imperfection.'[9]

Although Stevi discusses her work in terms of exploring 'imperfection', this is only meaningful in terms of traditional conditions and expectations of the Book. As interesting, is the way her inventive stitching, and investigations of the format and sequence of pages, open up the possibility of new functions: performative and interior spaces for the work to inhabit.

We can think of craft as reviving an enjoyment in materials and rediscovering skill... but the difference now is, that it's application that is important. The skill and act of making are not a determined end product, context or condition of use: '...the craftsman looks for what else he can do with the tools at hand'.[10]

See full responses + carry on the conversation here
http://tiny.cc/chapter3_2

Reader credits
1   Julia Moszkowicz 19/05/2009

References
1   Peter Dormer, *The Culture of Craft* (Manchester: Manchester University Press, 1997), 147.

Juicy Fruit by Karen Reimer (1999).

Partial copies of newspapers
by Karen Reimer (2000-2).

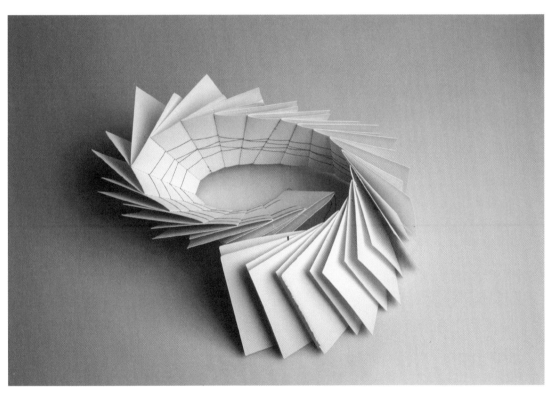

The Spine by Sofia Stevi (2009).

2   Richard Sennett, *The Craftsman* (London: Penguin, 2009), ix.

3   Malcolm McCullough, *Abstracting Craft: The Practiced Digital Hand* (Cambridge, MA: MIT, 1996).

4   In an email exchange with the authors about this response, she explained her thinking draws on Immanuel Kant, *Critique of Pure Reason* (1781), where Kant distinguishes between Empirical and Architectonic modes of knowledge production. The Tacit here fits with the Empirical.

5   Karen Reimer in an email exchange with the authors (2009).

6   Paul Carter, 'Material Thinking: The Theory and Practice of Creative Research' quoted in Carole Gray and Gordon Burnett, 'Making Sense: "Material Thinking" and "Materialising Pedagogies"' in *Interactive Discourse*, November/December 2007, Vol.1, Issue 1, 23.

7   Richard Sennett, Op cit., 11.

8   Ibid., 10.

9   www.sofiastevi.com/index.php?/the-spine/lordosis/ (accessed 15/07/09).

10 Richard Sennett, Op cit., 273.

Gestalt offers an effective way of approaching the notion of process that lies at the heart of contemporary discourse around creative endeavour, and could assist in the process of communicating memorable, figural experiences for audiences. In particular, the 'zones of awareness' and the notion of figure/ground relations could provide a useful corrective to current emphasis, within semiotics, on the production of meaning within structured, syntactic and predominantly formal relationships.

Finally, I would suggest that revisiting Gestalt methods of analysis – first explored by pioneering designers such as László Moholy-Nagy and György Kepes in the interwar years – would complement the currently retroactive tendencies of graphics practice, where the context of production is momentarily privileged over the context of consumption and/or post-production. Gestalt can reconfigure the notion of 'touch' graphics in terms of being touched by or feeling with such objects of design.

See further images here
www.limitedlanguage.org/images

References

1   Matthias Hubner and Robert Klanten, *Tactile: High Touch Visuals* (London: DGV, 2007).

2   Rita Street and Lewis Ferdinand, *Touch Graphics* (London: Rockport, 2003), 11.

3   Matt Soar, 'It Begins with "Ill" and ends with "digital": The Riddle of Illustration's Declining Fortunes' in Steven Heller and Marshall Arisman (eds.), *The Education of an Illustrator* (New York: Allworth Press, 2000).

4   For instance, see David Crow, *Visible Signs: an Introduction to Semiotics* (London: AVA Publishing, 2003), 31-61.

5   Audrey Bennett (ed.), 'Design Studies: Theory and Research' in *Graphic Design, A Reader* (New York: Princeton University Press, 2006), 5.

6   Judy D'Ammasso Tarbox, 'Activity Theory: A Model for Design Research' in ibid., 74.

7   Matt Cooke, 'Design Methodologies: Toward a Systematic Approach to Design' in Bennett, Op cit., 131.

8   Joseph Zinker, *Creative Process in Gestalt Therapy* (London: Vintage Books, 1989), 123.

9   Ibid., 126.

David Crowley

Boredom, b'dum, b'dum...

Communication. It is an easy word. It slips off the tongue without a thought. It is with us all the time; the scribbled note pinned on a door to say 'back in 5', the jerky prose of the txt, or that blinking on-off banner advertisement on every website (but not www.limited-language.org...).

But what does it take to slow us down? Or look hard and think carefully? In a world of fast communication, words and images seek us out. They seem to be irrepressibly alive. Writing about the ability of a young office worker to sing the tin-pan alley hits of the day, Siegfried Kracauer observed, 'But it is not she who knows every hit, rather the hits know her, steal up behind her and gently lay her low.'[1] That was 1929; today our pop commodities are more aggressive. Do you recall the 'accidental' exposure of a pumped-up breast during the 2004 Super Bowl intermission? Or the 'spontaneous' outpourings of emotion triggered by the death of Pope John Paul II the next year?

Communication is now the business of shock and awe. But of course real affect cannot be pre-progammed. It acts by accident and with stealth. Think of those snapshots of American soldiers in Abu Ghraib with the instinctive 'thumbs up and smile' gesture hovering over a corpse.[2] The awful pixilated blur hiding a beaten face. The shock lay in the apparent innocence of these products of the photographic reflex.

So in a world of visual noise, where might we find a quiet invitation to look and to think? Might it be possible for graphic design to operate as a system to slow down perception, to create silences in the noisy media world? Or perhaps even stillness? This is simply just another tool, another technique. What is the alternative to the heady stimulation of communication? What happens, asked Kracauer, if we allow ourselves to become truly and deeply bored: 'if one has the patience, the sort

Boredom to freedom

The original essay asks if boredom can be the refuge for creativity and, in the replies, Lisa asks: '...we are a bit bored ..., but what are we waiting for?'[1] But, for boredom to act as a catalyst it is important we do NOT know what we are waiting for. It is the anticipation of inquiry which is the root to the possibilities of boredom's creative potential.

Today, mass communication is awash with the 'next big thing' or what we should be doing with our lives; fashion, employment and recreation time, are all accounted for. The action of not doing, of not knowing what comes next, is liberating for an individual but terrifying for a government, corporation or media empire. Boredom separates the individual from the masses.

In his essay on boredom, Siegfried Kracauer worries that modern life has compartmentalised (commodified) our lives to such an extent that every minute is accounted for. Life, in a sense, has become a conveyor belt of products and information. We remain static whilst our consumer lifestyles continually revolve around us, taking on greater and greater significance as we sink deeper into the hustle and bustle of the day-to-day until, Kracauer comments, '[we] no longer know where [our] head is'.[1]

The modern world, according to Kracauer, is configured to negate a state of boredom. Even when we are alone we are worrying about what we should be doing, what we are missing. The omnipotence of modernity is beautifully captured in the comment: 'Everywhere in the city, adverts on the tube, bus, shop windows... Walking down the street, leafleters trying to hand you out all sorts of eye catching flyers'.[II] On the Limited Language website, Bervas' post captures the essence of Kracauer's observation that the city plugs our eyes and ears with stuff until, 'one is banished from one's own emptiness...'[2] The sensorial is important here, as the city leaves no room for any of our senses to roam free from the sonic, aural, visual and olfactory output of urban living. Darkness, like boredom, is banished from the modern metropolis.

Waiting at a bus stop might be the ideal place to be bored, standing still but awaiting a journey. Indeed expectation, for Walter Benjamin,[3] is an active partner to boredom. But the modern bus shelter is now a shell made of advertising hoardings (the bus itself is usually a moveable feast of images promoting consumerist gluttony). Added to this the bench is made narrow and uncomfortable, intended for the briefest respite and to discourage the comfort of daydreaming or an idleness that might nurture boredom.

The modern bus stop is designed to move us on. It provides an excellent example of how 'problem solving' design leaves a product which is not-fit-for-purpose. These are bus shelters designed with the emphasis on deterring vagrancy over giving shelter to commuters.

How can design nurture the emancipatory elements that Kracauer seeks in boredom? Architecture might provide spaces that offer solace to the continuum of distractions of modern life. The airport is a structure that is born out of modernity but riven by a postmodern need to fill our time with a mix of architectural style and commerce: the fashion of Guccio Gucci and 'star' architect Norman Foster vie for our attention with the latest glass-architecture engineering housing the current fashion in outfits and interiors. But the airport can be a place that might allow the spirit to daydream, as an anthropological 'non-place'.[4] It is ideal territory for us to be freed from the tyranny of the day-to-day.[III]

Gardermoen Airport in the Norwegian capital Oslo is one such place. Built in 1995, the design was not a lone architect's inspiration, but created by a collective of architects,

of patience specific to legitimate boredom, then one experiences a kind of bliss that is almost unearthly...in ecstasy you name what you have always lacked'.[3] What is it that you have always lacked? Have you ever been bored enough to find out?

See further images here
www.limitedlanguage.org/images

References
1 Siegfried Kracauer, *The Salaried Masses: Duty and Distraction in Weimar Germany* (London: Verso, 1998), 70.
2 These were photos, taken with the soldiers' cameras, of prisoners being abused at Iraq's Abu Ghraib prison in 2003 and which came to public light in the following year.
3 Siegfried Kracauer, Op cit., 304.

Fast communication?
Billboard, Elephant and Castle, London.

Wayfinding system and identity for
Gardermoen Airport, Oslo, designed
by Per Mollerup and DesignLab.
(Airport completed 1995).

http://bit.ly/oslo_airport
http://bit.ly/oslo_airport_interior

Webcam images from the terminal building at Oslo
Gardermoen Airport, Norway, updated every 15
seconds.

engineers and a local government insisting on design planning which would reflect the culture and economics of Norway. Thus the advertising for Norway's wood and pulp industry is embedded in the building rather than in bright lights and logos; for instance, the building uses massive beams of nationally sourced wood. Supported on thirty concrete columns, the large wood beams quietly stretch out above the passengers' heads from entrance hall to departure lounge. The sensorial effect of the building, which is made of glass, concrete, wood and aluminium, deliberately captures the tactility of craft and, by extension, Norway's craft industry. Per Mollerup's Design-Lab designed the wayfinding system within the building (including the corporate identity). Mollerup believes in simple structures: 'A comprehensible structure may depend on such factors as pattern, sequence, grouping, and procedural flow.'[5] This system means the signage does not interrupt the building but seamlessly appears in the eye-line when seeking direction. The Frutiger typeface dominates the typography used in the building and, although originally designed for Paris' Charles De Gaulle International Airport in the late 1960s, in itself it is shaped by the modernist concept of typography; to be a kind of 'transparent' vessel for imparting information.[6]

This notion of simplicity is central to the work of Jasper Morrison and Naoto Fukasawa whose product design has been called *Super Normal*. Their design aims for simplicity, not distraction. Fukasawa comments on their aims: 'Super Normal is less concerned with designing beauty than seemingly homely but memorable elements of everyday life. Certainly nothing "flash" or "eye-catching".'[7]

Their work has an ethical nature too. Designing 'pretty things', Morrison observes, feeds into the consumer cycle: 'The virus has already infected the everyday environment. The need for businesses to attract attention provides the perfect carrier for the disease.'[8] *Super Normal* work registers on the consumerist psyche in its use rather than any

Drinking and wine glasses,
sketches by Jasper Morrison.

Alessi, *Op-La Tray Table* sketch
by Jasper Morrison (1998).

fashionable sense of prettiness.

It's the way that Morrison and Fukasawa's work moves away from the in-your-face product and provides equilibrium between the tactile and the visual that is interesting. For instance, eating with super normal products – knife, fork, plate – the design is in the weight of the cutlery and the pressure of the bowl or of a glass in your hand. It is the 'atmosphere of the table' to which the design belongs.

Products like these are not merely confined to the designer commodity; super normal products can be found in shops like Muji and other commercial manufacturers like Rowenta. They help make the everyday of products and utilitarian objects a quieter place. All of these design products are not afraid to be ordinary.

Ordinariness allows us to be whimsical, to be bored.

See full responses + carry on the conversation here
http://tiny.cc/chapter3_3

Reader credits
I   Lisa 16/05/2005
II   S Bervas 16/12/2005
III Simon 18/05/2005 – Simon gives one example (by
     default…) 'I was on the tube yesterday and there
     was a poster for some Microsoft Office connectivity
     package that said, 'The "I'm out of the office and
     out of the loop" era is over.' The picture was of a
     businessman in an airport lounge relaxing with
     a latté and a dinosaur's head really badly photo-
     shopped on…contemporary life…is…set on
     stealing any last possibility for 'slow' moments that
     we have…I think this tendancy is going and will
     hopefully produce the opposite reaction and elevate
     boredom to be seen as the new freedom.'

References
1   Siegfried Kracauer and T.Y. Levin, *The Mass
     Ornament: Weimer essays* (Cambridge, MA: Harvard
     University Press, 1995), 332.
2   Ibid., 331.
3   'Looking at someone carries the implicit expectation
     that our look will be returned by the object of our
     gaze. When this expectation is met (which, in the
     case of thought processes, can apply equally to
     the look of the mind's eye and to a glance pure and
     simple), there is an experience of the aura to the
     fullest extent…' From Walter Benjamin, *On Some
     Motifs in Baudelaire* (1939), 338.

4   This term can be explored in Marc Augé, *Non-places: Introduction to an Anthropology of Supermodernity* (London; New York: Verso, 1995).

5   www.permollerup.com/designlab/english/design_research.html (accessed 07/04/09).

6   For instance, see Beatrice Ward, 'The Crystal Goblet or Printing Should Be Invisible' in Michael Beirut et al. (eds.), *Looking Closer: Classic Writings on Graphic Design* (New York: Allworth, 1999), 56.

7   Naoto Fukasawa and Jasper Morrison, *Super Normal: Sensations of the Ordinary* (Baden: Lars Müller Publishers, 2008), 16.

8   Ibid., 16.

Part of the process

The comment '...anything that cannot be marketed will inevitably vanish'[1] comes from the French art critic and curator, Nicolas Bourriaud. In his 1998 collection of essays, *Relational Aesthetics*, he captures the mood of much visual communication today, which oscillates between the brand consultant's wet dream and the critic's worst nightmare.

For Bourriaud, spontaneous social relations are vanishing in the information age as communication becomes restricted to particular areas of consumption; coffee shops, pubs and bars, art galleries and so on.

Relational Aesthetics explores art that concerns itself with creating more spontaneous encounters or moments of sociability within these 'communication zones'. One of the artists Bourriaud invokes is Rirkrit Tiravanija who created two identical versions of his New York apartment in London's Serpentine Gallery in 2005. Here, visitors could make themselves at home; put on the kettle, take a shower. It was not the flat that was offered up for contemplation but the way people inhabit the space. This process was made more noticeable in the move from one apartment to its identical, but uncannily mirrored, twin. Scribbles and Post-it notes accumulated spontaneously on the walls like graffiti on a toilet wall, one saying 'Not for me, sorry...', and below it, an illegible reply.

Relational refers to art that not only situates itself within the 'inter-human sphere' but is 'a formal arrangement that generates relationships between people'.[2] A unifying principle of relational aesthetics is that they are open-ended, negotiating relationships with their audience in a way that is not prepared beforehand. It is in this way that they resist social formatting, unlike the kind of scripted conversation that is designed to end in a sale or the more didactic form of a poster.

The term relational offers a more complex understanding than the simple oppositional binary of much

Community service

To start from design at all, when looking at social relationships (which includes the role of communication design[1]) is perhaps to start from the wrong end. New areas of conviviality and community are continually emerging: from 'experiments' in mobile living from senior citizens in Recreational Vehicle (RV) communities in the US[2] to evolving SMS languages. Where these organic communication networks differ from traditional systemic design/networks is how previously unimaginable communities have emerged: undesigned.

A pre-digital world, the world of (mass) communications, is predominantly rhetorical – what Bourriaud calls looped information – and demands no response other than that you follow. It is a system of communication of one to many; rather than today, where the possibility of many to many networks can drive much communication and design (or at least provide the possibility for a rupture from the top-down approach of so much design!).

Going back to SMS messaging for a moment, we can look to see how this works in two communities. In East Africa, a grass-roots, alternative economy began to emerge after Vodafone set up their pay-as-you-go mobile network. This simply started with users sending cash to each other and comparing market prices by phone – fruit and vegetables for instance – from one market to another (in a sense the technology was utilised to provide a commodities market). A technological network was put into place and the local community intervened to create a network contingent to their needs.

More broadly, SMS has become a predominant form of mobile communication where teenagers, first in Japan, followed by Europe and eventually the USA, took up SMS, originally a by-product of mobile telephony; it is now the predominant form of communication across a wide demographic of all ages.

The examples given above are driven by a many-to-many network rather than communication design or marketing strategies (although it has now provided opportunities for both).

Processes like these have been well-documented and informs much current thinking about design and the real world; like John Thackara who comments: 'we know what new technology can do but what is it for and how do we want to live?'[3]

The questions, What is it for? and How do we want to live? in a sense can be used as a catalyst to help focus the ideas put forward in relational aesthetics. Bourriaud's key terms, relational, open-ended, everyday micro-utopias, social interstices, communication zones, looped information, and micro-community, have been much discussed but for the sake of our argument here it boils down to the role of process and community: what and how do we create in a community sphere?

Community itself can be problematic. Community separates out, so you are defined by being in one and not the other. In simple terms, design community, art community but in more radical cases it can be situated outside of systems, capitalism, religion, national boundaries etc.

'Community is posited as particular where capitalism is abstract. Posited as its other, its opposite, community is often presented as a complement to capitalism, balancing and humanizing it, even, in fact, enabling it.'[4]

Design has a role in the 'balancing and humanizing' of the culture it acts within, but needs to focus on the 'What is it for?', 'How do we want to live?' Before it can radically do this. It requires an understanding of the minutiae of the subject-at-hand which provides assistance in answering these questions.

In an analogue context, much research in community/urban development (where a art and design as either socially active or not. So, are the processes at play in relational art practice, as Bourriaud sees them, also active in communication design?

From 2002-7, a talking point of the UK's Turner Prize at Tate Britain was the exit point. This was not the usual retail snare of postcards but a space for reflection; a room for visitors to linger in, debrief, pass comment and swap notes. Created by graphic designers A2/SW/HK, the room was walled by wooden panels with rows of loose-leaf A6 writing paper, hole-punched and hanging from what looked like pieces of dowel. These revealed themselves to be the pencils with which to write thoughts about the exhibition.

The Turner Prize's raison d'être has always been to generate debate, but the 'controversial' image attached to the prize quickly became jaded marketing rhetoric. This project aimed to reinvigorate a public discussion about art, but more intimately within the gallery rather than the tabloids and, crucially, with discussion directed by the visitor. A2 combined the structure of art debate with the traditional comments box and this then became something else as people scribbled on other's comments to reply, correct or agree. This was more than a simple method of feedback; more like meeting and creating a live community?

Spaces of encounter and the formation of micro-communities, even if only in text, are fundamental in giving value back to the unmediated consumer experience. In a sense, A2's was a different exhibition; less curated and independent of the show. One note said, 'The comments are more interesting to read than half that bombastic [unreadable] that we've all paid to marvel at.'[3]

This kind of work not only involves the audience, but is also made real or materialises in and with the audience (however this is not to be confused with work that is 'interactive'). This could also be seen in *Cracked*, a 24-hour show at La Vianda gallery in 2005, put on by students from the London College of Communication.

People were encouraged to come in with everyday problems from their work environment, by a team of sixteen graphic designers who provided them with solutions to walk away with, free of charge. The upstairs space provided a constantly updated display of these 'problems + solutions' for perusal, building up a while-u-wait portfolio/gallery. Downstairs, it was the client-designer relationship and the creative bustle of the working studio, always a process of dialogue both complex and fluid, that was offered up for contemplation. What made this relational was that it was the actual event that curated the work, not the other way around.

These examples provide moments or possibilities for social relationships that Bourriaud calls 'social interstices', a term borrowed from Karl Marx.[4] In contrast to a traditional leftist position, Bourriaud insists that these interstices co-exist and live within the branded environment, rather than acting as 'culture jamming', which aims to disrupt capitalist activity.

The world of mass communications, which Bourriaud calls 'looped information', is predominantly rhetorical. In many contexts this can be an alienating experience, compounded by a didactic signage system. A relational stance can work in this sphere, too. Kenya Hara's signage for the Umeda Maternity Clinic in Osaka, Japan uses the traditional visual language of information design – pictograms, symbols, typography, etc. – but the signs are printed onto white cotton cloth. These are detachable, allowing the signage to become part of the day-to-day running of the clinic; washed and recycled along with the laundry. Here, the conviviality of much relational aesthetics is not literal. It is the cyclical nature of the signage, which inhabits what Bourriaud calls the 'minute space of daily gestures', that is of interest. The signage makes the impersonal world of a large hospital more human or personal. Moreover, it is a more open-ended process in that the signage is perceived to come to life, not deteriorate, when washed. The signage has not been a target for graffiti, unlike the usual

transformative engagement with community is called for) the minutiae can be a critical catalyst in informing the design process and the eventual material outcome. Jodi Polzin who recounts her experience of working with design students and the local community in inner city St. Louis eloquently captures the problem of a one-to-many approach to design in her paper *Reconsidering the Margin: Relationships of Difference and Transformative Education*:

'The disparity between how the students and the residents experienced the same neighborhood was exemplified by the eventual selection of a site which the students described in a written presentation as "a trash-strewn vacant lot of no present value." The site turned out to be an important baseball field where the neighborhood children played and which had significant meaning to many in the community. The children, with whom the students did not consult, maintained that they did not want it touched because it would attract the older youth and no longer be theirs. This exasperated the students who felt that the residents did not appreciate something better in their neighborhood, a design which had been highly lauded by design faculty during in-house reviews'.[5]

In a different context, up until recently, social networking and 'tweeting' online has been derided precisely because its content is considered 'minutiae'. However, this is to think from a privileged (one to many) position.

For instance, the Baghdad Blogger was simply putting his diary online during the war in Iraq hoping a friend in Turkey might log in. Instead, to the world's press, starved of insider information, it became a mainframe for disseminating information.[6] At the time of writing the newspapers speak of the 'Twitter revolutionary'.

Community can't be prescriptive or pre-defined; but in any given context will see design as a starter-kit that can become something else. Metaphors still frame these spaces on the Web, so the user 'knows where

toilet
for
ladies

Signage for the Umeda Maternity
Clinic, Osaka, Japan by Kenya Hara.

modernist street signage which is prone to the taggers' aerosol wit. To graffiti Hara's signage, would that be like tagging the back of someone's shirt as they sit in the emergency waiting room?

A more literal engagement with conviviality – creating and relying on human relations – are the experiments in traffic relations which were originally devised in Holland and are now seen around the world. In some areas of Holland, traffic engineer Hans Monderman oversaw the removal of traffic lights, signage, speed-limit signs, speed bumps, bicycle lanes and pedestrian crossings. In his view it's when 'drivers stop looking at signs and start looking at other people, that driving becomes safer ...all those signs are saying to cars, "this is your space, and we have organised your behaviour so that as long as you behave this way, nothing can happen to you" ... That is the wrong story.'[5] The primacy of the traffic world is interrupted by repositioning the relationship between cars and pedestrians, making them aware of operating in a shared space. Drivers can no longer merely act on signage or a green light automatically, but have to act and react as part of a momentary micro-community of pedestrians and other drivers at each road junction.

Dubbed a Dutch 'naked road' experiment by the media, the *Shared Space* initiative in Wiltshire, England soon reduced accidents by 35 per cent on removing the white lines that separate drivers on one side of the road from the other.[6] In London's Kensington High Street, there was a 69 per cent reduction in accidents in three years through the removal of railings, pedestrian guard-rails and signs.[7] In a telephone interview, Ben Hamilton-Baillie, a British architect and advisor for *Shared Space*, suggested this makes the street 'legible', not through signage but as an elegant, live urban environment. 'Signage is, contrary to popular belief, a very poor way to influence behaviour. It may work in a car-only space like a motorway, but it's the least subtle and effective form of communication in the public realm. When we are talking about complex communication

they are'; the browser home page and computer Desktop bookend any computer mediated experience.

In a sense, Design has long been impotent in the networked city, whose institutions/ edifices – business centres, banks, airports, classrooms – are essentially nodal points that organise the exchange of information, capital and power in what Manuel Castells calls the 'space of flows'.[7] Today's Web 2.0 technology allows the opportunity to focus upon interpersonal communications; often the minutiae of social communication and, as such, can provide a shift in emphasis when thinking about 'network building' in design more broadly.

Following on from Castells, 'liquidity' is the dominant metaphor in a relational community orientated design environment, where in the realm of digital networks, 'Social structures are dissolving into "streams" of human beings, information, goods and specific signs or cultural symbols.'[8]

But is it the end of design as we know it... it will be for some!

Carry on the conversation here
http://tiny.cc/chapter3_4

The original article was not posted on the website and responses come from formal settings including *Multiverso* – Icograda Design Week. Torino. Italy. 2008.

References
1   Our original article *Part of the Process* – written between 2005-6 – looked for the relational in visual communication. In 2009 the article 'Strained Relations' the design writer Rick Poynor returned to Relational Aesthetics suggesting the line of enquiry didn't convince within the context of communication design: 'While it's possible to find graphic design projects that offer some degree of interactivity or draw people into a relationship with a space, projects that promote social relationships between people are rare.' Rick Poynor, *Strained Relations*, Print, April 2009, www.printmag.com/design_ articles/observer_strained_relations/tabid/519
2   In America, although the mobile elderly communities are clearly nomads by leisure and not through need, this meant they were amongst the first to arrive as volunteer aid workers after Hurricane Katrina, when

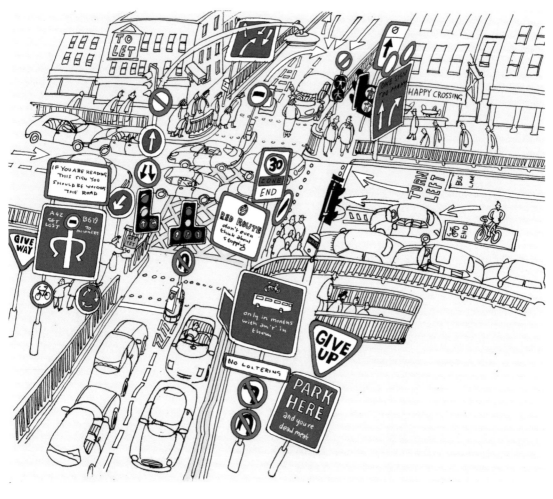

The shared space concept. The impact of traditional engineering measures on the urban environment by Ben Hamilton-Baillie.

A post-9/11 community in New York – but still with a commercial edge? (2005).

New Orleans was shattered in 2005. See for instance, Deane Simpson, *RV Urbanism*: Nomadic Network Settlements of the Senior Recreational Vehicle Community in the US, www.holcimfoundation. org/Portals/1/docs/F07/WK-Temp/F07-WK-Temp-simpson02.pdf, (accessed 08/05/2009).

3   John Thackara, Director, *Doors of Perception*, Competitiveness Summit '06. http://bit.ly/Thackara

4   Miranda Joseph, *Against the Romance of Community* (Minneapolis, MN:, London: University of Minnesota Press, 2002), 1.

5   Jodi Polzin, *Reconsidering the Margin: Relationships of Difference and Transformative Education* (Saint Louis: Washington University in Saint Louis, Sam Fox School of Design & Visual Arts Graduate School of Architecture & Urban Design, College of Architecture, 2009), 4.

6   Baghdad Blogger: 'In the run-up to war, a Web diary from the Iraqi capital captured an international following as its author, writing under the pen name Salam Pax, charted the daily lives of a people caught between a feared regime and a foreign invasion force'. www.guardian.co.uk/Iraq/blogger/0.,1018987,00.html

7   The economist Manuel Castells uses 'space of flows' to refer to the system of information, capital and power that structures societies and economies regardless of location: 'The space of flows, superseding the space of places, epitomizes the increasing differentiation between power and experience, the separation between meaning and function.' Manuel Castells, 'European cities, the Informational Society and the Global Economy' in Richard Le Gates and Frederic Stout (eds.), *The City Reader* (London: Routledge, 1996), 483.

8   Scott Lash and John Urry referenced in Ulrich Beck, *The Cosmopolitan Vision* (Cambridge: Polity, 2006), 80-81.

between two people, everyone knows that the more indirect communication is, the more effective the message. Women know that. Musicians, artists and architects know that.' In lectures, Hamilton-Baillie illustrates this point by describing a road accident where a car is wrapped around the cause: a street sign saying 'Thank you for driving slowly'.

Scenarios that foster spontaneous human relations are what Bourriaud would call 'microtopias'. For him, this is the core political significance of relational aesthetics and his most contested claim for them. In contrast to a classic, Utopian/Marxist stance that strives to change the world, Bourriaud argues that relational aesthetics create achievable micro-utopian moments, embedded within the everyday to make the now more pleasurable.

The examples here go beyond a simple diagnosis of design as good or bad, socially responsible or not. They might not be socially active in the sense of a protest poster, but can they still be seen to activate the social?

The relational model of enquiry is broadening in its remit as its approach expands beyond the sphere of contemporary art. Much of this is already going on in the design sphere at the operative level, but the core concepts are useful to provide a language for thinking about it. For design and visual communication, how might they come into their own to develop these ideas beyond the aesthetics of the relational?

See further images here
www.limitedlanguage.org/images

References

1   Nicolas Bourriaud, *Relational Aesthetics* (Paris: Presses du Réel, English translation 2002), 9.

2   Ibid.

3   These cards immediately caught the imagination of the public and press. We can see this in the way individual images of the comments cards were used in the British press as if to speak, by proxy, for the public at large. See, for instance, Nigel Morris, 'Conceptual Bull: Culture Minister and his Critique of the Best of British Art' on the cover of *The Independent*, 31 October 2002.

Farmers Market, Lincoln Boulevard,
Los Angeles, California (2009).

4   The term 'interstice' was used by Karl Marx to describe trading
    communities that operated outside the law of profit.
5   Hans Monderman quoted in Sarah Lyall, 'A Path to Road Safety
    With No Signposts' in *The New York Times*, 22 January 2005, www.
    nytimes.com/2005/01/22/international/europe/22monderman.html
    (accessed 05/04/2009).
6   These statistics come from a telephone interview with Ben
    Hamilton-Baillie (2006). Updated information can be found here;
    www.hamilton-baillie.co.uk (accessed 5/4/2009) A summation of
    findings can be found here; *Urban Design International: Special
    Issue: An International Review of Liveable Street Thinking and
    Practice*, Vol. 13, No. 2 (Summer 2008).
7   Ibid.

Slow times...

The slow fast

Being modern has long been associated with speed. In the 1920s the leader of the Futurist art movement, Filippo Tommaso Marinetti, asked his fellow Italians to stop eating pasta as it would slow them down.[1] Later, the architect Le Corbusier would comment that a modern city was a city built for speed.[2]

Latterly, the architect/theorist Paul Virilio has written about 'Dromology'[3] which, rudimentarily, is the study of speed. Part of his investigation is the differences between the digital and analogue world. The digital is screen-centred whilst the analogue is more analogous to a human, or natural, 24-hour cycle. Virilio's distinction came to mind when someone, who was going away for a long weekend, said she had Googled 'cheap places to eat in Athens'. Google returned over one thousand suggestions in a second. 'But I am only going for the weekend,' she bemoaned. This is a dilemma increasingly faced everyday. The instancy of digital, screen-based time changes the way we experience the world. Exacerbated by a lack of filtering or reflection, we lose the more fragile, day-to-day, bodily experience that helps us make sense of things.

One reaction to this process of speeding up is slowing down. A slow food movement emerged over twenty years ago in Italy as a reaction against speed and the accompanying globalisation which follows (Virilio sees that one effect of speed is geographical contraction). This movement has spread across Europe and influenced other areas. Now there is slow architecture too.

How, if at all, does this manifest in design, a profession now synonymous with screen-based culture?

Ironically, it's surfing the net that throws up many possible examples of 'slow design'. *PostSecret*[4] is a website which asks you to reveal your secrets to be displayed on the site. The idea is not a new one as there are many confessional sites with varying amounts of vitriol. The striking factor is the way the site engages

In the novel *Dombey and Son*, the writer Charles Dickens gives a sense of the great hopes for the innovations of the Industrial Revolution. Describing the railways being built out of London's Camden in the 1840s, he writes: 'In short, the yet unfinished and unopened Railroad was in progress; and, from the very core of all this dire disorder, trailed smoothly away, upon its mighty course of civilisation and improvement. But as yet, the neighbourhood was shy to own the railroad.'[1]

Trains were, of course, not of communities. In contrast to the stagecoach (and the way the horses had to be changed at each Inn), the rate at which the new locomotives steamed across the countryside effectively 'shortened' the distance between towns. Trains, democratic and speedy, connected them.

A marker of this new logic was the way time had to become standardised, so people didn't miss their connections. Time, until then measured locally by the passing of the sun through the sky, became 'railway time observed in clocks, as if the sun itself had given in'.[2]

In the novel *Hard Times*, written much later, Dickens evoked a different sense when he wrote of the lights in the great factories, 'which looked, when they were illuminated, like Fairy palaces – or the travellers by express-train said so –'.[3] These factories were of course the 'melancholy-mad' engines of the Industrial Revolution, with their monstrous serpents of smoke and monotony of labour. What we see here is how speed distances and disconnects.

In our fast times, high-speed rail has largely been superseded by a high-speed Internet connection, opening up the whole world as a 'global village'.[4] And, for the global digerati, there is Internet time.[5] However, all these new connections ('friends') operate in what Walter

Ong has called the 'second encounter'; at one remove.[6] It's immediacy that's experienced here, rather than a depth of connection.

Slow Times picked up on an increasingly commonplace thought that, to re-engage with the natural world, we might need to go slow. Replies to the article drew attention to a difference in contemporary experiences of speed. As David suggested: 'Computers that operate at speeds unimaginable a few years ago are used to type letters and to look at the Web. Jet planes are used for journeys better suited to trains. Those who walk around in trainers, seek to remind us that the possibility for speed is latent within them'.[I] This latency becomes literal in the congested London at the time of writing, where a car that can travel way beyond the limits of the law averages eleven miles per hour; the same speed as the carriage and horse.[7]

This excruciating experience, is hardly what we might call slow. Adriana points out how these two cultures of latent speed – analogue and digital – come together: 'News slides by on screens, we slide by billboards...'[II] She suggests that although at times we might be, 'shaken from this monotony by failures of the system... These raptures don't lead to productivity or poetry, but only to frustration and negative processes'...[III] For Adriana, the problem with latency is that when the body becomes disengaged, it becomes uninspired. Drawing on the philosophy of Maurice Merleau-Ponty,[8] she continues: 'For the body generates ideas not only with its mind, but via and in relentless dialogue with its senses over the entire physical landscape... The body innately houses potential for creative action; but it is the engaged, active body that creates. We need to bring the whole body back into the action if we want to spur on creative activity.'[IV]

This interest in the natural metabolism means that much of the slow movement is focused on an active and human-centred engagement with the environment. For instance, *Slow Down London*, a 'project to inspire Londoners to improve their lives by slowing down to do things well, rather than as

with its audience, the way it asks people to submit their secrets: rather than the immediacy of traditional digital blogs which lend themselves to a more instant outlet of emotion ('xxx is a shit' etc.), you are asked to produce a card, 6"x 4", and to send it in. Only then is it scanned and uploaded to the site. Here we see a blending of temporal modes, where the digital is counter-balanced with the analogue requirements of making the card. It is the act of 'design' which makes this a reflective, rather than a reactive or instant response (click here).

Is this an embryonic notion of slow design? We would like to propose this as platform to create a manifesto of sorts...

Proclamation one...

See further images here
www.limitedlanguage.org/images

References
1   Filippo Tommaso Marinetti, *La Cucina Futurista* (1932).
2   Charles A. Jencks, and Le Corbusier. *Le Corbusier and the Continual Revolution in Architecture* (New York, NY: Monacelli Press, 2000), 63.
3   See, for instance, Paul Virilio, *Speed and Politics: An Essay on Dromology* (New York: Semiotext(e), 1977).
4   http://postsecret.blogspot.com

Nike window display, Lillywhites, London (2009).

fast as possible'[9] started with a sixty minute walk over Waterloo bridge – usually a five minute dash or an interminable traffic jam.

When (slow) design does enter the frame, its role is to facilitate slowness and to renew the phenomenological richness of people, places and things. The focus here is the enjoyment of the lived and developing moment. A point of reference for the Slow Design movement is Bruce Goff, an American architect, who noted in the 1950s that: 'history is past and the future hasn't arrived but that the "continuous present" is always with us.'[10]

The knowledge gained here cannot be mentally deduced or visually accrued. It is tacit knowledge which only materialises in the act of doing.[11] As Katy puts it: 'Tactile over projectile – always!'[V] where projectile 'alludes to all these icons of speed; women descending staircases, sculptures of men ripping through space by the futurists and [...] hurling paint at the canvas... A cheap shot really, nothing more tactile than a Pollock painting... It is what you fixate on; the "action" or the thing it creates?'[VI] It is therefore, not action – speeded up or slowed down – per se that's important, but what it creates.

And here is the crux: how do we stop slowness becoming like speed? Where, as Paul D puts it: 'speed is one more product on the shelves of western excess'.[VII] For him what is crucial is that: 'Slowness is not about the temporal alone. ...The slow movement is about a way of thinking, of providing a platform for identity, nuance and investigation'.[VIII] For instance, we can see this 'way of thinking' in the collected works of SlowLab, a New York based design group, who offer six principles for Slow Design: to reveal, to expand, to reflect, to engage, to participate, to evolve.[12] To return to Paul D: 'Reflection is more than a slowing down, it is situating yourself in a world of latent speed'.[IX]

This situated position becomes the platform for a positive engagement with a world of literal and latent speed and, crucially, without destroying our own temporal rhythms.

Emil Gutman House, Gulfport, Mississippi – Bruce Goff (Blueprint, 1958).

'Bruce Goff, an American architect, noted in the 1950s that: 'history is past and the future hasn't arrived but that the "continuous present" is always with us.' Goff was interested in the many languages of architecture design – creating projects from petrol stations to museums. His phrase "continuous present" has become a mantra for the slow design movement. http://bit.ly/slow_design

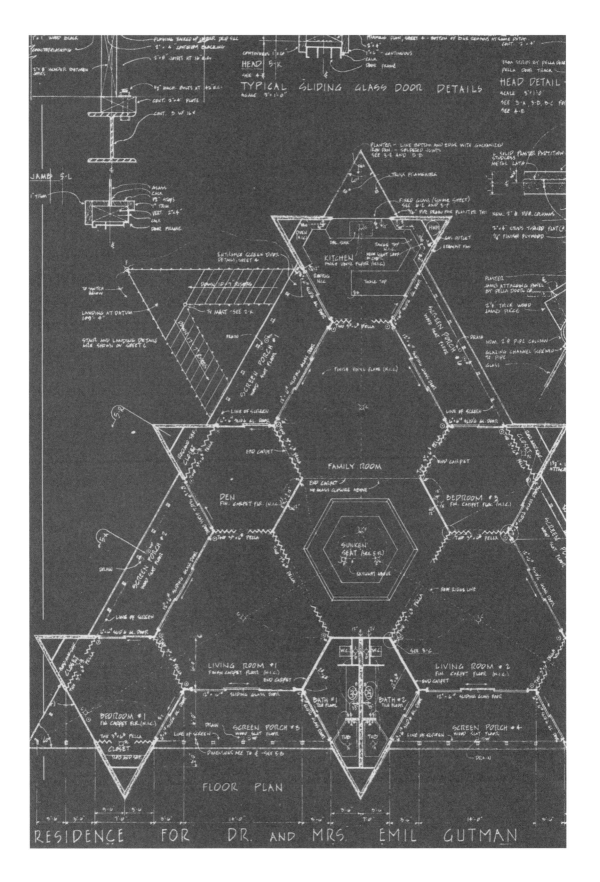

RESIDENCE   FOR   DR.   AND   MRS.   EMIL   GUTMAN

In *Looking Awry*, the cultural critic Slavoj Žižek makes a powerful analogy, drawing attention to what happens when you look out the window of a moving car. When the window is up, it separates you from a reality that can only be observed. With the window down, the rush of stimuli (the sound of the wind and the world flashing by) is overwhelming.[13]

We can make a connection back to Dickens' observations – at a distance – through the (closed) train window. However, the added dimension here is psychological. Winding the window back up from its state of immersion is also a conscious way of 'taking stock'. Physical or temporal distance, in this psychological sense, allows for a depth of reflection unavailable when one is all-immersed, overwhelmed.

In this alternative reading, the window wound down gives a sense of our experience in the digital Google, Twitter and blogging world of continual renewal. The digital world's fast connections make for a fairly fluid-feeling discursive space. For instance, it's no coincidence that the original Italian Slow Movement now proliferates online, but in a looser, more experimental and generative sense. However, when we click for too long through the infinite list of Web-links that Google generates and lose the thread of the search, we might download to reflect in peace. Here, it's the distance that allows us a welcome moment of rest, reflection and synthesis. This is one way that the analogue and the digital co-exist: inter-dependent yet separate.

Finally, the great invention of the Victorian era was arguably the train station. Today it's the airport and the screen interface[x] which mediates between the fast (of flying/searching) and slow (of waiting).

How might design mediate the relationship between the different intensities of the fast and the slow as the pace of consumption becomes ever more critical?

See full responses + carry on the conversation here
http://tiny.cc/chapter3_5

Reader credits

I   David 18/06/2005
II   Adriana 22/06/2005
III Adriana 22/06/2005
IV Adriana 22/06/2005
V   Katy 11/06/2005
VI Katy 17/06/05
VII Paul D 20/06/2005
VIII Paul D 20/06/2005
IX Paul D 20/06/2005
X   Anonymous 30/08/2006 – 'As someone who works on the usability of technology, some days it made me feel as if I had the most important job in the world… as we all know simplicity is the key in design. Can we not start to design "slow technology" that fits with the pace of life of the majority.'

References

1 Charles Dickens, *Dombey and Son*, The Oxford India Paper Dickens, Volume VI (London: Chapman & Hall and Henry Frowde, 1901), 92.

2 Ibid., 266. By the 1840s the railways, the telegraph companies and the Post Office were all suffering because of non-standardised local times and it was the Great Western Railway that first lobbied for 'railway time'. Leeds in the North of England, for instance, ran 6 mins 10 secs behind London time. It took until 1880 to introduce 'standard' time across the whole of Britain. www.carnforth-station.co.uk (accessed 03/04/09).

3 Charles Dickens, *Hard Times* (Harmondsworth: Penguin, 1969), 103.

4 The phrase 'global village' was first used in Marshall McLuhan, *Understanding Media: The Extensions of Man* (New York: McGraw-Hill, 1964) to describe the world as enabled by TV. This metaphor is usefully updated for the digital age in Paul Levinson, *Digital McLuhan: A Guide to the Information Millennium* (London; New York: Routledge, 1999).

5 'Digerati' is a term for the elite of the computer industry and online communities, whilst Internet Time is a 'new' way to tell time, the same all over the world and with no time zones or daylight saving time adjustments – as invented and marketed by the Swiss watch company Swatch!

6 Walter J. Ong, *Orality and Literacy: The Technologising of the Word* (London: Routledge, 1991).

7 This is ironic, when we think that the word 'car' is a shortening of its first denomination, 'horseless carriage'.

8 See for instance, Maurice Merleau-Ponty, *Phenomenology of Perception* (London: Routledge Classics, 2002).

9 *Slow Down London*, 24 April–4 May 2009, http://slow-downlondon.co.uk/about/

10 Alastair Fuad-Luke, 'Reflective consumption: Slowness and Nourishing Rituals of Delay in Anticipation of a Post Consumer Age' as part of the *Design for Durability* Seminar at the Design Council, 11 April 2006.

Clifton Suspension Bridge, Bristol, UK.
This 'slow' photograph was taken between 17
December 2007 and 21 June 2008. Pinhole Camera.
Pinhole photography by Justin Quinnell.
http://bit.ly/pinhole_photo

11 For a discussion of this see Peter Dormer, *The Culture of Craft* (Manchester; New York: Manchester University Press, 1997).

12 http://www.slowlab.net/slow_design.html (accessed 5/6/09).

13 See for instance, Slavoj Žižek, *Looking Awry: Introduction to Jaques Lacan Through Popular Culture* (Cambridge, MA.: The MIT Press, 1992).

Topophilia

Skyline and cityscapes / The bumps of flatness – the terrain of design
Analogous cities / Capturing the imaginary
Exposing the line in film and video / The curve of imagination
Report from the Hawk-Eye camera / Soft form
Kodak moments and Nokia digits / Used condoms and forgotten names

This chapter explores the topography of the
city as it is walked, mapped, drawn, surveilled,
photographed and branded.

Keywords
Image (898,000,000)
Imagination (13,300,000)
Literature (75,200,000)
Memory (130,000,000)

Keywords and their Google hit rate in conjunction with the word design.

Alexa

Skyline and cityscapes

A while ago, the Sunday supplements had a holiday advertisement for Ontario, Canada, with the by-line *The Towering Beauty of Ontario*. The accompanying photograph showed a benign public park with a trellis of trees supporting the skyline. The image is meant to portray an iconoclastic representation of the modern city. What caught the eye was the way the skyline, although augmented with trees, clearly opened into a vista of the CN communication tower. The 'Communication Tower' became a ubiquitous symbol of technological virility in the 1960s and 1970s. Cities from Moscow to London erected these modern day obelisks. East Berlin, in particular, gave the West 'the finger' when it erected its 365m tower in 1969 (its observation platform swivels to this day).

The architectural posturing that accompanied the cold war years has ceased. The silhouette of architectural figures on the postmodern visual landscape today relate more to commerce than ideology. Now, in this globalised environment, some of the traditional roles of architectural semiosis have changed: the Christian church spire no longer has to reach out to its parishioners and likewise the skyscraper to its investors. The former has satellite TV and the latter is exposed on market screens 24/7.

The Global city is, as Manuel Castells[1] points out, 'a process' rather than a physical space. And here is the rub: the city, so long the hub of capitalist production, is now dormant, in this guise at least. We live in a world of 'flows' both literal and metaphorical. Refugees (if the rabid tabloids are to be believed) and data stream from one capital to another.

In one promotional video Hong Kong branded itself as a 'portal city'. Of course, this city branding is not a new phenomena. In the 1970s, New York's tourism bureau turned casual references to the 'Big Apple'[2] into a brand and Milton Glaser's *I love New York* became

The bumps of flatness – the terrain of design

The original article stemmed from a perceived tension between the experience of a city imagined looking out of a hotel window when visiting abroad and that imagined at home, sitting in an armchair reading the newspaper. In one reply on the Limited Language website, Trin described the effect:

'As cities become plucked from any sense of the "real"; to become tick boxes in the glossy pages of *Wallpaper** and other magazines which document the state of global flows.'[1]

Both vantage points are influenced by the context of viewing, and we represented the city skyline through this contextual framework. The essay was trying to trace the relationship between emotional mapping, geography and memory.

A photograph in a newspaper advertisement provides the documentary evidence of the modernity of a given place, be it Ontario or elsewhere. The other framework, peering through a hotel window, provides a live image, one which is almost cinematic. But, as the sight pans the skyline it conflates with the memories of moving images seen on TV news bulletins and cinema: memory re-edits, splicing the real with the mediated.

Be it Tel Aviv, New York, Beirut or the rural slopes of Tuscany...each image, like a rollover button, has a composite beneath where the imagination acts as the hyperlink to broader emotional and cultural maps.

Although the original essay is about the topology of the city, the role of height or elevation, to be above, is not directly addressed. Height, both metaphorically and literally, is used to forge the modern experience: from 'towering beauty' to 'communication towers'. The vantage of height is used to impose and separate urban experience. We look down on

Giraffe, Portugal
(2005).

Manhattan Portage shopfront, New York (2004).

DKNY advert on the side of a New York
building (2004).

Hoardings as the Swiss Re building (the
Gherkin) is under construction, London
(2003).

a design icon. Branding now increasingly uses the NY skyline; the profile has become both the 'synecdoche and the swoosh'[3] of the city. We can of course look at the biography of individual buildings and see how 'cathedrals to commerce' are commissioned, built and embedded with meaning. However, these individual architectural statements are merely silhouettes of commerce as the physical work of 'old' cities transfers to the new 'edge cities' of call centres and Internet bubbles.

This process of transference of work from branded city to periphery is a phenomenon well documented in the market of brands. The President of Landor Branding Agency quoted in Naomi Klein's book *No Logo* states: 'products are made in a factory...but brands are made in the mind'.[4] This dynamic is reflected in the use of the city skyline as logo or trademark. Cities produce aspirations, the soft bedding for brands. For instance, September 11th reminded people just how potent the city skyline has become and after the event, the space left, ached in the news footage and photojournalism flowing out of the mourning city. One passenger on the Staten Island Ferry, looking up at the skyline, spoke of the city losing its two front teeth. This reaction can only be dreamed of by a brand manager and it is a brand loyalty exploited by both politicians and corporations.

The medium for super brands, television, has been quick to exploit the branding potential of the city skyline. New York features heavily in sitcoms, not only as a narrative context but the skyline is used as an editing device. *Friends*, *Sex and the City* and *Becker* all used the NY skyline as a 'sting' between edits. Sometimes, like the notorious subliminal advertising of the 1960s,[5] in a nanosecond. Sometimes a more leisurely pace allows an indulgent sweep of Manhattan holding up the New York skyline.

There is one final strand of the skyline, the skyline that is mediated through news coverage. Gaza and, earlier, Beirut have all become fragments in a skyline spliced with conflict. Staring out from a hotel room in central

people, the camera crane swoops to capture the close-up, we rise to the top, we bring people to their knees, and in an ironic homology, we raze things to the ground.

The spatial dynamics of cartography are commented on by Jess: 'maps are cutouts without skylines; we look at them as if from above'.[11]

The totalising effect of a map is, in part, brought-about by this privileged position of the viewer; above and detached. This is an elevated position allowing the flat, mapped, geography to become a place for the beholder's imagination to colonise.

It is the very flatness of the map which, we would argue, is instrumental in perceiving the map as a benign structure, to which we can attach our imagination. Flatness, like erasure, creates a visual realm ripe for subjugation. Enlightenment Euclidean geometry, where perspectival space extends infinitely in three dimensions, demoting flatness to a pre-modern anachronism.

We live in a world dominated by the architectonics of power and spectacle. This often materialises in the buildings that puncture the skyline of major cities worldwide; itself, a physical act of rupture from flatness.

Maps only provide an idea of space, because 'our body is not in space like things; it inhabits or haunts space...it is our expression in the world'.[1] In one way the map is the mechanical abstraction of what Merleau-Ponty calls 'the platitudes [and flatness] of "technicized" thinking'.[2] Here, our world becomes a series of one-dimensional, mechanised events: simple pins in a map.

So, how does this graphic space translate into the real world? The map is never the sphere of the cartographer alone. Artists and designers have explored and exploited the totalising language of mapping. The London Underground Map, which dates from the early 1930s and was almost avant-garde in its representation of non-Euclidean space, exploits the flatness of mapping to provide an abstracted iconography of place names to demarcate routes.

Another iconic representation of London, the A-Z map, is used in the work of the artist Lars Arrhenius. His facsimile of the London map is 'animated' with vignettes of people going about their daily business on the streets. Arrhenius provides the possibility for phenomenological interventions, simple narratives, into the non-space of maps.

How might designers, especially in the digital sphere, replicate the haptic? How might they conjoin lived experience with empirical information design? Interactivity, in one sense, allows the re-establishment of the sensorial within flat screen-based visual cultures, whilst Google Earth allows for tagging and annotating with your own images.

If the above is a positive spin on the mapping of territory, then many of the comments on the original essay explore the darker side of Skyline and cityscapes. They hint at the role of memory in constructing narratives and how visual mapping can, mistakenly, make the world all-too easily digestible. For instance, Toby Todd commented: 'Cities compete on image production rather than industrial production. The city skyline or panorama are the modern day "satanic mills"?'.[III]

And Steven added: 'A problem of visual culture exposed: images conflate and depict a "total" world rather than the Diaspora, which is the real one. The *I love New York* phrase/logo came out when the city was experiencing high levels of crime and deprivation. The question should have been "who loves New York?"'[IV]

So, in conclusion, what happens when abstractions return as lived experience, in Jess' words as: 'bodies to the graphics of territory'.[V]

What happens when we bring together map, memory and the material world?

Although the map is a symbol of the rationalising process, collecting empirical information to be transposed into visual form, it is always encoded with cultural and ideological meaning. The work of the Israeli designer David Tartakover provides an example. For Jess, 'Tartakover repeatedly uses an image he calls The

Tel Aviv, it's hard not see the skyline (like the colours in the Israeli flag; blue against white) without the scene conflating with the images from all the newsreel footage in recent times. The skyline, like a doppelgänger, becomes a composite or double exposure depicting smoke rising, pockmarks and sirens. This is the collateral damage of too many visual-bites on CNN, CBS, BBC and Al Jazeera.

The skyline, like any logo or sign, becomes part of the visual mapping we use to (mis)understand the world. Often, fatally, it can make the world seem easily digestible.

See further images here
www.limitedlanguage.org/images

References
1   For instance, see Manuel Castells, 'The Rise of the Network Society' in *The Information Age: Economy, Society and Culture* Vol. I (Cambridge, MA; Oxford, UK: Blackwell, 1996).
2   This term is first found in journalism and literature of the 1920s.
3   Synedoche is a figure of speech where a part is put for the whole. Here we are thinking that the skyline can both be convenient shorthand for a living, breathing, dynamic city or it can reduce the complex to visual sound bite.
4   Naomi Klein, *No Logo* (London: Flamingo, 2000), 195.
5   See Vance Packard, *The Hidden Persuaders* (First published by Pocket Books in 1957 and re-issued by Mark Crispin Miller as a 50th anniversary edition in 2007).

A-Z by Lars Arrhenius (2004).

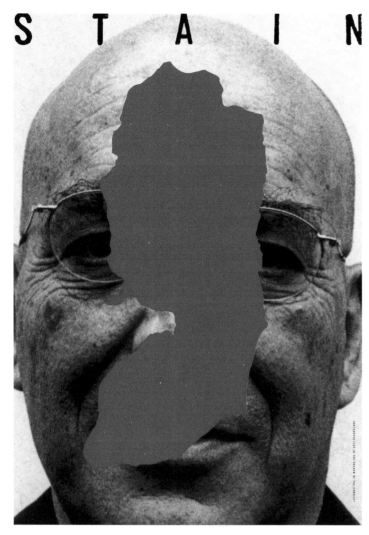

A portrait of the founder of Zionism, Theodor Herzel with the stain by David Tartakover.

Stain by David Tartakover, Poster (2002).

Stain; a solid red shape of the West Bank map. He uses it to "brand" portraits of politicians and public figures. He started with himself. Maps are cutouts without skylines; we look at them as if from above. Tartakover's use of this ragged silhouette – opaque, wet, indelible – returns bodies to the graphics of territory'.[VI]

This reading of mapping sides with the postmodern belief of the totalising effect of the map, rather than the emotional, relational mapping discussed earlier.

The flatness of the map and the totalising effect of the privileged 'view from above' has a literal translation in the Israeli-Palestinian conflict. The metaphorical stitch (the Israeli term used for the green line which notionally separates the two territories) is traversed by the Israeli army by air and on land. The invasion in Gaza in 2009 was, in part, retaliatory for the missiles fired by Hamas. The map-less trajectory of the missiles mean they fall inside Israeli territory haphazardly, but with monotonous regularity.

The flatness metaphor of the map and the literal power of elevation come together in the construction of the segregation wall and the destruction of Palestinian towns. Sharon Rotbard, in *A Civilian Occupation: The Politics of Israeli Architecture*, comments how the dividing wall illustrates that 'the actual object is more powerful than any image or metaphor'.[3] Conversely, Palestinian towns are bulldozed and razed to the ground:[4] reduced to the flatness of a map.

See full responses + carry on the conversation here
http://tiny.cc/chapter4_1

Reader credits
I   Trin 12/12/2006
II   Jess 19/12/2006
III Toby Todd 11/01/2007
IV   Steven 10/12/2006
V   Jess 19/12/2006
VI   Jess 19/12/2006

References
1   Thomas Baldwin (ed.) *Maurice Merleau-Ponty: Basic Writings* (London; New York: Routledge, 2004).

2   Ibid.

3   Sharon Rotbard, 'Wall and Tower (Homa Umigdal)' in
    Rafi Segal and Eyal Weizman, *A Civilian Occupation:
    The Politics of Israeli Architecture* (London: Verso,
    2003), 54.

4   BBC News Website, http://bit.ly/razed_town
    (accessed 18/08/09).

David Phillips
Analogous cities

Capturing the imaginary

'With cities, it is as with dreams: everything imaginable can be dreamed, but even the most unexpected dream is a rebus that conceals a desire or, its reverse, a fear. Cities, like dreams, are made of desires and fears, even if the thread of their discourse is secret, their rules absurd, their perspectives deceitful, and everything conceals something else.'
(Italo Calvino, *Invisible Cities*, 1972)[1]

Sometimes I feel that our physical experience of the city is less clear and comprehensible than the image or idea of the city. The complexity of cities makes them difficult, if not impossible, to fully understand. We prefer, instead, to understand their images. We favour a city constructed not from brick, stone and glass, but from memory, association and history.

Nicholas Roeg's 1973 film *Don't Look Now* is a favourite of mine, and I have seen it many times. I also love Venice, the city in which it is set and which I visit regularly. Each time I see this film I am intrigued by its fragmented juxtapositions of space and time. As the actors move through the city from location to location, there is no regard for geography or journey. They pass a palace on the Grand Canal and then seconds later they are outside the Biennale gardens. This fragmentation of location is, however, only evident if you are very familiar with Venice. Roeg has constructed a new Venice, an identified city, suited to his purpose.

This type of collaged continuity is not uncommon in cinema. We have all seen films shot in cities that are well known to us, where the director is keen to emphasise the location of the action and has, therefore, staged a car chase that passes, in no logical order, every landmark building in the city. As we watch we realise that this is another London, Paris or New York. A perfect condensed city of images, a place in which everything is near. I love the opportunity these false

Rereading the essay, what is notably absent from David Phillips' original article are people: a populace. It's in the responses to the article that we find them. In a sense he provides the mise-on-scene and the comments enter stage-right...

Where-upon we are immediately snapped out of the imaginative sphere of film and its concomitant; memory, to the external world: 'What I like about my adopted city (Toronto) is that most of the memories get swept away with the grime of the streets, on a cyclical basis, or built over and upon'.[1]

And other commentators join the quest to populate the imagined space created by the author, Adriana: 'the tour guides point out spots in the city, directing the gaze'.[II] Homeira Nekkui: 'Local people are wearing traditional dresses, men and women working shoulder to shoulder...'[III] Wei-Chun Kao: 'In reality I'm most comfortable in the crowded concrete city,'[IV] and so it goes on.

And it is in this realm, between the imaginary and the real, that design and visual communication operate. Policing and mining its creative potential, the creative process both erases and redraws how the city is configured: billboards, shopping malls, street furniture all serve to direct, collate and make the city a visceral place.

But it must be understood that the city, as it is explored in the original essay with its filmic and imaginative quarters, is a city of plenty, of excesses. James Souttar points out that the choice of Venice provides the potential for metaphor and symbolism because: 'Venice ...[is] a city built not on earth, but on water (fluidity? life?) – [which] has captured so many imaginations'.[V] An alternative view might be that Venice is built on the flows of capital rather than the poetics of its engineering alone.

Oshiage, Tokyo.
Photograph by David Phillips.

cities gives us to separate the real and the analogous city. I sometimes feel these comprehensible cities are better, more identifiable, than actual places.

In Aldo Rossi's seminal book, *The Architecture of the City*, he shows us a painting by Giovanni Canaletto seemingly of Venice, in which Palladio's unbuilt project for the Rialto Bridge, the Basilica of Vicenza, and the Palazzo Chiericati (also in Vicenza), are all arranged as if they were an actual part of a real city. It looks like Venice, but it is not. It is more than Venice; it is an analogous city, a city that expresses the idea of the city more perfectly, but less factually, than the actual city. Rossi says, 'Athens, Rome, Constantinople, and Paris represent ideas of the city that extend beyond their physical form, beyond their permanence; thus we can speak in this way of cities like Babylon which have all but physically disappeared.'[2]

Now we have another Venice within a hotel in Las Vegas. It is a city of paper-thin façades set around a crystal-clear canal. It is a strange, ugly copy that makes little attempt to replicate real places or forms. Unlike the other Venice the sky is always blue and very clean. It is banal, vapid and clichéd. And yet, when I saw this Venice it surprised me how it caused me to recall in detail the charm and intricacy of the real city, by way of its inaccuracy.

This got me thinking about other cities, the cities that I have never visited. When I imagine these cities I see all the great buildings gathered together along one street or around a single square. I know that when I do visit it will not be like that, but, for now, this will have to do.

In the 1970s the station identity for the London's Thames Television featured all the major buildings: the Palace of Westminster, St Paul's Cathedral, Tower Bridge etc. They were all grouped together in an impossible silhouette. I always loved the fact that this perfect London, a London that does not exist, should be the image of London. To those who knew, it was a fabrication and to those who did not, it was perfection. Quoting again

The architect Rem Koolhaas is a useful contemporary figure when tracing the relationships between architecture and economics. In *Junkspace*,[1] Koolhaas' broad critique of the postmodern urban experience, he comments: 'Junkspace thrives on design, but design dies in Junkspace.' And later in the same essay, he criticises our digital, Photoshopped, step-and-repeat existence when commenting: 'Regurgitation is the new creativity; instead of creation, we honor, cherish and embrace manipulation…'

But the city is more than a sequence of manipulations. It is made malleable – like the *Here & There* maps of Manhattan, a project by Schulze & Webb exploring speculative projections of dense cities. The projection begins with a three-dimensional representation of the immediate environment where close buildings are represented normally, and the viewer is shown in the third person, exactly where she stands. The projection connects the viewer's local environment to remote destinations normally out of sight. *Here & There* maps allow the city to uncoil in front of us; 'putting the viewer simultaneously above the city and in it where she stands, both looking down and looking forward'.[2]

And, the city is a series of narratives too. The notion of a city which unwraps in front of us is poignantly observed by the actress/director of *The Unloved* (2009) directed by Samantha Morton. This film centres on a young girl growing up in a children's home and, as such, takes a look from a 'child's-eye view' at the UK care system. Morton talked about her experience of being a child in-care and how walking home from school was a rare moment of being alone which she would stretch out by taking the longest route home. Lovers use the same strategy, prolonging the piquancy of a first date. Equally, taxi drivers, cyclists or those looking for shelter from a sudden cloud burst, look for the shortest route. In this way the city expands and contracts according to use or need.

In the pragmatic territory of design,

Here & There maps of Manhattan by
Schulze & Webb Ltd (2009).

from Calvino we can see that a city can be whatever you can imagine it to be, but only that.

"'From now on, I'll describe the cities to you," the Khan had said, "in your journeys you will see if they exist." But the cities visited by Marco Polo were always different from those thought of by the emperor.

"And yet I have constructed in my mind a model city from which all possible cities can be deduced," Kublai said. "It contains everything corresponding to the norm. Since the cities that exist diverge in varying degree from the norm, I need only foresee the exceptions to the norm and calculate the most probable combinations."

"I have also thought of a model city from which I deduce all others," Marco answered. "It is a city made only of exceptions, exclusions, incongruities, contradictions. If such a city is the most improbable, by reducing the number of abnormal elements, we increase the probability that the city really exists. So I have only to subtract exceptions from my model, and in whatever direction I proceed, I will arrive at one of the cities which, always as an exception, exists. But I cannot force my operation beyond a certain limit: I would achieve cities too probable to be real."'[3]

(Italo Calvino, *Invisible Cities*, 1972)

See further images here
www.limitedlanguage.org/images

References
1   Italo Calvino, *Invisible Cities* (First published in Italy by Giulio Einaudi Editore, 1972), 44.
2   Aldo Rossi, *The Architecture of the City* (Cambridge, MA: MIT, 1982), 128 (First published, 1966).
3   Italo Calvino, Op cit., 69.

the city always exists in the haptic realm. J.J. Gibson comments: 'The haptic system... is an apparatus by which the individual gets information about both the environment and his body. He feels an object relative to the body and the body relative to an object. It is a perceptual system by which animals and men (humans) are literally in touch with the environment.'[3]

The haptic bridges the external and internal, the material (substance) and perceptual (imaginative). So, the world comes alive in the touch of things – our physical environment – but also the movement of the body through space, of cognition and perception. The latter could be seen as analogous to the imaginary.

This capturing of imaginary space and movement is seen in the work of Lia Halloran. Her photographs, in a sense, capture the immateriality of imagination (and movement): the erasure of the gesture. In her *Dark Skate* series of photographs she photographs the non-spaces of skate culture; a light strapped to her wrist (or head?). The camera captures trajectories rather than material presence.

This outside/inside is the place design needs to mediate. Paul Rodaway, in *Sensuous Geographies*, explains how it provides a conduit between the three elements of environmental experience; 'Simple contact; the juxtaposition of two surfaces against each other..., exploratory activity; an agent actively investigates the environment...' and finally, 'Communication; the contact is actively intended by one party or both, but each party responds specifically to the other's tactile stimulation and messages are exchanged.'[4]

Our experience of urban living is a combination of these elements and design, from architecture to visual communication, provide the coefficients for these experiences – walkways, billboards, bus stops or the city square.

People are needed in design – not as audience alone but as user/consumer. Communication, for Italo Calvino, is the ability to open up the interiority of city living:

'[In] a great city, the people who move

Dark Skate | LA River Bridge by Lia Halloran (2007).
48 x 48 inches.

The artist Lia Halloran captures both geographic place, and imaginary spaces, in her photographs of Los Angeles. In her *Dark Skate*
series of photographs she captures the non-spaces of skate culture;
a light strapped to her wrist (her head?), the camera captures trajectories rather than material presence. (Lia Halloran is represented by
DCKT Contemporary New York.)

through the streets are all strangers. At each encounter, they imagine a thousand things about one another; meetings which could take place between them, conversations, surprises, caresses, bites'.[5]

Should design look to capture the imagination of the encounter? Shouldn't it look to foster that which could take place, and instigate a catalyst for such opportunities? That is, design as synapse between the space of motion and the places of touch.

In *Space and Place* Yi-Fu Tuan writes; 'Touch articulates another kind of complex world'.[6] It is a world that is in tension with, if not opposition to, the postmodern city of 'strange new feelings of an absence of inside outside, the bewilderment and loss of spatial orientation'.[7] This world described by Fredric Jameson is one dominated by the visual. It is a world of bricolage and fragmentation, a place obsessed with image.

Why does design have to belong to this monoculture, this one dimensional, touchless, world?

See full responses + carry on the conversation here
http://tiny.cc/chapter4_2

Reader credits
I   Anon 16/10/2005
II   Adriana 31/10/2005 – 'Tour guides point out spots in the city, directing the gaze. They walk on paths that contain the densest information of interest for tourists, adjust[ing] and updating their routes to integrate new attractions. On a tour in Berlin, after talking about the Brandenburg Gate, the tourguide turns to point at a window of the nearby hotel Adlon; the site of the infamous Michael Jackson incident.'
III Homeira Nekkui 29/11/2005 – 'This article reminds me of a village in the Middle-East that i went to a few years ago…'
IV   Wei-Chun Kao 07/12/2005 – 'Lewis Parker a musician from Camden creates beautiful soundscapes where my initial thoughts are that of an imaginary city. Not a perfect one or a 'New Jerusalem' just a genuine isolated area for myself when I have spirited away from the mundane monotony of modern life. The time periods change and I have a particular liking for Alexander the Great. Science fiction and retro Space Age cities are in the back of my mind sometimes. In reality I'm most comfortable in the crowded concrete city of London or Taipei. Quite a contrast.'
V   James Souttar 17/10/2005

References

1   Rem Koolhaas, *Content* (Köln: Taschen, 2004), 544.

2   http://schulzeandwebb.com/hat/

3   J.J. Gibson, *The Senses Considered as Perceptual Systems* (Boston: Houghton Mifflin, 1966), 335.

4   Paul Rodaway, *Sensuous Geographies: Body, Sense, and Place* (London; New York: Routledge, 1994), 198.

5   Italo Calvino, *Invisible Cities* (New York: Harcourt Brace Jovanovich, 1974), 165.

6   Yi-Fu Tuan, *Space and Place: The Perspective of Experience* (Minneapolis, MN: University of Minnesota Press, 1977), 235.

7   Fredric Jameson, *Postmodernism, or, The Cultural Logic of Late Capitalism* (London: Verso, 1991), 438.

Adam Kossoff

Exposing the line in film and video

There's a nice moment in Wim Wenders' film *Wings of Desire* (1987) when Peter Falk, previously an angel and now an ordinary mortal and an actor who spends his spare moments drawing, is standing at a mobile food stall drawing in the Berlin cold. Falk, feeling an angel's invisible presence (Bruno Ganz), says that it's good to be mortal, '... just to touch something, feel the cold, to smoke, have coffee, and if you do it together it's just fantastic. Or draw – you know you take the pencil and you make a dark line, then you make a light line, together it's a good line...'

At the centre of the mainstream moving image lies a technological desire for transparency, a need to obliterate a consciousness of the 'line' in order to veil the viewer's awareness of the technology that allows the two spaces, that of the cinema and that of the spectator, to merge into one; removing actual physical presence in order to promote the more illusionary presence of the moving image. By contrast, one can see that modern art rooted much of its practice in revealing the line or the edge, of exposing its duplicity in the production of presence. The force of modernist art – Sergei Eisenstein's *Battleship Potemkin* (1925) – serves as a filmic example. It made lines and edges apparent, boundaries were put under stress, where the line split and gathered together images, engaging with its production of meaning.

How does the moving image deal with the line? Although David Lynch uses the familiar elements of popular narrative cinema, one could summarise Lynch's oeuvre as an attempt to overcome the obvious linearity of mainstream cinema. The title sequence and first shot of *Lost Highway* (1996): car headlights illuminate a yellow dashed line along the middle of a motorway. With the forward movement of a car, the low angled shot picks up the dashed line in the middle of the motorway. This dashed line reappears at crucial points in the story.

The curve of imagination

The original article by Adam Kossoff, in one sense, plots a history of the ambivalent relationship between the senses and more specifically, the tensions brought about when sight is prioritised above others – in film especially.

The article eventually comes to rest by placing the problematic relationship at the centre of his own work via a cinematic history of Russian Realism, German New Wave and American Neo Art House, all peerlessly attached to their philosophical underpinning: Structuralism to Deleuze, spectatorship to art.

The responses themselves took issue with the notion of 'meanings', bluntly asking: 'I'm inclined to wonder where all this talk of lines leaves us.'[I] Another response simply dissolved the article into a literal sequence of lines.[II]

And in a sense, you do need to be 'in the moment' if not 'in the know' to follow the trajectory of articles like Kossoff's which try to excavate meaning beyond the common sensible and readily authenticated (the whole Limited Language website is party to this). It is like the language of technology manuals – you need to know what an 'ON' button is, otherwise a DVD player becomes a box covered in hieroglyphics, a paper weight maybe.

What is important in abstracting the notion of the 'line' for instance, is how it allows a serendipitous journey of how the mark or inscription, both literal and as metaphor, intersects and influences day-to-day practice. For many, the line – drawn, animated, digitised or mathematical equation – is the bedrock of practice.

Before Modernism's 'technological desire for transparency' (which Kossoff speaks of), the mathematical line as represented in perspective drawing was important in elevating

Train Lines by Adam Kossoff (2008).

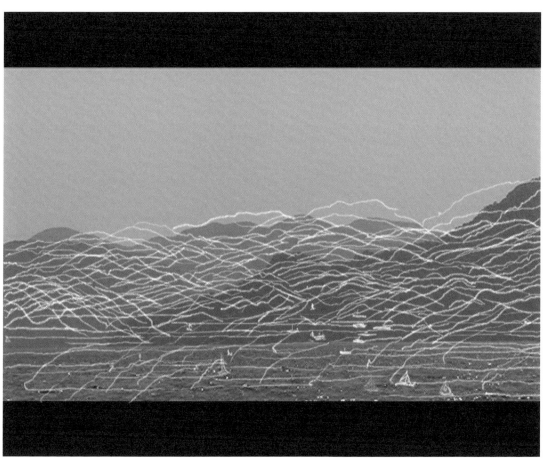

Chalk Lines by Adam Kossoff (2009).

the artisan to the classically defined artist. It literally separated the artist from the mechanical processes of doing to the cognitive world of mathematics. The Renaissance followed the Classical precedent where mathematically informed disciplines from astronomy to music were seen as the apex of liberal arts. Leonardo da Vinci's *Vitruvian* figure,[1] as well as being linked to symbolic measures and significance, quite literally transforms man into a series of intersecting lines.

This binary is still with us today; its embers enflame arguments between craft and art, science and culture.

It is Modernism that translates the line into the spaces of modular furniture and interiors where the physical line dematerialises into plains of colour or glass. The interior designs of De Stijl architecture in the 1920s show this well. Gerrit Rietveld's *Schröder House* is a classic De Stijl example of how surface and colour are used to create domestic spaces. Designed for Truus Schröder-Schräder in 1924, it is an example of a functionalism used to erase the more doctrinaire – physically demarcated – space making of architecture.

The building, similar to the methodology of Sergei Eisenstein's film *Battleship Potemkin* as discussed by Kossoff, makes explicit its production. Through a series of architectural edits – jump cuts – a structure is formed that both emphasises and erases the orthogonal. The line is perceived in the tension between structure, colour and light.

In the example above, we see architecture opening up as part of a narrative. Rather than simply reading books, texts and other linear forms of information-gathering about a building (or any other designed artefact), the building becomes known to us by walking through it. This is, if you will, a phenomenological twist to the Renaissance belief in the relationship between body, architecture and proportion.

Architecture gives us a clear methodology with which to explore the workings of the line. From childhood

Lynch's film, the story of a man accused of murdering his wife, who is then jailed, only to morph into someone else, follows this immanent trail of fragmented and rhythmic linearity, one which tempts but, simultaneously denies, meaning.

At the beginning of *Lost Highway*, the main character, Fred, hears the front doorbell ring. We see him look at the intercom. Cut to the intercom in big close-up. Fred is mysteriously informed that someone called 'Dick Laurent is dead'. He looks out the windows of his house to try and see the deliverer of this strange message. They obscure his view directly downwards. From the outside we see him staring out the windows, trapped behind the glass of his modernist house (a potent reminder of another non-linear film, Maya Deren's *Meshes in the Afternoon* (1943)). Via composition, framing and the sequencing of the shots, a straight line is drawn between Fred and the intercom, but that line is then interrupted by the obtuseness of the narrative and the shots of him trying to see onto the street below. A line is also drawn between the beginning and the ending of the film. Once Peter Dayton has morphed back into Fred, and the Mystery Man and Fred have disposed of Dick Laurent, Fred returns to his house and announces in the intercom at the front door, 'Dick Laurent is dead'. The narrative line follows the inside-out line of the Möbius Strip, where identities are switched imperceptibly.

How much is the line in the moving image drawn, how much is it given? The shot-countershot, the eyes of one character meeting another within the film, entrapping the spectator in their identificatory looking, is premised on an orientable 'straight-line' vision. Within Althusserian ideological terms, apparatus theory sought to condemn Hollywood, because it supposedly used the linear Renaissance perspective system of centralising the spectator, causing them to watch the film in an enraptured state of forgotten consciousness and unshackled desire. In Lynch's cinema, in contrast to say Yasijuro Ozu's films for example, the 180 degree line is never crossed; shot and counter-shot sustain a normative consistency that serves to sustain the audience's spatial orientation. Through careful continuity, sustaining the body's orientable asymmetry, characters will always remain on the same side of the screen. On the other hand, the narrative line in *Lost Highway* is assured where male hysteria, based on the desire and complete control of 'woman', causes the psyche to circle round and round itself, and the line, broken as it is, is both drawn, by the narrative, and given by the deranged subject.

Christian Metz,[1] one of the prime movers behind post-structural film theory, investigated the nature of film as a symbolic medium and a language. But theorising film as a language had its problems, namely whether there is a minimal unit or not on the level of the signifier. Perhaps another way of approaching the question of cinema as language would be to speculate about the role of the line in the cinema, sometimes a given, sometimes possibly even actively drawn. The line occupies a space between the imaginary and the symbolic. It is that boundary that divides them and, at the same time, makes them possible; image making/writing at its beginning. The line brings the image into play, is the image itself and connects images together. The line in cinema exists on two levels. There is the mimetic level, that is what is seen on the screen, the lines of represented reality, the lines inferred by camera movement, the lines designed to guide our vision of the unfolding drama or vision. And then there are the lines inherent to the technology; I'm thinking of the line that surrounds the celluloid frame, the lines, the black bars, that divide one still frame from another, to many – the life of film itself.

There is a body of cinematic thinking that has focused in on what Dziga Vertov[2] termed the 'interval'. It's a term that revolves around the gaps between the shots, an inherent measure of the cut, which allows one to edit in the manner of musical phrasing. The interval, the facilitator of cinematic movement itself, also occurs, if one follows Vertov's thinking, within the shot, in terms

drawings of a house with smoking chimney to sophisticated CAD drawings, we understand the relationship between line and form.

However, the original text by Kossoff develops beyond natural associations between line and form and, in doing so, presses a new 'ON' button – words and associations and how they influence our creative thinking.

Think of the desktop metaphor/symbol and how it transformed the way we relate to our computer? It's the essence of the office desktop transferred to a digital environment. This is an example of how visual symbolism can translate, or conceal, technology and become a generative model for creative output.

Semiotics describes how words and associated meanings are arbitrary: dog = furry four legged friend (and not a cat), for instance, is a culturally defined association. This arbitrariness leads to an unstable language. Meaning might be fixed to time as much as anything. Thus symbols, whether a red rose or a revolutionary Cuban hero, are in flux – meanings detach and reform as time passes – so a revolutionary figure like Ernesto "Che" Guevara can come to represent anti-authoritarianism in general, or equally, a decorative element on a T-shirt which appeals to the fashion-conscious. This to-ing and fro-ing of meaning is at the centre of our semiological consciousness.[2]

Design (and design thinking) appropriates and remixes the visual world until 'all this noise begins to mean something'.[3] New meaning(s) become visible in this mixing process. In this way, design functions to fulfil Maurice Merleau-Ponty's comment about 'meaning arising at the edge of signs'.[4]

This creative element of meaning-making is captured in Roland Barthes' essay *The Imagination of the Sign*, where he delineates upon the creative possibility of the imagination in creating the sign:

'The...imagination no longer sees the sign in its perspective, it foresees it in its extension: its antecedent or consequent links, the bridges it extends to other signs...hence the dynamics of the image here is that of an arrangement of mobile, substitutive parts, whose combination produces meaning, or more generally a new object; it is, then, a strictly fabricative or even functional imagination.'[5]

The original article picks up the dynamics of the scratch as an extension of the line; as Kossoff puts it, the most ignored event in the history of cinema. The scratch exists, but is dormant, in the phenomenological experience of cinema. A cinematic experience described by Siegfried Kracauer in the 1920s as a 'fragmented sequence of splendid sense impressions', where 'The stimulations of the senses succeed each other with such rapidity that there is no room for even the slightest contemplation to squeeze in between them.'[6] He invokes a spectator weaned on narrative and, more specifically, the spectacle. The scratch, as such, was technological, aberrant and invisible.

With analogue technology, such invisibility is culturally conditioned (the line and the scratch are there, we are simply schooled not to see them). For instance, the picture plane 'is required to be read as mute and empty of characteristics, over and above that required to allow line centre stage as the apparent site of all meaning'.[7]

Today, in a digital world of CDS, MP3s, DVDs and Blue-ray, technological production is literally invisible. This provides a desensitised sonic or visual experience where mechanics are largely replaced by algorithms. As Lucy Kimbell, in *New Media Art* comments: 'Computers are "chameleons" capable of combining media, sampling, morphing appearance, and working in invisible ways'.[8]

The increasing invisibility of technological production creates a need for a visible ontology of production, in such a scenario the scratch becomes a trace of authenticity. The scratch has become the pixellated image in the digital world.

And finally, the scratch emulates a patina of use and authentication; it provides the provenance of its technological heritage.

of a change in emphasis in the camera movement, for example. The idea of the interval was important amongst structural filmmakers, for example Tony Conrad, whereby cinema stressed its materiality and its rhythms via the idea of the flicker film. In Hollis Frampton's *(Nostalgia)* (1971) one is forced to contemplate the lines in the image and the edges of the images, amidst the self-containing temporality of the interior spaces of memory. The horizontal lines in video usually reveal themselves when the image is re-filmed or re-photographed. I'm not qualified to pass comment on High Definition video, albeit to say that it's higher in its definition because it uses many more lines per image. Mobile phone videos are of such low quality that they have an aesthetic of their own, one of blocked out spaces, jumpy and pixelated; images with a peculiar lining. But the most obvious point of contact with the line, when watching a film, is the edges of the frame. This line that demarcates the image is supposed to remain invisible, demarcating the space of the screen, allowing the flat plane of the image to be transcribed into a three-dimensional space.

Which brings me to the most ignored event in the history of cinema: the scratch on the film. The scratch, usually vertical but sometimes horizontal depending on how the damage is done, is largely invisible, apart from the odd experimental film that has drawn attention to this 'material inscription'. Unfortunately, digitising and transferring to DVD mark the natural end to this celluloid enemy that has, in its time, served to 'authenticate' many a documentary film or archive footage. This is the line, sometimes even drawn before our eyes by a poorly maintained projector, that marks the limits of the image, the materiality of film, that leaves scars and mementos of the passage of time on an object that is primarily mimetic and archival. Sadly, as cinema dies, so does the scratch (and other miscellaneous marks).

Recent thinking has misspent a lot of energy on refuting the straight line and linearity; the straight line represents a form of incarceration. Gilles Deleuze in

*Rietveld balcony. The Schröder
House* by Gerrit Rietveld (1924).
Photograph by Expectmohr.

See full responses + carry on the conversation here
http://tiny.cc/chapter4_3

Reader credits
I   Tony Todd 07/11/2007
II Border Patrol 14/11/2007 ·
    '|
    || As interesting as discussions such
    ||| | are, or may be, I'm inclined to won
    |||| | | where all this talk of lines leaves
    |||||| |...'

References
1   The *Vitruvian Man* is a drawing created by Leonardo
    da Vinci which dates from the end of the 15th
    century.
2   Roland Barthes, *Critical Essays* (Evaston, IL:
    Northwestern University Press, 1972), 206.
    Here we are placing the designer as 'analyst' rather
    than the 'user' in the manipulation of sign making.
3   M. Merleau-Ponty, G.A. Johnson, and M.B. Smith,
    *The Merleau-Ponty Aesthetics Reader: Philosophy
    and Painting* (Evanston, IL: Northwestern University
    Press, 1993), 78.
4   Ibid.
5   Roland Barthes. Op cit., 210.
6   Siegfried Kracauer, *The Salaried Masses : Duty and
    Distraction in Weimar Germany* (London; New York:
    Verso, 1998), 13.
7   Gordon Shrigley, *Spatula: How Drawing Changed the
    World* (London: Marmalade, 2004), 10.
8   Lucy Kimbell, *New Media Art: A Practice and Context
    in the UK 1994-2004* (London: Arts Council England,
    Cornerhouse Publications, 2004), 277.

his *Cinema 1* and 2 (1986 and 1989)[3] celebrates the
time-image of post-war realism and European art house
cinema, arguing that it utilised the non-linearity of the
Bergsonian concept of time. There are many issues that
one could take up with the Deleuzian theory of the
cinema and time, where the line, perhaps a spatialis-
ing term, undeservedly suffers. The line in the cinema,
the scratch, a drawn line in an animation film or early
abstract cinema, causes the surface of the screen to
become apparent and so disturbing the assumed depth
of the moving image. The line brings to the fore cinema
as a technics – the line that emerges from the surface of
the screen foregrounds the process of viewing itself and
reveals the spatial materiality of the medium. Walter
Benjamin wrote that the graphic line is 'determined by its
opposition to the surface'.[4]

This leads towards an understanding of my own
work, *Train Lines* (2008) and *Chalk Lines* (2009) for
example, where the line provides the satisfaction of
bringing together a recognised absence in the present;
a melancholic pleasure that the line is in a position
to acknowledge as well as a mapping of immanence,
whereby the viewing experience is one of sensory accu-
mulation made visible, where the line draws on the
interval between the surface and the deep space of the
moving image.

See further images here
www.limitedlanguage.org/images

References
1   See for instance, Christian Metz, *Film Language: A Semiotics of the
    Cinema* (New York: Oxford University Press, 1974).
2   The idea of the interval appears across a range of Vertov's writing. See
    Dziga Vertov, 'We: Variant of a Manifesto' in Annette Michelson (ed.),
    Kino-Eye; The Writings of Dziga Vertov (Berkeley: Pluto: 1984), 9.
3   Gilles Deleuze, *Cinema 1: The Movement-Image* (London: Athlone
    Press, 1986) and *Cinema 2: The Time-Image* (London: Athlone Press,
    1989), translated by H. Tomlinson and B. Habberjam.
4   Walter Benjamin, *Painting, or Signs and Marks, Selected Writings*
    (Cambridge, MA: Harvard University Press, 1996), 83.

Tom McCarthy

Report from the Hawk-Eye camera

Soft form

Some months ago, it was suggested by the Corporation of London that the best way of dealing with the pigeons fouling the high-rise on the twelfth floor of which the International Necronautical Society (INS) has its HQ was to drape netting over the whole building, cap-a-pied. Having spent a year researching the history of cartography with a view to mapping death, researching this history in all its details, from the variations between *Mercator*, *Petersen* and *Polar Gnomonic* map projections to the question of graticule to instances of blank and one-to-one scale maps (Lewis Carrol's oeuvre is awash with these) – INS staff were intrigued by the prospect of having a grid square superimposed over their splendid view of the world's greatest city. They were, however, even more appalled by the thought of working in what would effectively become a cage, and lobbied the Corporation to opt for an alternative method of pigeon control.

The INS has agents everywhere, and always gets its way. Arms were twisted, favours were called in, and as a result the building now enjoys twice-weekly visits from two hawks. Arriving in a Van Vynck van and launched from the leather-gloved forearms of their keepers, these austere birds patrol the skies above Golden Lane Estate, strangely anachronistic among the modernist fibre-glass and concrete as they sweep and turn in arcs and semicircles, Yeatsian gyres. Perhaps they're copying the markings on the tennis courts, across whose surface netball game-space codes are also taped, the overlay producing endless tangents, radii and incomplete circumferences, as on the taxi-ways of airports. The students on the four floors of the Italia Conti Dance school directly opposite HQ (an INS staff job has its perks) seem to be copying the hawks as they spin and pirouette. So, too, do the small aeroplanes that bank above Golden Lane to begin their descent into City Airport. Occasionally the hawks will break their pattern to plummet, thunderbolt-like, on a

Multiple cameras, montaged screens, manifold perspectives: the most ubiquitous example of this is CCTV, where recordings are collated by police to construct how a crime unfolds. Within the screen, moving images emphasise the development of events – narrative – over time. Now, imagine panning back out from the frame to take in the way a surveillance operator presides over a bank of screens. This offers several perspectives on the same moment. In another example, picture someone checking their mobile phone, its screen a grid of traffic-cam views streamed live from the requested route they're about to travel. In the original article, Tom McCarthy maps out many more such encounters.

In all these occurrences, the experience of space is transformed. Any old ideas about singular experience and continuous space become untenable: the self divides and space becomes discontinuous. How to respond?

One response is technophilia, a fetishisation of technology for its own sake – SatNav galore. Another response is a sense of loss. In a reply to the article, Helen Walker asks: 'Double vision, all vision, is life only complete when accessed from all angles? Why the thrill when life moves from one screen into our own screen of vision? What happens in between...?'[1] Walker is interested in what time has elapsed, what events go un-recorded. Although she's right to draw attention to the gap, what's missing is irrelevant. The thing that affects us is the rupture itself.

In another mediation, that Simon (a Motorola owner) draws attention to on the Limited Language website, is Danny Baker discussing the 'Curse of the Phone Cameras'[1] in *The Times*: 'Football grounds are getting quieter and the reason is because every...

One feedback loop we all participate in is government surveillance: CCTV. A mixture of street violence, post 9/11 paranoia and regulating car traffic, means many countries have seen an expansion of surveillance in urban areas. It has produced an industry of resistance – online and on the street.

Banksy, London (2008).

flock of pigeons, one of whom they'll off pour encourager les autres. It is an awesome spectacle.

No sooner had the INS installed its hawks than parliament followed suit. Since January Van Vynck birds have been keeping the exterior of the debating chambers and Big Ben pigeon-dirt free. During much of this period hawks have been outgunning doves inside the building also as the government prepared the approach-route to war against Iraq. Parliament is clearly visible from INS HQ, its left tower cut into tangents by the giant British Airways wheel known as The London Eye. The whole city is visible from INS HQ. During the huge anti-war demonstration in February it was suggested that the INS track and document the movement of police and news helicopters over London's airspace, but this proved impracticable as our own machinations had deprived us of a window grid-square within which to do so. Nonetheless, matching helicopters visible to the naked eye's horizontal plane with the overhead images that alternated with the worm's-eye ones on the TV set installed below the racked INS files turned out to be interesting.

When the war proper started, the stunning visuals transmitted to the same set by cameras attached to bombs inspired us to start lobbying the Corporation once again. This time we were demanding hawk-cams on the birds, with images relayed via a server to the laptop screens of subscribers in Golden Lane Estate, or, for that matter, worldwide. Nature documentaries provide this facility already; viewers can experience vicariously the pleasure of an Andean eagle's swoop and snatching of a rabbit or an African lion's rush and savaging of a gazelle. What neither nature documentaries nor CNN war footage yet provide is the reverse-angle shot, the victim's point of view – but this is perfectly feasible. Nick a gazelle's thigh muscle or slightly dope a rabbit so as to render it odds-on to fall prey to its pursuer, strap a small Sony to its flank and, hey-presto! – gazelle-cam. Give a spy coordinates for your next target and you could recoup expenditure on bombs by selling bunker or

nitwit fan in Britain now tries to capture even the most routine incident during a match on their rotten mobile phone cameras... As for penalties, just take a look at the "toward-goal" angle of a spot kick the next time one is televised. Behind the net, behold the solid wall of Nokia nincompoops. Thousands of jaded lunatics, not experiencing the real world in front of them, but collecting it preciously via a murky 1in x 1in screen. I have a friend who actually tries not to get too carried away when a goal goes in because he doesn't want to lose the framing on his shot ...'[1] Within the stadium, the loss of the crowd's roar is analogous to a loss of authenticity. There's no irony for Baker that he asks his readership to witness such inauthenticity via the 'toward-goal' shot on TV; the curse of their cameras long absorbed...

These multiplications and the experience of division, of splitting, are not the preserve of the technological age. In *Men in Space*,[2] Tom McCarthy's second novel, Anton Markov, a refugee, sits in a Prague café watching events before him rendered in triplicate by wall-mounted mirrors. 'Looking at the multiplying scene, Anton recalls his [football] refereeing days in Bulgaria: the trick was to see all the near-identical shirts, repeated runs, sudden departures, switches and loopbacks as one single movement, parts of a modulating system which you had to watch as though from outside, or above, or somewhere else.' Multiplications, loops, replays – these ruptures aren't a problem for Anton; they are the substance of the world.[3]

The discontinuity of space is addressed by Henri Lefebvre in *The Production of Space*. He suggests we might think of 'layers of space'[4] like flaky pastry, rather than the unified space we might more usually talk about. First printed in 1974, this provided a philosophical challenge, now visibly compounded by banks of screens, to the unifying logic of Cartesian perspective with its centred eye which has provided the dominant way of conceptualising space and subjectivity in the

Make'n'Shoot! *WiFi Camera Obscura* workshop by Bengt Sjölén and Adam Somlai Fischer with Usman Haque (2006 - ongoing).

Radiography prints can be created to reveal the various networks visible within a space as you move by.

hosp-cam pics to the world's media. We wanted pig-cam: hawk-cam, pig-cam, and the ability to switch between the two at will. Our moles within the Corporation tell us that the proposition is unlikely to succeed so we are currently approaching the Arts Council of Great Britain, who tend to go more for this kind of thing.

Parliament sits to the left side of INS HQ's ungridded window. To the right is Lord's Cricket Ground. I mention this fact not because during the five-day long Test Matches played there you can also match blimps and helicopters with the TV images they transmit (which you can), but rather because media coverage of cricket is one step ahead of everything else. While Formula One racing has embedded cameras in drivers' helmets, cricket's tech-boys have managed to worm these into the very stumps at which the bowler aims. It's hard to avoid flinching when, each time a batsman is clean-bowled, the tragedy is replayed through the stump-cam. Stump-cams have been in operation ever since Channel Four took over television coverage of cricket from the more sedate BBC. Along with these came the snickometer, a device which uses a visually-rendered sound-line to determine whether or not a passing ball has touched the bat before being caught by the wicket-keeper (if it has the batsman's out). Best of all cricket's new visual plug-ins, though, is the system known as 'hawk-eye'. Available both on TV and over the Internet either in real-time or as an archive, hawk-eye allows you to sort deliveries by pitch, speed, movement off the ground and consequence, and to view results in a variety of display modes, from 'normalised past stumps' to 'wagon-wheel'. Hanging beside this data on the webpage, as beside parliament, is the station's logo; a large eye made of spokes. Perhaps it's no coincidence that Channel Four also hosts *Big Brother*.

Cartographers of event-space tend to be continental thinkers: Virilio, Lyotard, Blanchot, Badiou – essentially sub-Heideggerian phenomenologists. It never ceases to amaze me that these people (not being British Commonwealth subjects) have never been exposed to

West, from the Renaissance through Le Corbusier.[5] A line can be drawn from Leonardo da Vinci's *Vitruvian Man*[6] to the Corbusian conception of the body as a module that space should wrap around. ...and its resulting architecture which would/should shape, even rationalise, experience.

Many practitioners have challenged this logic. In *Far From Equilibrium*, Sanford Kwinter highlights architects like Rem Koolhaas and Diller, Scofidio + Renfro for whom: 'The logic that determines our routines of inhabiting the world [are] seen to exist at the level of buildings only in the most secondary of ways.'[7] For them, one of the primary influences on our behaviour are these technologies of vision – from the eye to the screen.

The performative effects of cameras can be seen in TV's *Big Brother*, where people living in a house are filmed 24/7 for a national audience and, with each series, their behaviour has become increasingly bizarre. Performativity becomes a point of exploration for Rem Koolhaas in his use of ubiquitous screens in the *Prada Epicentre* store.[8] In the changing rooms plasma screens are built into mirrors so customers can capture and play-back images of themselves trying clothes on. RFID tagging provides a databased inventory of clothes and so the experience can be extended to their website where customers can access a 'history' of all the clothes ever tried on. Back in the changing room, the doors are made of glass with a liquid crystal film which becomes opaque to the touch. Like a two-way mirror, you can see out, but do you trust the technology that they can't see you?

Total entertainment/total surveillance?[9] Either way, it's a paradigmatic example of how 'humans are invariably the prey caught in an ecstasy of self watching'.[10]

And it certainly compounds Koolhaas' insight, 'that it is soft form, not hard, that bears the maximum of active structure'.[11]

'Soft form' incorporates networked connections between screens, satellites, servers, websites, databases, distribution systems etc. It also includes their articulated connections: to advertising, branding, merchandise, ad infinitum. We might more readily think of this as infrastructure. Of course Modernists always understood infrastructure to be important: subways, motorways, sewage systems, distribution hubs etc. Today, it's not only the extent of the soft form that's different but its relative instability: fluctuations, interferences...

Taken as a whole, advertising and branding have inserted themselves more consciously into this realm. The problem with advertising is that it seeks to loop the effects back to its own ends – Love Prada, Love Big Brother... For instance, although it was mooted on the Limited Language website that a camera's 'worm's-eye view' has the potential to subvert a dominant view, once integrated into the infrastructure such potential is equally easily lost, with multiple views compounding, not subverting, each other. When design ends up glorifying the technology and reproducing the zeitgeist, Kwinter calls this *thinfrastructure*.[12]

A more robust approach, he suggests, is for architects and designers to engage with infrastructure as research. That is, not just fetishise, but understand it: its brute materiality, the effects and how we might account for its consequences.

Can't this ethos be seen in the work of the burgeoning new 'research labs'? Just two examples are the affiliated Kitchen Budapest[13] and Aether Architecture[14] who explore the effects of converged communication and urban space. For instance, in one project by Kitchen Budapest, walking by a wall projection, makes hanging dolls, dressed in designer clothes, mimic your movements. In another, Aether Architecture use *WiFi Cameras* – hand-made, using familiar materials – to capture the Wi-Fi networks and radio signals to play them back as live images. But it remains to ask what or how this acts as research.

Invariably 'research' – or simple experimentation – becomes literalised, for commercial ends. What's interesting is the cricket. The game is the most precise mise-en-scène their thought could ever hope for. It's about repetition, information, geometry, history, stylised violence. How can Badiou understand Beckett without realising how indebted the latter's plays and novels are to cricket, from the stones that Molloy circulates between his pockets (the trick umpires use to keep track of the number of balls bowled in an over) to Hamm's insistence that he be placed in exactly the right position, shifting first a little right and then a little left (the scene is modelled on a batsman taking his mark) to Clov's slow intuition that, even though not much action ever seems to happen, nonetheless 'something is taking its course'? On the top of Lords, ninety degrees round from the new media stand, is a weathercock depicting Father Time, a crook-backed old man with a scythe. It gently turns beneath the curved vapour trails that light up when the sun descends towards the horizontal axis as each day progresses, reminding the more astute spectators what the philosophers already know; that all space-based events (and what other type is there?) play themselves out beneath the sign of death.

Two summers ago I was sitting in HQ transcribing for the INS archive an interview with the post-Situationist artist Stewart Home about the nature of the spectacle while simultaneously watching the Test Match on TV and glancing out of my window to see if any rain clouds were nearing the stadium. From behind the London Eye, two massive brown Chinook helicopters rose and started heading north. George Bush was visiting the Queen that day. 'It's him,' I thought. I tracked them as they swept hawk-like above the city, then, when they passed the blimp above Lords, looked back at the TV. There they were on the screen, being tracked from the ground camera. 'President George Bush,' the scrolling text announced. Moments later, a rain cloud loomed above the stadium and play stopped. To fill the air-time, Channel Four showed a previous match – one I myself had attended.

I'd started out in the cheap seats but had eventually managed to make phone contact with an INS associate who I knew was being entertained by the Lords Treasurer. The associate invited me to join him in the Treasurer's box, where liveried waiters served cucumber sandwiches, cakes and champagne. Towards the end of play a Pakistani batsman hooked a rising ball that started heading straight for our box. It continued rising, hitting the apex of its curve as it passed high above the boundary rope, and as it did I realised that it was heading not only straight towards the box but, more precisely, directly for me. I stood up to catch it. Now, back in HQ, as Home repeated electronically the phrase 'the spectacle is the order of power', I watched on the TV what I had already experienced from the reverse angle: myself flinching and closing my eyes and the ball kinking at the final instant, missing me and smashing into the neatly-ordered trays and glasses, cakes and sandwiches. Collateral damage, I suppose. While well-groomed ladies and gentlemen all dived for cover, cream came showering down onto their upturned legs, like so much pigeon crap.

First published in *RBS Gazette*, New York, 2003 © Tom McCarthy 2003

See further images here
www.limitedlanguage.org/images

way that the development of these technologies – this infrastructure – is use-led. This differs from police or retail operations which tend to loop their effects back to a particular end. Whilst Aether Architecture wish 'to expose the invisible "information landscape" of today's urban and public environments,'[15] when they release details of how to make their WiFi cameras using old pea-cans on their website, a new opportunity to ask 'what for?' opens up for each new use.

See full responses + carry on the conversation here
http://tiny.cc/chapter4_4

Reader credits
I   Helen Walker 28/11/2007
II   Simon – Motorola owner 05/09/2005 from *Kodak Moments and Nokia Digits* http://tiny.cc/chapter4_5

References
1   Danny Baker, 'Curse of the Phone Cameras' in *The Times*, 9 September 2005.
     http://technology.timesonline.co.uk/tol/news/tech_and_web/personal_tech/article562810.ece
2   Tom McCarthy, *Men in Space* (London: Alma Books, 2007), 3.
3   McCarthy's thinking, here, is extended in the various outputs of the International Necronautical Society, the semi-fictitious avant-garde organisation of his creation. The INS inhabits various artistic sites, moments and cultural forms, including the way the organisation parodies corporate and secret societies and all their manifestations of propaganda: reports, broadcasts, committees and sub-committees. For instance, in the INS 'Declaration of Inauthenticity', presented in its latest incarnation at the Tate Britain on 17 January 2009, inauthenticity is 'the core to the self, to what it means to be human, which means that the self has no core, but is an experience of division, of splitting'.
4   Henri Lefebvre, *The Production of Space* (Oxford: Basil Blackwell, 1991), 286.
5   See for instance, Lorens Holm, *Brunelleschi, Lacan, Le Corbusier: Architecture, Space and the Construction of Subjectivity* (London: Routledge, 2009).
6   The *Vitruvian Man* is a drawing created by Leonardo da Vinci dated from the end of the 15th century.
7   Sanford Kwinter, *Far From Equilibrium* (Barcelona; New York: Actar, 2008), 19 (inset). See also www.dillerscofidio.com
8   This is often called 'augmented space'. A discussion of this project and other examples can be found in, Lev Manovich, 'The Poetics of Augmented Space', *Visual Communication* journal (London; Thousand Oaks, CA; and New Delhi: Sage Publications, June

2006), Vol. 5, 219.

9   Michel Foucault in his influential book *Discipline and Punish* (1975) outlined the psychological dimension of panoptic surveillance whereby the surveilled internalise surveillance and so have already adjusted their behaviour. In the Prada store, this is the pre-existing, but invisible counterpart to the retail performance. Interestingly, the OMA website archives this; 'In 1979 OMA were asked to "study" the possible renovation of a Panopticon prison – one of the three ever built on the principle in its pure form: a circle of cells with the all-seeing "eye" of the observatory as its centre. The 100-year-old building had to be equipped "for at least another 50 years" and "to embody present day insights into the treatment of prisoners…". Now, for a variety of reasons it was decided that perhaps it should not continue to exist.' http://www.oma.nl/

10 Sanford Kwinter, Op cit., 19 (inset).

11 Ibid., 132.

12 Ibid., 69.

13 This was part of the show *Soft Is the New Cool*, at the Hungarian Cultural Center during New York Design Week, 2009. www.kitchenbudapest.hu/en

14 www.aether.hu

15 *WiFi Camera* is an ongoing research project initiated by Bengt Sjölén and Adam Somlai Fischer with Usman Haque: http://wificamera.propositions.org.uk/Panoramic-Wifi-Camera. It analyses the Wi-Fi spectrum (around 2.4GHz). This is also called 'hertzian space' and a broader study of it can be found in: Anthony Dunne and Fiona Raby, *Design Noir: The Secret life of Electronic Objects* (Basel: Birkhäuser, 2001).

Kodak moments and Nokia digits

Used condoms and forgotten names

The photograph, the journey and the travelogue are the traditional triumvirate of the holiday experience. But how do we evaluate the memory today. How do we capture it?

The Greeks first listed the Seven Wonders of the World.[1] These were icons which celebrated religion, power, art and science and served to demarcate the Mediterranean landscape from the uncivilised world beyond. Now, the Seven Wonders include the Taj Mahal and The Pyramids. A recent addition to one version of the list is the Eurotunnel. This wonder, which cannot be seen, is phenomenological. That's to say, the experience is the travelling through. Indeed, the way the Eurotunnel only becomes 'visible' for us once it fails, acts as a metaphor for contemporary travel.

For tourist travel to be successful, the speed and comfort of the trip is paramount. Inconvenience must be minimised. The bump and grind of the journey is skipped over in travel-brochure tourism, in favour of the attractions at the other end. In luxury travel, it is smoothed by the attractions on board: Internet access, full waitress-service and the rest. With bargain-bucket air travel, one might say that the idea a journey's worth anything has disappeared. And yet, doesn't easy travel feed nostalgia for the days when 'the passage' used to be, in someway, special?

Today, travel is made up from units of consumption, from the tourist's Duty Free shop to the way off-the-beaten-track travellers say they have 'done' a country, as if ticking it off a shopping list.

This collapse of A to B, is a modern phenomenon. In part it is explained by the 'constant now' of today's living and the speed of distance travelled. In part by the way identity, ritual and artefact have all become mobile, often spliced with whichever economic environ they find themselves in.

Arguably, it is now impossible to experience 'anew' the places we visit. The anthropologist James Clifford, in

'I found a used condom under the bed' reads a review of a hotel in the West Midlands, England; one of twenty reviews for the hotel on an Internet discount-booking site whose by-line is, 'Happy exploring!' This is one site amongst hundreds, one review among thousands.

This is a rather graphic example of how travel is experienced today. We arrive at our destination with the experience already part indexed: travel as archive.

The cyber traveller, or virtually enhanced tourist (VET)[1] increasingly replaces the 'armchair tourist': the cognitive reader has been usurped by a corporeal, but pre-packaged experience.

John Urry in a seminal text, *The Tourist Gaze*,[2] identifies the multifarious nature of the tourist and comments on the impossibility of identifying a unified notion of the traveller. This is particularly true as the idea of travelling has become another product of our globalised commodity culture. The photographer Michael Hughes unites the commodity with the gaze in his work. He creates photographs, usually of kitsch tourist artefacts: a model of the Brandenburg Gate, the Eiffel Tower etc. He photographs these souvenirs in front of the real building or object conflating the real and the artefact. This is a process that undermines (or underlines?) the process of re-remembering; the role of the tourist artefact.

In one image, Hughes holds up the CD case of The Beatles' *Abbey Road*[3] album, so that the infamous cover image of the four striding over the Abbey Road crossing, taken in August 1969, animates the contemporary streetscape. Today this zebra crossing is a tourist destination in itself, and you can 'visit' the spot yourself 24/7, from anywhere in the world, via the Abbey Road webcam.[4]

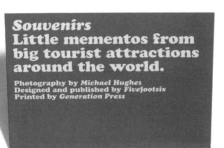

Souvenirs
Little mementos from big tourist attractions around the world.
Photography by *Michael Hughes*
Designed and published by *Fivefootsix*
Printed by *Generation Press*

My souvenir adventure began in 1999 on the Loreley Cliffs near Mainz, Germany, when I realized I was standing in the exact spot depicted on a postcard I'd purchased. Over time, I discovered that I was not only poking gentle fun at souvenirs, but at the very attractions they represent. So many of these monuments and icons have become mere signifiers of place – ubiquitous symbols in the parlance of world culture.

The best thing about souvenirs is that they let us take home a piece of our adventures. Like photography, they capture tiny moments of our experience and give us the feeling, however fleetingly, that we're in control of our life's journey.

Michael Hughes

Loreley cliffs on the Rhine near Mainz in Germany (1999).

Souvenir project Concept and photographs by Michael Hughes. Presentation booklet design by fivefootsix.

The Predicament of Culture, writes: 'An older topography and experience of travel is exploded. One no longer leaves home confident of finding something radically new, another time or space.'[2] Previously he had pointed out that the 'exotic' is uncannily close. So, the European eye which once unpicked the fabric of foreign lands such as India, Africa or The Middle East, can now experience the 'authentic' at home. Local market stalls, grocery aisles and the Discovery Channel all provide the contemporary exotic...

That the aesthetic of travelling is now pre-experienced is also due to the legacy of cinema, advertising and early 20th century photographers like Henri Cartier-Bresson. Bresson's black and white photographs made icons of Mexico, New York, London and Paris. We might say that these were all delineated into simple tones and shapes. Later photographers, advertising and film have added local colour to form the composite now transferred to anything we look at on our travels.

Travelling is always about looking. And whilst this provides a constant train window of change, with the tourist brochure photograph or the snap-shot, the temporal nature of change that is the crux of travel is frozen. It is replaced by a series of representations of 'I am here'. Clock towers, feats of engineering, historic relics all become stereotypical representations which confirm and sustain understanding of any given place. Photography, from social index ('travel broadens the mind') to confirmation of ritual ('can we have the bride and groom here please?') to captioning experience ('it's a Kodak moment'), lost its claims to objectivity long ago.

If we accept this prepackaged summation of the photograph, both politically and aesthetically, what now?

Increasingly we see people with a camera-phone that, on taking a picture, gives the option [send?] before [save?]. This conflates the digital realm of email (data flow) with the more temporal (and analogue) photo album. And so a woman, being pulled along by a crowd, holds the camera phone high to capture for herself what she is missing. This provides a new perspective of the

For Hughes, his work is a way of saying; '"Look at this thing in front of you, it used to have a function, it was part of a town and used to have a purpose but it's now just a sign that everyone looks at and plays around with." It has no meaning other than the fact it's visually important.'[5] However, he is wary of elitism, which he also spies in the original article.[6] For Hughes, it's a conflation of the critical position with a respect for 'the way people put meaning in their lives by associating themselves with things they know other people have seen,' where, 'everyone has a right to feel that their lives have been meaningful'.[7]

One criticism of John Urry (and contemporary theory in general) is its privileging of the visual. This essentialising of the visual is questioned by Gemma Owen in a reply to the original article: 'No, No, it is not just about the seeing, it's about the smelling, the touching, the hearing...the feeling. And besides, every travelling experience is different.'[1]

This more sensory element of the traveller is part of what has been called the 'immersive' typology of the tourist. André Jansson, in the article 'A Sense of Tourism',[8] looks at the changing role of the Western tourist in a wired world and identifies four typologies: immersive, adventurous, traditional and performative.

The adventurer has a tenuous link to real adventure, following instead the route of packaged 'adventure holidays' and often relying upon the photograph to authenticate the adventure, the encounter with the exotic.

In a European context the 'adventurous spirit' would seem to emulate the Victorian notion of the explorer as adventure hero. A post-colonial critique has identified one effect as the colonisation and eroticisation of difference.

In contrast, the immersive traveller is more prone to look for inclusivity, wanting to embrace difference. Connecting with the surroundings of his/her travels and to be seen as the same and equal. The immersive traveller is less likely to document the experience with the photograph or other digital media but rather, rely on the oral traditions of story telling and anecdote. This might simply be keeping a journal, which becomes a 'priceless souvenir' on the return home. However, in doing this they still can't help but place the experience of the encounter in the framework of 'one's own society'.

The traditional tourist will literally make the transference of normal social patterns of home, to a holiday resort. Here, personal photographs of friends and family enjoying themselves document the holiday. The traditional holidaymaker will make use of the places where, already: 'the countries or holiday destinations have pinpointed a specific place for the best photo, [or] "photo opportunities"'.[11] The emphasis in this comment from Nathalie Francis is not on new experience and the encountering of difference, but on relaxation.

The performative tourist is an extension of the traditional typology but the variant is the need to engage with a more public narrative of 'being on holiday'. This will include the use of technology to document the experience such as mobile phones with text and picture messaging often uploaded onto video and social networking sites. It is a narrative that is relayed 'live' via phone or Internet. This presents a 'co-ordination of social activities within the tourist setting, and the desire to immediately narrate and share memorable moments and bodily performances with family, friends, and potentially a wider audience'.[9]

The more sexualised version of the performative tourist is the 18-30 holiday. The Club 18-30 website comments:

'Club 18-30 is what the summer is all about. Best mates. All in one place. No ties. No responsibilities. No work for a couple of weeks. Warm waters. Hot sun. Cool tunes. Great clubs. The ultimate holiday experience...'

It continues: 'There comes a time in life when you need to do it for yourself. A time to break free, break rules and break the mould. To explore, leave the map at home and find

scene to be assimilated into the individual's experience.

The mobile phone has become an extension of ourselves, a sixth digit between thumb and index finger. Is this the closest we have come to media theorist Marshall McLuhan's 1960s prophecy of technology becoming a natural extension to the body?[3]

The camera has always been hailed as a mechanical eye, yet you might hand it to a passer-by to take your picture in front of the Taj Mahal. With a camera phone, would you do that? The low-pixels hardly lend themselves to the iconic photo, but it also feels as if there is also something else going on. It's the personal relationship we have with the mobile phone which, when coupled with a camera and an Internet connection, requires a very different understanding of the personal photograph. Intimate and transient, it is as lacking in fidelity as memory.

The fact that the mobile phone photograph is completely different from a traditional photograph is important because this epistemological split is mirrored in how travel is often perceived; as if we were moving from photograph to photograph...

See further images here
www.limitedlanguage.org/images

References
1   The Seven Wonders of the Ancient World was based on guidebooks popular among Hellenic (Greek) tourists and only includes works located around the Mediterranean rim, constructions of classical antiquity.
2   James Clifford, The Predicament of Culture (Cambridge, MA: Harvard University Press, 1988).
3   See Marshall McLuhan, Understanding Media: The Extensions of Man (New York: McGraw-Hill, 1964).

yourself. To find that one moment and make it last a lifetime. That time is now. Sunrise to sunset. Sunset to sunrise. This is the time of your life. Love every single second of it.'[10]

The emphasis is on hedonism rather than place. Digital technology extends the social networks of home to the new/same places of tourism: Ibiza, Koh Samui or Blackpool. The performative tourist is born out of a digitally mediated world. A narrative is produced, not of travel but instant experience without reflection. Social networking sites enable a continuous stream of communication which is placeless, if not timeless. The tourist gaze has become a refugee, exiled by narcissism,[III] reverie and digital communication.

The performative tourist thus described counters the premise put forward by Urry in *The Tourist Gaze* that 'When we "go away" we look at the environment with interest and curiosity...we gaze at what we encounter.'[11]

The VET arrives without curiosity, but rather, a bag full of expectations (...of condoms?). This is informed by the narratives which mix social networking sites like Facebook with Lonely Planet travel guides.[12] Consumption with The ultimate holiday experience...

See full responses + carry on the conversation here
http://tiny.cc/chapter4_5

Reader credits
I   Gemma Owen 13/12/2005 – Gemma precedes the point with this; 'I'm going to have to say I disagree on the fact that the aesthetic of travelling is pre experienced due to the legacy of cinema and the likes...'
II Nathalie Francis 16/12/2005
III Gemma Owen 13/12/2005 – For instance: '...only today I had a picture sent to me by a friend asking my thoughts on her new haircut, which got me thinking...does this new age of communication tools promote narcissistic values?'

References
1   Virtually enhanced tourist (VET).
2   John Urry, *The Tourist Gaze: Leisure and Travel in Contemporary Societies* (London: Sage, 2002). Urry explores how the tourist gaze orders and regulates the relationship with place.

'ben with... O, I have forgotten her name'
http://bit.ly/m8t2z

3   This photo was taken outside the Abbey Road
    recording studio on 8 August 1969. The cover
    designer was Apple Records' Creative Director,
    Kosh. The cover photograph was taken by
    photographer Iain Macmillan.
4   www.abbeyroad.com/visit/
5   Michael Hughes interviewed for *It's Nice That*, 2009.
6   Email exchange with Michael Hughes, 2009.
7   Michael Hughes, Op cit.
8   André Jansson, 'A Sense of Tourism: New Media and
    the Dialectic of Encapsulation/Decapsulation' in
    Tourist Studies, Vol. 7, No. 1, 5-24.
9   Ibid.
10 http://bit.ly/18_30
11 John Urry, *The Tourist Gaze: Leisure and Travel in
    Contemporary Societies* (London: Sage, 2002).
12 The *Lonely Planet* series' first book was Tony
    Wheeler's *Across Asia on the Cheap* (1973) which
    followed, and made classic, the 'hippy route' through
    Turkey, Iran, Afghanistan and Pakistan, to India or
    Nepal.

Sensibilities

The sacred and the holy / Transient urban spaces
The extra ear of the other: on listening to Stelarc / The parasitical and the para-critical
Earlids and brainlids: on thoughts and sounds / Sound Polaroid
White cube noise / Between the gallery and the street
Images of images: photographs of pain in war / The slow look

This chapter explores the senses and emotions in design:
from Sonics to touch, sacred space to performance.

Keywords
Curation (221,000)
Sacred (8,540,000)
Sound cultures (28,000,000)
Temporality (84,100)

Keywords and their Google hit rate in conjunction with the word design.

The sacred and the holy

Transient urban spaces

In the modern metropolis, architecture is often employed to mask death. This happens either through its formal language, metaphor or simple physical opacity. It leaves only an anthropological vestige – a ghost – of ritual and performance in the 'absolute space' of cemetery landscapes. The visceral burial pits of earlier times (and diseases) are, if still present at all, now formal neo-classical gardens[1] or part of an analogue database of 'parish records: burial registers, vestry minutes, and churchwardens' accounts'.[2]

The increasing forces of secularisation have transfigured the urban environment. The 17th century outbreak of the Plague in London is an example of the temporal clash between modernity and tradition, secular government and religion. Here, the 'popular attachment to traditional practices: the individual funeral and interment, in which the family played an important role' were in conflict with the 'Plague Orders...which aimed to restrict public assemblies and processions'.[3]

This collision between the new Plague Orders, which advocated immediate burial, and society's need for 'commemoration' represents a process where Governments began to exert power over societies through legislation and administration. This was a practice that was particularly effective in the realm of health and the Polis.[4]

Historical place is equally susceptible to change. Richard Sennett in *The Conscience of the Eye: The Design and Social Life of Cities*,[5] eloquently explores how the grid is used in American urban design to erase past histories and sacred spaces; a clean sheet, literally. In European cities new burial sites are banished from the centre to the periphery of modern life.

In part, the Romantic Movement is a correction to the rationalising forces of modernity (Enlightenment thinking). In the 18th century one witnesses a transference of the sublime, the infinite and a sense of awe from

Modernity has kraaled sacred space into particular sanctioned places like the cemetery. In contrast, in the original piece, Ground Zero in New York after 9/11 became a paradigm for the temporary sacred space. Developing on from this idea, here we look at the way contemporary urban culture has reintroduced the idea of a transient holy or sacred space into everyday experience. In part, this is inspired by white bikes – literally old bikes, painted white – which have started to appear by the sides of roads where cyclists have died. Called 'ghost bikes', they form part of a coordinated action from Austria to New Zealand. This piece explores how sacred spaces are being created which both intervene in the urban landscape and provide an interstice for political action. In this instance it's bike safety, but this can also be seen in the markings used to reaffirm identity in the case of gang-associated violence.

Writing from the UK, over the last year it's hard to ignore the media attention given to knife crime in inner cities, London especially. This has accompanied the increasing visibility of locations of fatal car crashes, hit-and-run accidents and gang violence. As happens elsewhere, each place is demarcated with tributes to the victim whereby flowers, notes, mementos and articles of clothing are tied to lampposts and road railings.

There were twenty-five stabbing fatalities in London in 2008.[1] The victims of stabbing fatalities are, more often than not, young male teenagers who have either belonged to a gang or have been caught up in inter-gang turf wars. The social backdrop to many of these sites is one of social exclusion; class, ethnicity, economics.[2] All play a part in the biography of the victim.

Spatially, the sites are often in areas like

high streets around nightclubs and late night eateries where natural surveillance is minimal, if not absent; thus 'escaping informal social control'.[3] In a census of urban street gangs in the 1920s, sociologists from the Chicago School found gangs were prevalent in the 'interstitial' sites of the city. This is a spatial observation still relevant today. Furthermore, neighbourhoods that suffer gang violence are linked to areas of 'social disorganization'.[4] It is within these boundaries that crime is carried out as part of a performative relationship between authority and peer group, where the 'excitement, even ecstasy (the abandonment of reason and rationale), is the goal of the performance' and 'excitement is directly related to the breaking of boundaries, of confronting parameters and playing at the margins of social life'.[5]

Following the tragedy of each stabbing, a temporary occupation of the murder scene is witnessed. The boundaries, originally marked by the police crime scene tape, are replaced by the portable architecture of grief, memory and celebration: commemoration. The bolt-on of a sacred space is a collective event. This is not the transport trucks and air balloons of Archigram's[6] 1970s conception, but a relational, interpersonal construction of space. The site is policed and bounded through a sequence of transgression, social semiotics and occupation: graffiti; school ties hung up on railings and lampposts; flowers and, finally, peers of the victim who police the site.

The site becomes demarcated spatially via inscriptions, tags and general graffiti in honour of the deceased. In these sites there's an inversion of techniques (which corresponds to the inversion of centre/periphery at Ground Zero in New York, as addressed in the original article). Thus a 'remembrance book' is created through the use of pavement slabs, inscribed with tags and personal statements of loss or celebration. Graffiti is an important element of boundary. It 'challenges the dominant dichotomy between public and private space. It interrupts the familiar boundaries of the public and the private by

God to Nature. In the urban environs of the 21st century an equal process, or correction and transference, can be seen to take place as people construct or claim space as sanctuary, an extra-home: a transient sacred space. Sacred space allows (momentary) ownership for the dispossessed: the teenager or the grieving for instance.

Religion, for the purposes of this essay, is a 'collective experience' and the definition of the Sacred comes from Durkheim, where: 'Individuals...experience the sacred as an integral aspect of their innermost being and as a source of joy, peace, and strength.' And furthermore, 'The circle of sacred objects...cannot be fixed once and for all; its scope varies endlessly from one religion to another'.[6]

Modernity has kraaled the notion of sacred space into a sanctioned topography, and now we see how contemporary urban cultures are providing resistance to these structures by reintroducing the idea of holy/sacred space into the everyday experience. Namely, a transient urban sacred space; providing spaces in opposition to 'the sacred precincts of the last global religion – capitalist consumerism'.[7]

The immediate response to 9/11 can be seen as a paradigm for the creation of the temporary Sacred in the non-places of late capitalism. This historical moment realigned the idea of 'centre' and 'periphery' both spatially and ideologically. The ideological dimension is articulated by the following observation:

'...the attacks in New York and Washington provisionally, but dramatically, reversed the dominant space-time[8] of the "centre" (that of safe viewing) and the "periphery" (the space-time of dangerous living). On 11 September 2001, the "centre" and only contemporary superpower entered the space-time of dangerous living [periphery]. It became the sufferer.'[9]

Its spatial ramifications are witnessed in the transference of the centre of Capital as symbolised by the World Trade Center Complex (WTC), where the Twin Towers stood supreme to the peripheral – the spectator/mourner/New Yorker. This reverse of the centre/

The corner of North Road & York Way in Islington, North London, where
people have paid tribute to murdered teenager Ben Kinsella (2008).
Photograph by Rhodri Jones.
http://bit.ly/Rodrico
http://www.benkinsella.org.uk/

declaring the public private and the private public.[7] Here, public space separates into private/sacred space. The site composes a strategy of 'inversion and hybridization'. That's to say that the socio-political position of the murdered and bereaved is reversed in the temporary sacred space through what David Chidester and Edward T. Linenthal describe as 'mixing, fusing, or transgressing conventional spatial relations'.[8] Chidester and Linenthal's broader work identifies three typologies of sacred space: inversion and hybridisation are part of this triumvirate together with the strategy of exclusion discussed in the original article.

This process is akin to Homi Bhabha's observation that hybridisation 'terrorizes authority with the ruse of recognition, its mimicry, its mockery'.[9] The ruse in the spaces thus described is the very temporality of the event; the interruption of the flows of city experience and making visible the irony that 'a space or place is perhaps revealed at its most sacred when people are willing to fight, kill, or die over its ownership and control'.[10]

If the sacred spaces related to gang killings are transgressive, seeking to provide 'resistance to domination' and an alternative to the traditionally state endorsed memorial space, then the Ghost Bike movement provides more traditional networks of memorial and sacred space.

The movement's website informs the visitor: 'The Street Memorial Project honors cyclists and pedestrians that have been killed on New York City's streets. We seek to cultivate a compassionate and supportive community for survivors and friends of those lost and to initiate a change in culture that fosters mutual respect among all people who share the streets.'[11]

The movement has developed, since its artistic inception in 2005, into a global campaign for change in road safety. The structure and ideology of the pressure group belongs to a modernist sphere of democratic protest. It does not call upon the carnevalesque and

periphery is based upon what David Chidester and Edward T. Linenthal, in American Sacred Space[10], call a 'strategy of exclusion', where sacred space is defined by its boundaries and its relationship with outside forces/peoples/dialogues. The site of the Twin Towers, an enclave for the upper echelons of US corporate culture, is transformed post 9/11. The boundaries that might have been policed by a particular hierarchy (of banks and corporate lawyers against anti-capitalist campaigners for instance or, equally, the separation of professionals from the cleaners and minimum-wage security guards who worked in the building) are reversed. The site became estranged from the sanctity of capital production and reconstituted as a place of mourning/memory/rebirth: sacred.

This overturning and re-centering of space, as sacred space, is captured by the curator and writer Jon Bird, who describes the days following 9/11:

'The next few days now seem like a disarticulation in the normal temporal flow: a transitory period between the before and after of a world-historical event during which all the familiar points of reference transformed into their opposites... And, wherever a wall or other surface presented itself, the messages, photographs, drawings and improvised memorials, a bricolaged anthem of tenderness and loss...'[11]

In the immediate post-attack, this 'disarticulation' of space, the WTC and its doppelgänger, Ground Zero, form a dialectical relationship in the creation of sacred space. What happens in this process is a re-imagining of the site. More generally, James Donald[12] describes how cities are articulated through the imagination. In creating the 'living city' he proposes a 'poetics of imagination': a mixture of politics, psychoanalysis and the phenomenological. The jarring of the imagination as the planes hit the buildings, created, in its aftermath, a dilemma of ownership; a conflict over organisation and control, but also imagination. In simple terms, the conflict between economics and an individual/collective need to create a narrative.

In a strategy of exclusion, Chidester and Linenthal comment that sacred place is contested and maintained through advocating the 'special interests of power and purity'.[13] In the aftermath of 9/11 this dynamic of 'special interests' informs the communities putting forward proposals for the WTC: art, business and blue-collar workers. Each proposes the site be redrawn to the blueprint of their imaginations (each group providing a claim for the purity of the site). The Director of the Metropolitan Museum of Art, Philippe de Montebello, commenting a matter of days after the attack captures the tensions of ownership:

'From many in the business community has come a plea to summon our most defiant optimism and erect a new skyscraper... At the other end of the spectrum, Pete Hamill, the *New York Daily News* columnist, has urged that a park be encouraged to blossom there. From others we hear an equally compelling proposal: Dedicate this now sacred ground to a work of art memorializing the thousands of victims of this month's horrors. Some have already begun speaking of commissioning such a work.'[14]

Montebello captures the ongoing battle to lay claim to a small area of downtown New York.

What we see in the following months after 9/11 is another disarticulation. This time it is the intervention to claim back or re-zone the area, to return it to the profane and the secular. Like the plague burial pits 400 years earlier, you see the conflicting temporal/spatial regimes of governmentality and individual agency. The brief separation of centre and periphery contracts and reasserts itself, like a cultural form of muscle memory.

Within weeks of the disaster, the footprint of the WTC was cordoned off. Walkways and one-ways, circumvented the area providing a homogenous, choreographed, experience to the visitor. The chain-link fencing had signs forbidding the 'messages, photographs, drawings' that had expressed the collective trauma of New Yorkers. The Port Authorities and Federal Government slowly but firmly

performative, nor a strategy of hybridisation as already discussed but, rather, a strategy of inversion; 'reversing a prevailing spatial orientation'. It provides a framework for symbolic gesture rather than the spatial intervention seen at Ground Zero or the bolt-on relational space commemorating the victims of knife crime.

The movement relies upon the symbolism and aestheticisation of the object: a decommissioned bicycle painted white. The problem of meaning – semiosis – and any slippage in connotation is countered by its presence on the World Wide Web: the Web coordinates meaning. Rather than a tool of radical communititive rupture to social action, the Internet provides a mapping tool.

The memorial project does not create a physical architectural space as in the other examples discussed in the original article, but instead provides a semiotic intervention. It allows death and its cultural associations with ritual and sacred space to be brought into urban living as a phenomenological experience. This forces the 'organization of these experiences into causal relations'.[12]

Ghost Bikes is part of a broader series of art practices, which have created a range of critical interventions in the everyday of urban living: the globally active *Reclaim the Streets Movement*[13] for instance, or the installation work of Cornford and Cross. In one project, the latter created a temporary peace garden over the entrance to a Cold War nuclear bunker in London's Southwark.[14]

The *Ghost Bike Movement* makes a co-ordinated, conscious intervention into the city/urban centre and, as such, draws upon a more traditional methodology – i.e. Religion and art practice – in creating an urban sacred space. Is it the one example which sits most comfortably in an organised, modernist typology of the sacred?

And finally...

This isn't a postmodern account of the sacred, living between the Mall and New Ageism. Nor is it to overturn the structures of modernity. If anything, the sacred is not

A ghost bike chained to a traffic light just north of Dupont Circle at the intersection of
Connecticut Avenue and R Street NW in Washington, DC, USA. It was in memory of cyclist Alice
Swanson, who died on 8 July 2008.
The bike was removed by the Department of Public Works in August 2009 and a protest 'memorial'
immediately took its place. In September 2009, a local artist struck back by putting up 22 bikes at
the intersection, one for each year of Alice's life.
Photograph: John Curran.
http://bit.ly/Alice_Swanson http://bit.ly/washington_post
A visit to the flickr pool for Ghost Bikes makes sobering viewing:
http://bit.ly/ghostbikepool

de-sanctified the area. In this mix of signifiers – sacred/ commercial, public/private – coalesces what Michel Foucault called a Heterotopia. That's to say, an environ 'capable of juxtaposing in a single real place several spaces, several sites that are in themselves incompatible'.[15]

The World Trade Centre, now reconfigured in the imagination, has re-entered the topography of New York. 'In the most intimate and personal sense, in the sense of an ache that cannot be salved, ground zero is not really downtown'.[16] The experience of 9/11 and its effect, how-ever ephemeral, on urban experience in the West...is this a paradigm for how the sacred, as a secular event, can be reintroduced into urban culture as a point of resistance?

See further images here
www.limitedlanguage.org/images

References
1 Broadgate, in the financial district of London, is one example of the gentrification of an original plague burial site.
2 Vanessa Harding, 'Burial of the Plague Dead in Early Modern London,' *Epidemic Disease in London: Working Papers series/ Centre for Metropolitan History; no. 1*, J. Champion (ed.), (London: Centre for Metropolitan History, 1993), 88.
3 Ibid.
4 See Michel Foucault, *The History of Sexuality* (London: Allen Lane, 1988).
5 Richard Sennet, *The Conscience of the Eye: The Design and Social Life of Cities* (New York: Alfred A. Knopf, 1991).
6 Émile Durkheim, *The Elementary Forms of the Religious Life*, Carol Cosman (trans.) and Mark S. Cladis (ed.) (Oxford: Oxford University Press, 2001), 358.
7 Fredric Jameson, 'Future City' in *New Left Review* (May-June, 2003), 21.
8 ...space and time must be considered relative concepts, i.e., they are determined by the nature and behaviour of the entities that 'inhabit' them (the concept of 'relative space'). This is the inverse of the situation where space and time themselves form a rigid framework which has an existence independent of the entities (the concept of 'absolute space'). Jonathan Raper and David Livingstone, 'Development of a Geomorphological Spatial Model Using Object-oriented Design' in *International Journal of Geographical Information Systems*, Vol. 9 (1995): 359–83.
9 Lilie Chouliaraki, 'Watching September 11th: The Politics of Pity' in *Discourse and Society*, Vol. 15, No. 2-3 (2004), 185-98.

attached to a grand-narrative, but rather, a sacred space which is 'rich, complex, open'.[15] It is one that is situated in a public sphere which is still susceptible to personal 'democracy'.

In *The Sacred & The Profane*, Mircea Eliade captures the spirit of how sacred (church) and profane experience co-habitat in the city: '...the threshold that separated the two spaces also indicates the distance between two modes of being [sacred and profane]. The threshold is the limit, the boundary, the frontier that distinguishes and opposes two worlds. At the same time, it is the paradoxical place where those worlds commu-nicate, where the passage from the profane to the sacred world becomes possible.'[16]

The transient nature of the sacred spaces and architecture provide this bridge. Not one between the fixed architecture of churches and memorials, but a relational infrastructure which can, briefly, embody the non-places of shopping areas, roadways and car-parks.

Carry on the conversation here
http://tiny.cc/chapter5_1

References
1 P. Allen, 'Teenagers Murdered in London in 2008' in *The Guardian*, Tuesday 18 November, 2008.
2 A. Topping, 'I Only Get Angry When the Police are Rude' in *The Guardian*, Friday 12 December 2008.
3 Marcus Felson, 'Those Who Discourage Crime' in John E. Eck and David Weisburd (eds.), *Crime and Place*, Vol. 4 (Monsey, NY: Criminal Justice Press, 1995): 53-66.
4 Luc Anselin et al., 'Spatial Analyses of Crime' in *Criminal Justice*, Vol. 4 (2000), 213-62.
5 Mike Presdee, *Cultural Criminology and the Carnival of Crime* (New York: Routledge, 2000).
6 'The first stage programme [of the Instant City] consisted of assemblies carried by approximately twenty vehicles....' and 'Instant City', see Archigram/Peter Cook (London: Studio Vista, 1972).
7 Tim Cresswell, In *Place/Out of Place: Geography, Ideology, and Transgression* (Minneapolis; London: University of Minnesota Press, 1996).

8   David Chidester and Edward Tabor Linenthal,
    American Sacred Space. Religion in North America
    (Bloomington: Indiana University Press, 1995).
9   Homi Bhabha, as discussed in ibid.
10 Ibid.
11 The Street Memorial Project
    www.ghostbikes.org/new-york-city
12 Maurice Merleau-Ponty, *The Primacy of Perception:
    and Other Essays Psychology on the Philosophy of Art,
    History and Politics*, James M. Edie (ed.), (Evanston:
    Northwestern U P, 1964), 228.
13 http://rts.gn.apc.org/
14 *Words Are Not Enough*, 2007,
    www.cornfordandcross.com
15 Graham Holderness, 'The Undiscovered Country':
    Philip Pullman and the 'Land of the Dead' in
    Literature & Theology, Vol. 21, No. 3 (2007): 276.
16 Mircea Eliade, *The Sacred & The Profane: the Nature
    of Religion* (London: Sheed and Ward Ltd,1957).

10 The strategy of exclusion is one of three typologies of sacred
    space put forward by Chidester and Linenthal; the others being
    inversion and hybridisation. See David Chidester and Edward
    T. Linenthal, *American Sacred Space: Religion in North America*
    (Bloomington: Indiana University Press, 1995).
11 Jon Bird, 'The Mote in God's Eye: 9/11, Then and Now' in *The
    Journal of Visual Culture*, Vol. 2, No. 1 (2003): 83-97.
12 James Donald, *Imagining the Modern City* (London: Athlone Press,
    1999).
13 David Chidester and Edward Tabor Linenthal. *American Sacred
    Space, Religion in North America* (Bloomington: Indiana
    University Press, 1995).
14 P.D. Montebello, 'The Iconic Power of an Artefact' in *The New York
    Times*, 25 September 2001.
15 Michel Foucault, 'Of Other Spaces' in *Diacritics*, Vol. 16, No. 1
    (1986): 22-27.
16 D.W. Dunlap, 'Renovating a Sacred Place, Where the 9/11
    Remains Wait' in *The New York Times*, 29 August 2006.

Joanna Zylinska

The extra ear of the other: on listening to Stelarc

The ear, as Jacques Derrida[1] poignantly observes, is uncanny: it is double in more than one sense. First of all, it is always that of the other (ear). The ear can also be open and closed at the same time. The only organ that cannot voluntarily shut itself, it always remains ready to hear, to receive, even if its 'owner' is not actively listening. The very possibility of speaking and writing and thus of communicating, exchanging and, more generally, of being with others comes from the ear. But what happens when the ear wanders down from the side of one's head to one's arm (as it does in the Australian artist Stelarc's 2006-07 art project, *Extra Ear: Ear on Arm*) and when it mutates from a receiving to a transmitting organ? Stelarc's *Extra Ear* mimics the actual ear in shape and external structure but, rather than merely hearing, it will wirelessly transmit sounds to the Internet, thus becoming a remote listening device. The *Extra Ear* inevitably draws in the observer's eye; it attracts a curious gaze while also encouraging a cross-sensual exchange between bodies and organs which goes beyond the functionalism of information exchange. But what is Stelarc trying to say with this *Extra Ear*? And what would it mean to really h-ear him, and respond to him?

Stelarc's recent visual and aural performances shift bodily architecture into the hybrid terrain of walking heads, hearing arms and fluid flesh (*Walking Head Robot* (2006) and *Blender* (2005), with Nina Sellars). Stelarc's invitation, extended to his audience, to open up to his reconstructive and often invasive bodily projects, at times seems to fall on deaf ears, which is why some responses to his work end up in a solipsistic, and often moralistic, position of not hearing him at all, and of deciding in advance what he is trying to say and why it is wrong. The artist's provocative statements that 'the body is obsolete' and that we need to devise alternate anatomical architectures which are not available in

The parasitical and the para-critical

Who's met a Cyborg? Cyborgs are hybrid life forms. They exist on the human-machine/physical-virtual threshold and, as such, they challenge traditional ideas of the body; even life itself.[1]

Walking through any city centre, taxi drivers can be seen talking to the ether, via a Bluetooth connection tucked behind their ear. Walk into any newsagent, and excessively beautiful women can be seen on covers of men's magazines – *Nuts, Arena, Zoo* – with their Silicone-breasts, Collagen-lips and Botox-youthfulness, tight skin – and should we imagine tight vaginas?

In *Bioethics in the Age of New Media*, Joanna Zylinska proposes these women as 'twenty-first-century neo-cyborgs bearing the marks of technology on their bodies'.[2]

Fashion has used technology to sculpt the body, covertly and not, from the 19th century corset to the late 20th century hosiery of Jean-Paul Gaultier. His infamous *Cone Bra* (as worn by Madonna) both extends the body as a series of impossible shapes and provides 'armour for a late 20th century cyber-woman out of a science-fiction cartoon'.[3] Naturalised, internalised or fragmented, disembodied: all are disciplined and pivot around certain positions of power and it's in this way that the body materialises in the work of Zylinska. In her work, extreme makeover for instance is understood, 'as part of the global biopolitics of life management'.[4] Power, of course, is also intrinsically to do with ethics.

Bioethics typically aims 'to maximise the general social welfare and to minimise harm'.[5] An example might be stem cell research for improving mobility after spinal cord injuries. Zylinska argues that, whilst bioethics emerged in the 20th century as a form of

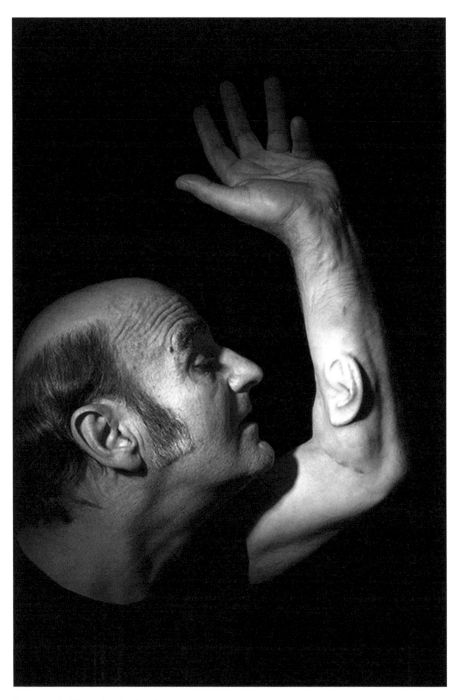

Ear on Arm by Stelarc. London, Los Angeles,
Melbourne (2006). Photography by Nina Sellars.

evolution but which become possible through engineering, are often interpreted as simply meaning that the body is both inadequate and unnecessary, that it is only an obstacle in our technological age. The French philosopher Paul Virilio even went so far as to accuse Stelarc of enacting a new version of 'clinical voyeurism'.[2] A dangerous strategy aimed at improving the human but, ultimately signalling, for Virilio, both the end of art and the end of humanity. So what does it mean to really hear Stelarc and respond to him? How can, or should, we engage with his *Stomach Sculpture* (1993), *Partial Head* (2006), or *Extra Ear*? On what grounds can Stelarc's projects themselves be described as responsible (or not)? What values does his reworking of the architecture of the body challenge, and does this challenge imply any broader epistemic transformation?

Stelarc repeatedly tells us that he has no ambitions to be a philosopher or a political theorist. He refuses to be prescriptive in his work and so will not instruct us as to how we should treat our bodies, or how we should coexist with technology. However, I believe listening to Stelarc will allow us to envisage a more effective politics and ethics. This will be a technopolitics of distributed agency and suspended command, informed by an ethics of infinite – and at times crazy, shocking and excessive – hospitality towards the alterity of technology (that is always already part of us). This is not to say that 'we are machines' or that 'we are all Stelarcs now', as Arthur and Marilouise Kroker put it.[3] As humans and machines are collapsed (as they tend to be in some current accounts of 'the network society') into a fluid epistemology in which difference is overcome for the sake of horizontal affective politics, it is not clear any more who encounters, responds to, and is responsible for whom in an ethical encounter. Or, what is more important, why it should matter at all. This is why I want to suggest that we need to retain, even if while placing it in suspension, this idea of the human (and that of the body). The narrative of seamless coevolution between different

(self)regulation on scientific and medical development,[6] her alternative ethics works towards a 'non-normative ethical responsibility'.[7] Put simply, this refuses to take a moral position (like the tabloid headlines) and also to engage in singular ethical positions which respond to particular real-world scenarios (should they remove hereditary genes from the baby-to-be?). It does not tell us what to think, but asks us to question how we think – and why. It's in this context that she invites us to explore the 'promising ethical ambivalence'[8] of the 'swans' (and 'ugly ducklings') of makeover culture.

To look at Stelarc's *Ear on Arm*, as introduced in the original article, is to face a more recognisable grotesque than the grotesqueries of everyday life. The article uses the device of the ear, not as a physiological or technological entity, but as a conduit for thinking about listening, with Zylinska asking: '...what would it mean to really hear him, and respond to him?'

This depends on who's listening... it's worth noting that this question is posed within a particular philosophical framework. Just as Stelarc's work provides a particular way of looking at the body. Stelarc's ear is Internet connected; to listen to him is to turn around ideas of the body as a closed, impenetrable, skin-tight container.[9] For Stelarc, 'Altering the architecture of the body results in adjusting and extending its awareness of the world'.[10] He seems to be asking us to listen to technology as counter-part. This resonates with Zylinska's bioethics, which ask us to face difference (alterity), say of technology, as we face others: hospitably, as equals.

Earlier, Judith Butler had introduced the body as a moral dilemma: 'There is always a risk of anthropocentrism [...] if one assumes that the distinctly human life is valuable... or is the only way to think of the problem of value. But perhaps to counter that tendency it is necessary to ask both the question of life and the question of the human, and not to let them fully collapse together.'[11] Zylinska's work follows Butler's trajectory for the body, but introduces it into a technologised and economic sphere. With this, comes the need to rethink ethical positions. It brings in the economics of the bioindustry.

Whilst Zylinska is critical of the disciplining nature of makeover culture, as already noted, she is also committed to exploring its 'promising ethical ambivalence'. This seems to be part of the bigger question; how can we embrace future forms if we are still using preconceived ideas?

The way that we name the (future) body/world is important because it determines how we use it. The body hears the environment in a different way than the eye sees it, and so it will make a different sense of it. Translating this to design and names/brands such as 'ThinkPad' and 'Laptop' are terms designed to make people comfortable with the computer as an extension of the body but they also frame the way we will think about it. There is a difference though, in naming, between art and design: whereas naming in design tends to minimise cognitive disruption for a new user, naming in art and philosophy enjoys it.

Herein lies a classical split between art and design. Art may invoke old ideas, but to ask new questions. Art asks questions to test new boundaries. Design concretises. It makes things understandable. It makes things utilitarian. It often makes them spurious.

The way that design concretises – makes literal – could be seen at the start, where design has already brought Stelarc's ideas into the world unremarked upon. However, whilst *Ear on Arm* is absurd, a Bluetooth connection fitted around the ear is not.

Design can also be a kind of pedagogy. In one example, bioengineers have worked with designers to bring tissue-engineering as a debate to the public realm. *Biojewellery*[12] became the conduit; asking six couples in to donate bone marrow, which could then be

biological and cultural entities that depicts the whole world as 'connected', it seems to me, threatens to overlook too many points of temporary stabilisation that have a strategic political significance. It is via these 'points of temporary stabilisation' that partial decisions are being made, connections between bodies are being established, aesthetic and political transformation is being achieved and power is taking effect over different parts of 'the network' in a differential manner. And yet at the same time, 'the human' should not be seen as an essential value or a fixed identity but rather as a strategic quasi-transcendental point of entry into debates on agency, human-technology, environment, politics and ethics. Ethical thinking in terms of 'originary technicity' (which brings forth the very concept of the human) allows us to affirm the significance of the question of responsibility, without needing to rely on the prior value system that legislates it or resort to unreconstructed moral convictions. This responsible response to the difference of technology (which is not all that different) is one non-didactic lesson we can learn from Stelarc.

This is an edited excerpt from *The Extra Ear of the Other: On Being-in-Difference*, an essay in a catalogue accompanying the exhibition of Stelarc's work (1-30 June 2007) at the Experimental Art Foundation in Adelaide, Australia.

See further images here
www.limitedlanguage.org/images

References
1   Jacques Derrida, *The Ear of the Other: Otobiography, Transference, Translation* (New York: Schocken Books, 1985), 32-3. See also Nicholas Royle, *The Uncanny* (Manchester: Manchester University Press, 2003), 64.
2   Paul Virilio, *Art and Fear* (London and New York: Continuum, 2003), 43, 93.
3   Arthur and Marilouise Kroker, 'We are All Stelarcs Now' in Marquard Smith (ed.), *Stelarc: The Monograph* (Cambridge, MA: London: MIT, 2005), 63-86.

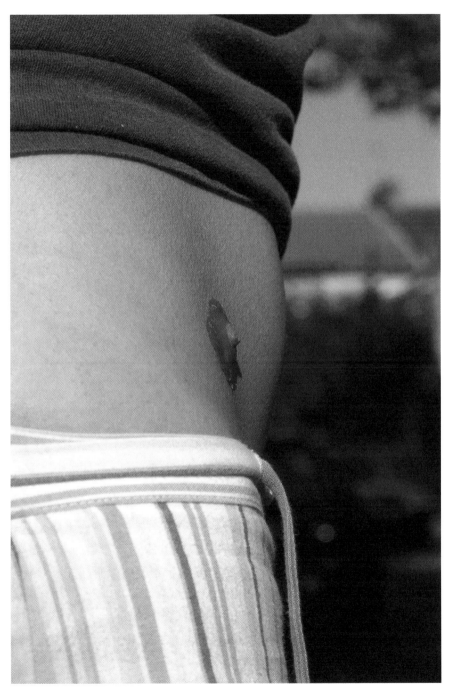

'Nipple' from *Body Modification for
Love* by Michiko Nitta (2005).

grown together around a ring-cast, sized for the couple. Here, an invasive medical procedure is made 'sensible' through a recognisable social custom. The role of prototypes/projects like these is 'to help imagine what the social dimensions might be, even though the eventual applications of the science aren't yet clear'.[13]

These social/psychological dimensions were central to *Design and the Elastic Mind*,[14] an exhibition looking at collaborations between (bio)science and (bio)design where Biojewellery featured. Another piece, the *Body Modification for Love* project by Michiko Nitta, used in-vitro cultured meat production technologies to grow selected extra body parts on the skin to emotional ends. Would you want an extra (ex-girlfriend's) nipple for instance? Or your mother's hair – which of course will grow! Will memories, embedded in the body like this, remind us that they need care and attention like the rest of us?

Also on show at *Design and the Elastic Mind*, was *Typosperma* by the Israeli typographer Oded Ezer. This is a spoof project, where supposedly cloned sperm hypothetically have typographic information implanted into their DNA to create new transgenic creatures, half-(human)sperm/half-letter... But, what for? Is this a potent reminder of the power invested in both scientists and designers?

Finally, this brings us back to why ethics are important. Design, art or science – literal, utilitarian or spurious – at worst, any of these projects can have a parasitical role in relation to biotechnology. That is, they can unquestioningly fetishise it. The design historian David Crowley makes a useful distinction here where, at best, the parasitical could be transformed into the para-critical.[15] By this he means they deliberately feed off bio-developments, in order to call them into question. If we look back to the kind of beauty body modification discussed at the start, we can see that this is called up for debate in the surgical 'art' work performed on the body of artist Orlan[16] who has worked to, 'reveal the damaging impact of the pervasive images of

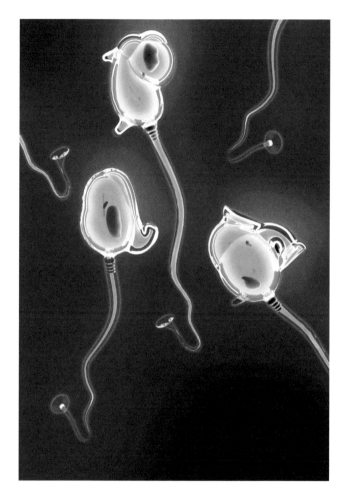

Typosperma by Oded Ezer (2007).

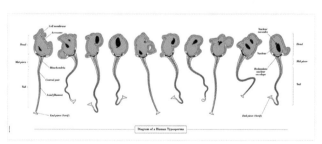

Site by Itamar Lerner; 3D rendered by Amir Lipsicas.
Photographed by Ruthie Ezer.
Scientific consultation by Hagit Gueta.
Assisted by Ifat Yairi.
http://www.odedezer.com/typosperma.html

female beauty in Western culture'.[17]

Surgery, as art, might be open to 'difference', but when it's invariably offered as the 'latest look', sold at reduced prices on the high-street and squeezed into the lunch break, it goes one step further to creating a world without difference.

So, what's wrong with a corset? Nothing of course, but it's a useful device to see how technology becomes essentialised: where a 19th century object designed to 'discipline' a woman's waist becomes a surgical procedure today.

Carry on the conversation here
http://tiny.cc/chapter5_2

References
1   This thinking is developed in Joanna Zylinska,
    Bioethics in the Age of New Media (Cambridge, MA;
    London, England: MIT, 2009) and was also discussed
    at Zylinska's Lecture on Bioethics as part of the 'New
    Nature' lecture programme at the Royal College of Art,
    London, 2008.
2   Ibid., 102.
3   See for instance, *All Tied-Up: The Corset in
    Contemporary Fashion* in http://bit.ly/alltiedup
4   Joanna Zylinska, Op cit.
5   Cary Wolfe in 'Bioethics and the Posthumanist
    Imperative' in Eduardo Kac (ed.), *Signs of Life: Bio Art
    and Beyond* (Cambridge, MA; MIT, 2007), 97.
6   Joanna Zylinska, Op cit. See Chapter One
7   As outlined in her Lecture on Bioethics, Op cit.
8   Joanna Zylinska, Op cit.
9   Joanna Zylinska used the term 'skin-tight container' in
    her Bioethics lecture, Op cit.
10 Stelarc, www.stelarc.va.com.au
11 Judith Butler, 'Undoing Gender,' quoted in Joanna
    Zylinska Op cit., 141.
12 The Biojewellery research project between designers
    Tobie Kerridge and Nikki Stott from the Royal College
    of Art in London and Dr Ian Thompson, a bioengineer
    from Kings College London. Funded by the EPSRC
    (Engineering and Physical Sciences Research Council).
    www.biojewellery.com See also www.materialbeliefs.com
13 Sociologist Robert Doubleday quoted in 'See through
    Science' (DEMOS) on www.biojewellery.com
14 See Hugh Aldersey-Williams, Peter Hall, Ted Sargent
    and Paola Antonelli, *Design and the Elastic Mind* (New
    York: Museum of Modern Art, 2008).
15 David Crowley in his introduction to the 'New Nature'
    lecture series: Royal College of Art, London, 2008.
16 www.orlan.net
17 Cynthia Freeland, *Art Theory: But Is It Art? An
    Introduction to Art Theory* (Oxford: Oxford University
    Press, 2001), 134.

Angus Carlyle

Earlids and brainlids: on thoughts and sounds

'"Can one think without speaking?" – And what is thinking? Well, don't you ever think? Can't you observe yourself and see what is going on? It should be simple. You don't have to wait for it as for an astronomical event and then perhaps make your observations in a hurry.' (Ludwig Wittgenstein, *Philosophical Investigations*, First published 1953).[1]

'Well these are the simple facts of the case – There were at least two parasites one sexual the other cerebral working the way that parasites will – And why has no one asked "What is the Word?" – Why do you talk to yourself all the time?' (William S. Burroughs, *The Ticket That Exploded*, First published 1962).[2]

A pale light eases its way through the white curtains, a brittle mixture of the nearby street lamp and the slowly brightening sky. I run my palm across the friction of four days of stubble and the image of a match being struck, surfaces then disappears like an ornamental fish. I hook my arm under the bed to retrieve the red bike lamp that is always there. Resting it, unlit, on my chest I grope for the travel alarm clock I bought in Berlin. Its luminous dial points to four o'clock.

Replacing the clock on the wooden floorboards, I switch on the lamp. The alarm clock now seems to have taken on a more strident tone, as if it, too, has been woken from a more dormant state. In the red glow of the bike lamp, the ticking mechanism seems irregular, shifting from faster to slower, as I move my head on the pillow. Intrigued, I attempt to manipulate this effect only to discover that with intensified concentration, the clock lapses into a stable tempo and then falls back into a more subdued participation in the bedroom's atmosphere.

In its place come other sounds. My wife's breathing struggles through the cold that she's not been able to shake; her inhalation the texture of pipes and drains, her exhalation like air from a balloon neck. A softer

Sound Polaroid

In his beautifully emotive essay, Angus Carlyle captures a Sound Polaroid[1] of a waking family. But it is a sonic landscape bristling with the visual, where 'a match being struck surfaces then disappears like an ornamental fish'; or 'luminous clocks' and 'the red glow of the bike lamp' illuminate, metaphorically and literally, the scene. Carlyle brings into focus the clash of two sensory cultures: sonic and visual.

Long before the 'visual turn' of Structuralist thinking,[2] there has been a sensory order. This includes the binary of inside/outside, between the thought and the spectacle. Here, inside means the psychological with the outside being the phenomenal world. Film has explored this relationship (especially in the genres of horror and suspense) where the three-dimensionality of sound is used to good effect, for instance approaching footsteps from behind a closed door or wind rubbing against a windowpane. The opening paragraphs of Carlyle's essay read like a Foley artist's[3] storyboard, connecting the visual experience to its sonic Other. The former is exposed in the light whilst the latter remains perceived – out of shot?

David Toop's response to the original article makes the outer/inner connection explicit when he comments on listening to the, 'clicking of our cat's claws on the wooden floor'[1] and how this ignites his later evocation of Edgar Allan Poe, who he read as a child. His comment encapsulates how the aural outer world ignites our psychological inner spaces.

When did creaking floorboards shift (as they did for Toop) from simple indexical link to presence and to a more, 'fearful listening'?[11]

Toop's comment specifically mentions *The Fall of the House of Usher*, the Edgar Allan Poe tale, which opens, 'During the whole of a dull, dark, and soundless day...'[4] The short story's protagonist is Roderick Usher, who lives within the confines of a decaying gothic country house, which bears his family name. The house is described as being in a grotesque state of decay, which is mirrored in the physical and psychological demeanor of Usher himself. Amongst other ailments, he suffers from a form of acousticophobia where it is, 'Only...peculiar sounds, and these from stringed instruments, which did not inspire him with horror'.[5]

In many ways Usher's 'morbid acuteness of the Senses' can be seen as an indictment of modernity. It is a story of the rational and irrational; where the latter, the ancien régime, is transformed by Enlightenment thinking.

The sociologist Fran Tonkiss in a contemporary context captures this relationship between sound and modern urban living:

'Cities, after all, insist on the senses at the level of sound. It is easier and more effective to shut your eyes than it is to cover your ears. Ears cannot discriminate in the way eyes can – as with smell, hearing puts us in a submissive, sensuous relation with the city'.[6]

Whereas for the Poe character the sonic clutter of encroaching modern life is a sentence of morbid horror, today we have developed strategies to perform in the sonic realm. Tonkiss calls one such strategy 'social deafness'. This is where people develop strategies to filter out sound and create personal aural spaces – it's a psychological space where 'no one is listening' creating an individual rather than a communal space. Think of someone speaking loudly into their mobile phone in an otherwise silent train carriage or coffee shop – oblivious to those around them!

This individuation is further fine-tuned with the technology of the iPod and Bluetooth headsets. We coexist in a stratified sonic territory, where the inner and outer, earlier described, is psychological and can provide a tension between individual and community.

In *Topophilia*, Yi-Fu Tuan's magisterial investigation of the material world, he observes how in small scale societies, as with forest

echo emerges from my young daughter's sleeping body, less troubled and more steadily rhythmic. From my son, sprawled nearest to me on top of the duvet, arm flung across his sister, hardly a sound escapes. No more than the rustles that accompany his shifts and turns and the occasional glutinous thumb-sucking that no promise of toys or adventures is incentive enough for him to relinquish.

Out in the street beyond the curtains, seagulls mark their temporary territory. The flying gulls offer their characteristic cry, rising and receding as they move between the terraced houses. Once settled on a rooftop, another call. This time an insistent 'ugg, ugg, ugg!' signals their presence.

Rubbing the beginnings of my beard again for comfort, without, this time, eliciting the image of a match, I switch the bike lamp off and place it on top of the small pile of autobiographies I keep on my side of the bed; guilty primers for a lived life.

A gentle rain has begun to fall, rustling through the early Summer leaves of the tree outside our window and tapping on the car roofs below. Another, smaller, but unidentifiable bird can be heard, a brighter refrain. Perhaps a starling? A blackbird? The bird song almost, but not quite, repeated, melodic variation withheld and then unexpectedly given. The window frames rattle percussively in response to the growing breeze.

Behind the sleeping family and the gulls and the birds and the gentle rain, traffic noise is now discernible. Not yet in the focused form of a vehicle in our street, but still there as an ambient backdrop of tyres on wet tarmac and ill-defined engine murmur.

I am conscious now of my own breath, a sharp release through my nostrils. Conscious too, suddenly, of the sounds of my body's movement in the bed, of legs drawn up then extended against the sheets, of my hair brushing against the pillow and my nails scratching the skin of my upper arms, of the cartilage in my finger joints as I snap them through a nervous routine. Listening below those surface sounds, a persistent hum

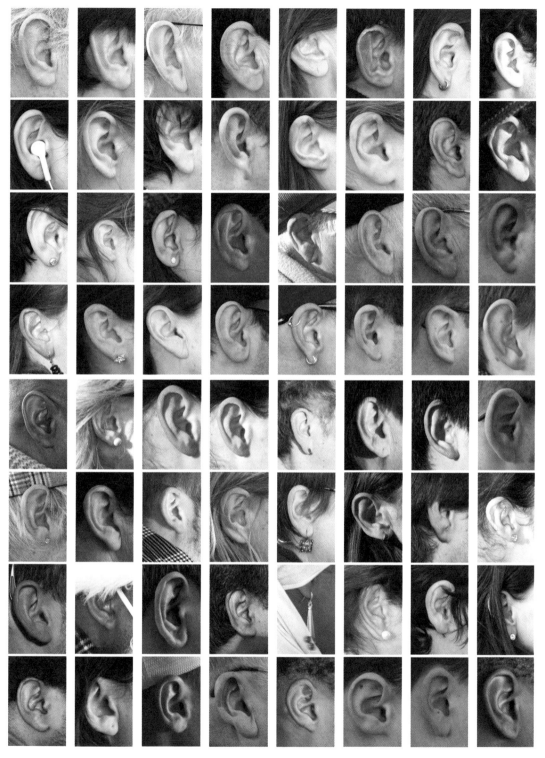

You Are Ear. Art Direction by Angus Carlyle (2009).
Photographs by Matthew Hawkins.

Motorsounds, BMW M Modelle,
Haus der Baureihe.

BMW Museum, spatial choreography by
ART+COM (reopened June 2008).

emerges at the threshold of audibility. It seems to come from somewhere inside. Maybe it is nothing more than the fridge downstairs or maybe it's an acoustic illusion born of excessive attentiveness combined with that special fatigue that is the privilege of those who should be asleep. Whatever its source, I try to grasp it and discern more of its shape and colour.

Before I can capture the elusive drone, I become aware of another noise – this time one that is unambiguously internal – the noise of my thoughts. This is not just the sound of nouns and verbs shadowing in distinct, then indistinct, ways what might have been spoken aloud; that is what happens when we are thinking as Wittgenstein might have said.

My thoughts now, with the bike lamp back on and my wife's snoring much gentler. My thoughts, as I write then pause, write then pause. My thoughts also consist of fuzzy renditions of associated ideas; forms of what has once been heard, but as might emerge from a turntable whose stylus has accumulated a little coat of fluff. The start of the match scrape; the wet ripple above the fish and a child's voice to the left; the thump of a snowball against my taxi in Berlin; the rush of water beneath a manhole cover and reverberation through a guttering pipe.

My brain is too active to let me lie any longer. I switch off the bike lamp and return it to the floor. I swing my legs out from under the duvet and rise, unsteadily, to my feet. One hand holds the pencil and paper, the other probes the beginning of a spot at the corner of my mouth. I creep out of the bedroom, like the worst actor portraying the worst burglar.

As Marshall McLuhan[3] once observed, there are no earlids. For the vast majority of human beings, there is no escaping the external sound world, even when asleep. Yet although complete escape is not an option, retreat remains a possibility, a possibility that seems everywhere to be readily grasped. The enduring derogation of sound in stubbornly visual cultures can be traced across a number of indices, too many to be captured in this

dwellers, sound becomes important in, 'a pervasive environment undistinguished by landmarks' and people will 'attribute special importance to the unfocused sound'[7] – of singing, chanting or musical instruments for instance. '[S]ound... serves to draw the attention'; this provides a mapping of the forest. This form of echolocation is reminiscent of the use of music in the large and featureless department stores where the escalator moves you from one sonic sphere to another, as if being drawn into the canopy of a stratified world of modern consumption. Moving from the jazz of the coffee shop to the post-punk of a Diesel© franchise, sound can fix you in the non-spaces of modern consumerism. A 'temporary territory' in the words of the original article.

Inevitably, it is often consumption (as the simple pulse of the everyday) that acts as a conduit between design and sound cultures.

The senses (including sound) are carriers of social values and not simply mechanistic receptors of information. This is well documented in visual cultures, in relation to cultural specificity of colour for instance, but the contingency of sound is less evolved in sensual discourse.

The psychologist Mark F. Zander, among others, has investigated how musical composition can influence our consumption patterns and, specifically, how musical tempo and rhythm can alter our perception of time: studies looking at advertisements and audience perception of their length found temporal awareness was influenced by the accompanying musical style when viewing.

In a broader context, 'The role music plays must be considered carefully because it attracts attention, transports implicit and explicit messages, generates emotions and helps one retain information.'[8]

To imbricate sound (with music being its dominant language) into the design-world is important in situating design into a broader immersive environment. Sound can be used as a vehicle for sense of self, place and imagination.

Interactive design is a natural home

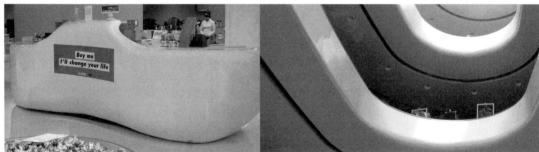

Buy me
I'll change your life

'..music in the large and featureless department stores where the escalator moves you from one sonic sphere to another, as if being drawn into the canopy of a stratified world of modern consumption.'

The Selfridges department store, Birmingham UK: Architects: Future Systems (completion 2003). 'The interior is planned around a dramatic roof lit atrium criss-crossed by a white cat's cradle of sculpted escalators and a smaller but equally powerful atrium'. http://bit.ly/dept_store

short article. As one brief measure of sound's marginalisation, it is worth conducting a concentrated listening experiment like the one described above, if only to compare your discoveries to the soundscapes conventionally represented in film and to hear what was once rich, dynamic and engaging, rendered banal.

Another dimension that emerges from such experiments is the extent to which a significant proportion of the soundworld we inhabit cannot be located externally. Sound-proofed windows and walls, ear-plugs and active noise reduction systems can muffle the sounds from 'outside'. Cranked-up headphones or stereo speakers may replace certain exterior sounds with others that have the values of having been chosen and being predictable. None of these systems, however, can drown out the sounds from within. The sounds of metaphor and association played through that dirty turntable I mentioned; the match scrape, the fish plop, the Berlin snowball, the gurgling pipes. That inner voice articulated by Wittgenstein and Burroughs at the start is also, I believe, a consistent contributor to our personal soundtrack. And finally, in this clamour, there are those mysterious hums and whines of obscure origin that emerge, paradoxically, both in moments of relaxation and of enervation.

Just as there are no earlids, nor are there brainlids. Nada Brahma: all the world is sound.[4]

See further images here
www.limitedlanguage.org/images

References

1   Ludwig Wittgenstein, *Philosophical Investigations* (Oxford: Blackwell, 2001), 327 (First published, 1953).
2   William S. Burroughs, *The Ticket That Exploded* (London: Flamingo, 2001), 144 (First published 1962).
3   Marshall McLuhan and Quentin Fiore, *The Medium is the Massage: An Inventory of Effects* (New York: Hardwired, 1996), 142 (First published, 1967).
4   Joachim-Ernst Berendt, *The World Is Sound: Nada Brahma: Music and the Landscape of Consciousness* (Rochester VT: Inner Traditions, 1987).

for this synthesis and design groups like ART+COM, an association of designers, scientists, artists and technicians have a twenty year history in this area. The BMW Museum in Munich is an example of an ecology of digital means and sensual needs where: 'Spatial choreographies of projections, light and sound create a dynamic backdrop for the seven "exhibition houses"'.[9]

The currency of zeros and ones, which is the inspiration for collectives like ART+COM, means all creative practice from typography to film, illustration to sonic arts is part of a new digital economy. Just as desktop publishing made people aware of typography (to a lesser or greater extent) or, likewise, editing software makes photo-manipulation second nature for the most amateur photographer; increasing access to sound software, from simple sampling to more sophisticated notation programmes, inevitably leads to sound gaining greater and greater prevalence in our creative lives. Sound has become one more digital tool for the creative impulse.

See full responses + carry on the conversation here
http://tiny.cc/chapter5_3

Reader credits

I   David Toop 12/07/2005 - 'Strangely, reading this coincides with a nocturnal listening experience of my own last night. I was woken by tiny sounds - the minute clicking of our cat's claws on the wooden floor - and as I lay awake, I remembered a kind of paranoid, hypersensitive listening from childhood, though which I would hear very small sounds - either internal or external - and develop these into a feeling of terror, going deeper and deeper into the sounds until they materialised in my imagination into physical presences in the room. To me, this relates closely to EA Poe stories such as The Tell Tale Heart and Fall of the House of Usher. I read these as a child, but I think the fearful listening preceded them. The nocturnal mix of heightened external sounds heard in extreme quiet and a site of physical restraint, microscopic listening, and those internal sounds which may be neural processing and other body functions with audio components is a unique moment in audition. The question is, does Nada Brahma take us forward or back in understanding this phenomenon?'

II   David Toop 12/07/2005

References

1   Interview with Scanner in *CMJ New Music Monthly* October 1999.

2   Structuralism developed the idea that human culture is to be understood as a system of signs and was heavily influenced by the work in linguistics led by Ferdinand de Saussure.

3   The Foley artist creates many of the natural, everyday sound effects in a film.

4   Edgar Allan Poe, *The Fall of the House of Usher* (New York: American Book Company, 1907).

5   Ibid.

6   Fran Tonkiss in Michael Bull and Les Back, *The Auditory Culture Reader, Sensory Formations series* (Oxford: Berg, 2003), 510.

7   Yi-Fu Tuan, *Topophilia* (Columbia University Press, 1990).

8   Mark F. Zander, 'Musical Influences in Advertising: How Music Modifies First Impressions of Product Endorsers and Brands' in *Psychology of Music*, Vol. 34, No. 4 (2006): 465-80.

9   ART+COM: www.shrinkify.com/tsk

Monica Biagioli
White cube noise

Sound has an amorphous quality about it that, when coupled with the word 'art', presents a very real and immediate problem in terms of presentation in a gallery space. In its pure, unfiltered form, sound has no tangible boundaries. It just is. Means used to create, capture, and transmit it often become the unwitting focus in presentations of sound-based works. Installation art approaches can engage audiences in active participation with the listening elements of the work. Yet, often, in the journey from sound to sound art, visual representations become more of the focus. How can we take attention away from the vehicles, trappings or visual representations of sound and place it back where it belongs?

Steven Connor has addressed this problematic head-on, in a talk at the *Audio Forensics Symposium* at the Image-Music-Text gallery (IMT) in London in 2008. His talk, entitled *Ear Room*, explored language as a container and argued for a more forthright approach to sound aesthetics through semantics. Why talk about sound and space? Why not give body and shape to these formless terms and refer to them as ear and room? He argues that this focus, this pinning-down, would provide sound art with a solidity it now seemingly can only find via its vehicles, trappings and visual representations. However, this assumes that fitting into a container is what sound art wants to do, and yet many of the manifestations of sound art avoid receptacles altogether via ambient strategies (radio and Internet transmission being two examples). But this does not solve the problem of the white cube. How to put focus on the sound in sound art within the gallery space?

If the amorphous and ambient elements of sound art are to be featured, any physical representation, be it object-based or installation, can draw attention away from the sound. A way of addressing this problem is to embrace sound's invisibility and place focus on its more

'What are days for?
Days are where we live.
They come, they wake us
Time and time over.
They are to be happy in:
Where can we live but days?'
(Philip Larkin, *Days* 1953)[1]

In Larkin's poem, the open and close of days provides more than the rhythm against which our lives are set. Days 'wake us'. They frame and inform human experience.

It's in this way that the temporal materialises in the curation of Monica Biagioli, author of the original article, which proposes that artists and visitors think about time in the gallery, and not the spatial experience alone. Biagioli worries that the visual trappings of sonic presentation detract from the experience of sound itself. She suggests that using less abstract, more visceral language is needed to provide an alternative to the visual conception of the gallery. Not sound, she suggests, but ear; not space but room.[2]

It is also useful to think about time in terms of days. Biagioli remarks 'On any day that you walk into a gallery, at that moment you will experience the space slightly differently – to the people that came in before you, or the last time you came in. You will only capture that moment'.[3] The gallery, here, is explored as a transient place – a series of moments – making the connection back to the outside world?

We can see this in *Sound Proof*[4] a series of yearly sound exhibitions Biagioli is curating over a five year period which focus on the transformation of the UK Olympics site in East London's Lower Lea Valley in the lead up to 2012. In one installation, Jem Finer's recordings create an audio cartography of the transformations, capturing the sonic changes of the conversion from waterways and marshland to building site to global tourist attraction. Just as sounds come and go, some will inevitably disappear. In 2008 at the E:vent Gallery, the exhibition comprised six one-hour sound recordings, a comfortable seating area and a set of visual maps of the soundscapes.

Sonic, as opposed to visual mapping, makes a different sense of things, expanding our experience. In *Ecology of Sound: The Sonic Order of Urban Space*, Rowland Atkinson explains,

'Sound...provides a means of exploring the more ephemeral and shifting elements of urbanism that often slip through our fingers when we try to give concrete assessment of its character... Apparently quiet urban oases and noisy spaces themselves often change according to other cycles, such as street festivals, nocturnal house parties or the daily flows and routes of commuting workers... This relative "stickiness" of sound in place, to take the example of urban commuting flows in cars, gives sound its ecology, or a relative fixity, even as its complexity and relatively unbounded nature need to be acknowledged'.[5]

Like Larkin's bounded Days, Biagioli and Atkinson capture the texture of time: time and time over. In replies to the article on the Limited Language website, Rachel Gray reminds us of other temporalities; '...the "opening" hours for spirituality have traditionally been marked by sound – the church bells which call Christians to prayer and which also mark out every hour of the day, and the Adhan, the Islamic call to prayer, five times a day. This is both immaterial (the ambient sound of spirituality) and the marking of time as it materialises in culture as hours of the day'.[1]

In the city, church bells and the Adhan synchronise (or asynchronise) with the daily flows of commuters etc. It is this ordering and layering (rather than a simple sequencing) of the urban soundscape which draws attention

salient qualities. One of these is its existence in a time-frame. Working with time, instead of space, in curation allows for sound's visual absence of boundaries to be expressed and, at the same time, provides a means for packaging the work within the gallery. It also places special emphasis on the sound properties of the piece, even with visuals present in the space.

This does not mean that a sound art exhibition would not have object or installation elements. David Toop speaking at the same symposium at IMT, explored the idea of using objects as a way of focusing on sound. Taking this approach would deal with our gallery-going expectations directly. So, by pinning down the visual language of sound (and getting that expectation out of the way) it frees us up to engage with the sound more purely.

Still, the focus needs to come back to sound and a good vehicle for doing this is time. Considering the gallery in terms of opening hours rather than cubic metres can help bring audiences to the sound element of the work. And, through the activity of listening, this can link up the gallery experience to a process-based approach that has body and form beyond the white cube.

See further images here
www.limitedlanguage.org/images

Jem Finer's audiocartography records transformation of the Olympics site in East London's Lower Lea Valley in the lead up to the London Olympics 2012.

Sound Proof at the E:vent Gallery, curated by Monica Biagioli (2008).

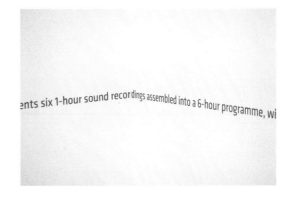

Close-up of *Sound Proof*.

to the social and political dimensions of everyday life, so that '[t]he city is not then simply an open sensory experience...but one which impacts on us in ways that perhaps we are only beginning to understand'.[6]

The visual, of course, is integral to the sensory experience of the city too, and many of the same anxieties arise. Design, and most recently graphic design, are enjoying increasing visibility in the gallery and museum. However, here, the visual ordering and layering of the urban landscape – its ecology – is easily lost. As the historian and philosopher Tony Fry warns, '...to reify design...which is to present it in an objectified form removed from its dynamic process, is to misconstrue the very nature of design'.[7]

Part of the problem for design is that the gallery or museum experience so often emphasises its visual aspects over this temporal dimension. Take the term 'impact': considered visually, it throws up discussion of aesthetics; form and colour or, in ad-speak, the wow factor. Considering how design impacts upon us in a temporal sense can start to take into account effects that can only be understood over time.

Recent examples of this temporal emphasis can tentatively be seen... For instance, when the Graphic Design Museum opened in Breda, Holland. Here, LUST created *Poster Wall* for the 21st century,[8] which automatically generated six hundred posters daily, using content gathered from various Internet sources.

Visually powerful, the LUST installation abstracts news feeds from any narrative context, providing a graphic interface, a moving wallpaper of information. But, when considered temporally, poster by poster, moment by moment, day by day, the project might, even if fleetingly, reframe the contents of the museum in relation to a larger dynamic process, out there.

And yet, in order to capture and interrogate the ways in which design exists within this larger dynamic process, isn't there still so much work to be done?

The *Journal of Popular Noise* is a periodical which comprises three seven-inch vinyl singles within a folded sleeve with accompanying contextual material.

The journal editor Byron Kalet observes 'recorded sound seems to have transcended its former physical manifestation and returned to its original formless presence, vibrating air'. The journal consciously attaches the sonic world with the artefact: a beautifully designed, letterpress sleeve.

The journal website comments: 'Dedicated to maintaining the highest quality in the physical manifestation of music and sound, all releases are issued in packaging and formats designed to maximize the listeners pleasure'. http://bit.ly/pop_noise_book
Image credit: Jeremy Balderson.
Design: Byron Kalet.

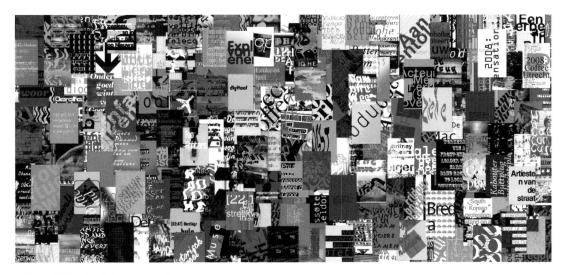

A Poster Wall for the 21st century for the
Graphic Design Museum, Breda, Holland.
Concept, Design and Programming: LUST 2008.

It is design's uses and effects, year in, year out, which are pertinent for thinking about its future.

Almost 40 years ago, Victor Papanek in *Design for the Real World*, was one of the first to advocate 'design thinking'. He called for '...a greater understanding of the people by those who practice design'.[9] Ecology is finally becoming a dominant conceptual framework in design.

In the 1970s, as now, this was prompted by an anxiety over the increasing power of design to shape tools, environments and by extension human experience: how we live.

Where can we live but days? Larkin reflected:

> 'Ah, solving that question
> Brings the priest and the doctor
> In their long coats
> Running over the fields.'[10]

When designers question the cycle of consumption...who will come running!

See full responses + carry on the conversation here
http://tiny.cc/chapter5_4

Reader credits
1   Rachel Gray 27/01/2009

References
1   Philip Larkin and Andy Ihwaite (ed.), *Philip Larkin: Collected Poems* (London: Marvell Press; Faber and Faber, 1998), 67.
2   Biagioli draws on Steven Connor's talk 'Ear Room' at the Audio Forensics Symposium, Image-Music-Text Gallery, London, 30 November 2008.
3   Telephone conversation with Monica Biagioli (2009).
4   *Sound Proof* (2008), http://bit.ly/soundproof2008
5   Rowland Atkinson, 'Ecology of Sound: The Sonic Order of Urban Space' in *Urban Studies*, Vol. 44, No. 10 (2007), 1905-6.
6   Ibid.
7   Tony Fry, *A New Design Philosophy: An Introduction to Defuturing* (Sydney: University of New South Wales Press, 1999).
8   See http://www.graphicdesignmuseum.nl/
9   Victor Papanek, *Design for the Real World: Human Ecology and Social Change* (New York: Van Nostrand Reinhold Co., 1984), ix-x.
10   Philip Larkin, Op cit.

Images of images:
photographs of pain in war

Regarding the Pain of Others,[1] was an extended essay by Susan Sontag written in 2003. It looked at how we experience photographs of war in the speedy digital age of 'shock and awe'. This included re-addressing two widespread ideas on the impact of photography: firstly, that the media direct our experience of war and, secondly, that people have become complacent or numbed by the sheer quantity of images of horror. For instance, revisiting the infamous 1968 photo of a Vietcong (National Liberation Front) suspect and his executioner at the moment when the bullet has been fired and the prisoner is grimacing but not yet fallen.[2] Sontag comments: 'As for the viewer, this viewer, even many years after the picture was taken...well, one can gaze at these faces for a long time and not come to the end of the mystery, and the indecency, of such co-spectatorship.'[3]

Regarding the Pain of Others marks a departure from the postmodern theorists of continental philosophy, particularly Jean Baudrillard and Jacques Derrida who had drawn attention to a de-centred universe made up of multiple meanings and manipulations to the point where reality recedes.[4] This is what Baudrillard called the simulacrum.

Thus a postmodern reading of the Vietcong execution mentioned above might be that it's no longer an image of pain, the degradation of man or even moral outrage but, instead, becomes part of a discussion of the 'authentic'. For Sontag, this postmodern denial of the notion of truth beyond a relative term in constructing the world is a bogus position. 'To speak of reality becoming a spectacle is a breathtaking provincialism. It universalises the viewing habits of a small educated population living in the rich part of the world, where news has been converted into entertainment'.[5] This is to the detriment of the many for whom there is real pain. *Regarding the Pain of Others*, then, is a reclaiming of

The slow look

Susan Sontag's, *Regarding the Pain of Others*[1] was written after 9/11, an event for which the 'image' was multiplied to infinity, via rolling news and global computer networks. The book's importance lay in the way it focused on how we experience photographs of pain in a paradoxical manner, where news from afar is brought to us as if at close proximity (which demands that we care) and equally, as info-tainment (which doesn't). It's this nearing and distancing of pain, both geographical and cultural that informs the cultural imagination of war.

Via the media, we enter into symmetrical and asymmetrical relations with the pain of others. We can empathise with the child made homeless by bombing whilst maintaining a critical distance from the mutilated body of a 'terrorist'. A moral position (with us or against us) allows the spectator a split personality when reacting to news footage.

This split personality became apparent in the 2009 war in Gaza, the context in which this response has been written. The original article was never posted as an article on the Limited Language website, but the context of rewriting has provided the opportunity to explore ideas which the original article couldn't account for.

Having argued in the original article that 'Western media outlets reduce pain to an editorial, rather than pictorial display', in January 2009, even if briefly, there was a shift in experience for the Western viewer as newspapers ran close-up images of the dead and dying. No foreign reporters were being admitted into Gaza and coverage of events relied on journalists already there, at the epicentre of the violence.

Anglo-American sensibilities of the image collided with those from the Arab community.

For a Western press, an event like this removes the possibility of framing a crisis within the image in the way explored in the original article. Instead, it has to be 'managed' outside of it; most obviously this is done in image selection, captions and length of editorial. These are factors always found in media framing.

We can see one distancing mechanism employed in image captioning from the *New York Times*; 'Men carried the bodies of Gazan children *they said* were killed in an Israel airstrike'.[2] (The italics are ours.) The ambiguity of guilt in the caption counters the documentary evidence of the image.

In the wider world, beyond Gaza, satellite television, Internet access and the searchability of the World Wide Web, has created an expanded media sphere.

News coverage once exclusive to predetermined geographic boundaries, is now readily available to an unbound – global – audiences. This means that a Western viewer is increasingly seeing death, war and suffering, filtered not through his or her shared codification and moral framework but rather, a myriad of social codes and ideological perspectives. Thus the visceral depictions of war casualties on satellite channels based in the Middle East, for instance, can be in direct opposition to the established 'norms' of showing the pain of others in the West.[3]

In *Regarding the Pain of Others*, Susan Sontag discusses how photographs invoke a shared experience. Whilst this might open up dialogue between the photographer and different viewing communities, from the start she reminds the reader: 'No "we" should be taken for granted when the subject is looking at other people's pain'.[4] By the end of the book, she notes that images of pain are characterised by a fundamental difficulty in communication; that this 'we' (which may or may not include the photographer) have not experienced the pain on view.[5]

When the photographer removes the urgency of the here-and-now of suffering, it pain *and* reality. This is a 'modern' view in response to her own experience of war in Sarajevo and 9/11 in New York. This modern view is forged out of the traumas of the First and Second World Wars and the development of documentary war photography into the language, the syntax, of war zones. For Sontag, photographs do have meaning and people don't become anaesthetised by the quantity of violent images, but by passivity.

Where this essay departs from *Regarding the Pain of Others* is in looking at how both the photograph and the response have become part of a culture of lifestyle consumption. A consequence of this is that, although context allows you to separate Diesel adverts from war documents, say, it is no longer possible to totally separate the language and textual framework used to look at them. Two examples immediately come to mind, although these aren't formally related. One is the series of Diesel clothing adverts which cemented their reputation as an 'edgy brand' in the 1990s with the tongue in cheek by-line, 'For Successful Living'. Bruce Grierson, writing in *Adbusters* magazine, called them 'cryptic ads-within-ads'; '...set in North Korea, [they] feature images of, for example, skinny models on the side of a bus packed with (presumably) starving, suffering locals. "There's no limit to how thin you can get," says the ad on the bus'.[6] Another image which troubles is from *The Times* newspaper. This one shows a Palestinian man carrying a wounded child moments after an Israeli strike on the Rafah refugee camp in the Gaza strip in 2004, with the caption underneath worded to this effect.[7] Viewing the image, it's hard not to notice the man's T-shirt, emblazoned as it is with the legend 'Urban Wear'. Can we stop this from providing an alternative caption?

Some time in the late 20th century, somewhere between the art exhibitions which endorsed the view of the extraordinary war photograph as 'beautiful' and the Hollywood war films which embellished and Americanised this aesthetic, a global brandscape of war has emerged.[8] This is a culture where the 'reading' of images

Feeding the Arab furies

The Iraqi war has been a gift to states looking for a reason to unite against their common enemies, writes **Colin Smith**

Shortly after midday two young men on a motorbike wove their way through the heavy traffic of Ramallah, the West Bank town that is the de facto Palestinian capital. The pillion passenger was waving a large Iraqi flag.

This was the signal for the arrival in Manara Square, the town's gathering place, of a cohort of about 100 mostly teenage schoolgirls wearing green-and-white-striped tunics over jeans. Perhaps half had covered their hair in the Islamic fashion with tightly knotted white scarves.

"Oh please, oh beloved Saddam," they began to chant, impish smiles on their faces. "Bomb, bomb, bomb Tel Aviv!"

A few held aloft portraits of the Iraqi leader. Most carried posters condemning the war, several written in English for the convenience of the international media. "Iraqi lives are also sacred," said one.

By the seventh day of the war they had a new slogan. "Oh please, oh beloved Saddam," they pleaded. "Bomb, bomb, bomb Kuwait and leave not a Cadillac standing."

Kuwaiti persecution of its Palestinian community following Yasser Arafat's ill-advised support of Iraq during the Gulf war in 1991 has made it the least popular of all the region's pocket eldorados.

As the current war entered its second week, rage against the British and Americans — and the governments that support them — had spread like a bushfire

America of returning the world to the law of the jungle, "where the mighty rule over the weak".

The Americans, however, had hoped would spare them such scenes. For as well as the predictable denunciation of "Bush barba-

police. The crowd was eventually dispersed with tear gas. Jordan and Egypt are Israel's only Arab

old city screaming: "With our soul and blood we redeem you Baghdad."

tory," said Abdel Moneim, a bank clerk in Cairo. "If Saddam succeeds, then nobody will trespass

al-Feqi, chairman of the foreign relations committee of the Egyptian parliament who regards himself as a friend of the United States.

Protests in pro-western Egypt, Jordan and Bahrain started with the first day of the war. For Egypt's president, Hosni Mubarak, the conflict is already disastrous, torpedoing tourism, which is his country's biggest hard currency earner.

Jordan, ruled by the Sandhurst-trained King Abdullah II, the son of an Englishwoman, is thought to have allowed the SAS to cross into western Iraq from its territory in order to search for Scuds that might threaten Israel.

Protesters' frustrations have focused partly on such leaders. In Syria, 100,000 demonstrators not only chanted anti-American slogans but also denounced King Abdullah as a "Zionist" and Mubarak as a "dollar worshipper". In Ramallah, the schoolgirls chanted: "Abdullah, your people don't want you."

There have also been demands for the kind of pan-Arab unity not seen since Gamal Abdel Nasser ruled Egypt. In both Amman and Cairo, the demonstrators taunt the police with their chant: "Where is the Arab army?"

By this weekend the nearest the conflict had seen to this was the arrival in Iraq of Arab volunteers who set off from Syria with the blessing of the country's president, Bashar al-Assad.

During the last Gulf War Syria, then ruled by Bashar's late father Hafez al-Assad, joined in with the Americans and sent troops to Kuwait. This time the Assad dynasty has let the Bush dynasty down. "We hope that they don't succeed and we doubt that they will," the Syrian leader, an ophthalmologist who trained in London, told a Lebanese newspaper.

Some of the volunteers passing through Syria may have been southern Lebanese Shi'ites, men who had been influenced by Sheikh Mohammed Hussein Fadlallah, the

Vahid Salemi

A placard raised during a demonstration in Tehran last week displays the anti-American feeling sweeping the Arab world in the wake of the Iraq attack

BUSH IS
CHILDREN
LLER

'Feeding the Arab Furies', *The Sunday Times*, 30 March 2003. Photograph by Vahid Salemi.

opens up what Lilie Chouliaraki refers to as, 'a space of analytical temporality'.[6] This is one in which events can be debated and reflected on and she refers particularly to the long shot. On the one hand, we can see this in images of a city-scape of smoke or the night-spectacle of bombings over Baghdad. These latter images, of course, are part of the rhetoric that allows death to be dispassionately rethought of as 'collateral damage'.

On the other hand, we can also see it in photographs taken 'in place', but after the event has occurred. This allows both empathy and indignation to be suspended for deliberation. With Gaza, although much of the daily and lead reporting used the close-up, the temporal/analytic space was often employed in photographs chosen for the inside (analysis) pages of the daily newspapers and in the weeklies whose role it is to summarise and reflect back on the last seven days' news. For instance, an essay in *The Economist* asking, 'Where Will it End?'[7] set the tone with a header image of the back of a man's head in silhouette looking out of a (glassless?) window and over the scene of a bomb-hit building. In this photograph, the exposed infrastructure of rooms and concrete stairways twist and hang off their steel innards. No longer connected, the scene served to remind us of the daily lives similarly fractured and dispossessed which were yet another casualty of this (any) war. In an image captioned, 'Too hard a lesson',[8] the viewer looks, through the eyes of the photographer, at a woman sitting on steps at the other end of an alleyway and she is facing back to the photographer/viewer. Between lie several charred pairs of shoes and soiled clothes. Other photos showed people picking through more strewn personal effects; books, papers and other remnants of once-daily life. The viewer, photographer and the person in the photo cannot connect through the pain of such loss. However, in implying, rather than depicting the human condition, these photographs demand a slower look.[9] These are the same minutiae that give nar-

has, over half a century, become so common place that the ability to analyse imagery is second nature for many in contemporary Western culture. Increasingly, this has become a culture where images are supplied to us with the analysis ready-inscribed. This phenomenon could be seen in the media analysis of the 2003 war in Iraq, which was raging as Sontag's book hit the shelves. Here, response to images didn't follow their reproduction in the media but came pre-packaged. For instance, the image of George W. Bush in full combat gear jumping off his fighter jet which had 'Commander in Chief' painted on the side to the backdrop of the u.s.s. *Abraham Lincoln* and a building-sized banner stating 'Mission Accomplished'.[9] Here the language of films like *Mission Impossible* and *Top Gun* and the historical document are all rolled into one.

Another piece of pre-packaged commentary was the British *Guardian* newspaper's G2 coverage which showed an Iraqi boy, looking out from the page and into the viewer's eyes. The pull-quote read: 'This is Sufian. He is 11. One evening, American soldiers hooded and hand-cuffed him, then took him to prison. For three weeks his parents had no idea where he was. Is this the way to police Iraq?'[10] This tale made the boy news worthy but what made it media friendly was his attire: an American Simpsons cartoon T-shirt, with Bart saying: 'I didn't do it. Nobody saw me do it. You can't prove anything'. The image was not simply reportage. One can recognise the horror of the situation but can more readily empathise with the knowing nod to the ideology of empire (of occupation and media empires and their homogenising effect) which is symbolised in the child's T-shirt.

Shot to commission, the photo agency Troika told us that the image was in no way orchestrated by the photographer. However, its context is a liberal broadsheet where journalists and editors are aware of the self-knowingness of a modern day audience. Could they be accused of providing editorial and images already aligned to these tastes? Doesn't the child's image read like a Kellogg's packet advertising its free gift; the bonus of an ironic statement for the audience's appreciation?

This 'relationship' is clearly illustrated by Anne Higonnet in *Pictures of Innocence: The History and Crisis of Ideal Childhood*. Higonnet, an art historian, comments: 'The Knowing idea belongs to our particular historical moment. Photography's fidelity is to the values of that particular moment, not to some "real" truth about children'.[11] In this mediated relationship, the photograph enters into a dialogue with the viewer which is more about a shared language between photographer and viewer and less about the pain of the child.

This cultural knowingness or relationship between news and audience is intrinsic to what we see and what we don't see. For instance, the Qatari television station *Al Jazeera* understands pain to be legitimate, visceral viewing. In contrast, Western media outlets reduce pain to an editorial, rather than pictorial display. Early on in the coverage of the war in Iraq, American *Time* magazine commentated on a 'PG-rated war'[12] in terms of images. It made a call for more 'real' images of devastation and death to wake us up from the stupor that led the West to war. A stasis, not induced by repeated exposure to pain and violence, but by its aestheticisation. One photograph from *Time*, that was taken during the fall of Saddam Hussein International Airport, shows two soldiers directed (as is the viewer) by the signage for Arrivals.[13] This image is a version of advertising's 'Big Idea'; the visual equivalent of the verbal soundbite.

And yet there is also another war aesthetic on view: one of *images of images*, as much of place as of people. For instance, after the Americans had taken Baghdad, Simon Norfolk photographed the bombarded Ministry of Defence, where a poster of Saddam Hussein hangs unscathed on the wall.[14] In the absence of the man himself, to capture any of Saddam's icons on film was a potent press image in itself. And the documentary mode discussed here soon becomes a visual trope when translated into new contexts. For instance, in a campaign by

rative to our own lives. Might there be some shared experience in the act of looking at these traces?

Eye-witness photographs in close-up can only present people as victims. In the more analytical, temporal mode, photographs do more than witness. Chouliaraki suggests they can ask us to contemplate the experience of those who witness events in reality, and also our own experience of witnessing through the image. The sufferers, as well as being victims, become: 'humanized and historical beings; as people who feel, reflect and act on their fate'.[10] In this way do they, momentarily at least, become people like 'us' who happen to live far away?

Carry on the conversation here
http://tiny.cc/chapter5_4

References
1   Susan Sontag, *Regarding the Pain of Others* (London: Hamish Hamilton, 2003).
2   'In the Fog of Urban War Crimes and Ethics Blur' in *The New York Times*, reprinted in *The Observer*, 25 January 2009, 2. Photograph by Hatem Moussa/ Associated Press.
3   For instance, Gaza Under Fire, Islamic Channel, Sky 813, 1 February 2009. Here, phrases such as 'genocide' slid across the screen as the camera panned in and out of pictures of children, injured and dead, their families mourning and buildings being bulldozed.
4   Susan Sontag, Op cit., 6.
5   Ibid., 113.
6   Lilie Chouliaraki, 'The Symbolic Power of Transnational Media: Managing the Visibility of Suffering' in *Global Media and Communication*, Vol. 4, No. 3 (2008), 337.
7   'The Struggle for Gaza: Where Will it End' in *The Economist*, 10 January 2009, 23.
8   Image captioned 'Too hard a lesson' in 'The Struggle for Gaza', *The Economist*, 10 January 2009, 25.
9   Peter Campbell, 'The Lens of War' in *New Left Review* 55, January-February 2009, 2 .
10 Lilie Chouliaraki, Op cit., 337.

Starter article Readers' comments Limited Language reflection   241

the German charity, Misereor, a mural of a family of workers in the fields which has been riddled with bullets in some unspecified conflict, is accompanied by the by-line, 'War Leaves Many Traces: War Orphans Need Your Help to Live in Peace'.[15]

In both of these, a move can be seen from direct representation or experience to the traces of the everyday. It's an aesthetic which Sontag's book can't account for as it so often precludes pain. But even when it doesn't, it's something she doesn't (encourage us to) look for. The capturing of traces keeps war at a distance, but it doesn't present us with a simulacra of the war like a movie might do. The trace, in a sense, becomes the indexical link to reality.

The trace can also present us with a more complex series of images which can't be reduced to soundbites for the next day's news. Instead, these need time to penetrate the depth of their possible meanings. Consider the following image, presented when the war was over: it shows Iraqi men eating outside a café in Baghdad with American soldiers patrolling in the background. On the café table stands a collection of fizzy drink cans. Look a little longer and one drink can, which at first glance seems to bear the Seven Up logo, on closer inspection reads, 'Cheer Up'.[16]

The layering of images and narratives (including the fragmentation and unremarkable nature of the images discussed at the end) is not to reinforce the postmodern, European position whose dislocation of truth and the value of experience has taken away from engagement with the image.

Instead: Is the trace now the same as the modernist idea of experience? Images not only have meaning but, in an over-saturated visual world, is it often the traces which give meaning? Images cannot compete with the SFX of movies, but traces are real and not just simulations.

See further images here
www.limitedlanguage.org/images

Baghdad Ministry of Defence. © Simon Norfolk (2003).

War Orphans Need Your Help to Live in Peace,
for the charity Misereor. By Kolle Rebbe
(2007).
http://bit.ly/Misereor

References

1   Susan Sontag, *Regarding the Pain of Others* (London: Hamish Hamilton, 2003). This was a revisiting of some of the ideas she had originally developed in *On Photography* (New York: Farrar, Straus, Giroux, 1977).

2   Photograph of an execution in Saigon, South Vietnam, 1 February 1968 by Eddie Adams, USA, for The Associated Press. The photograph won the World Press Photo of the Year: 1968. www.worldpressphoto.org

3   Susan Sontag, Op cit., 53-4.

4   This work is more particularly part of post-structuralist thinking. Two of its main protagonists were Jean Baudrillard and Jacques Derrida. Baudrillard proposed the 'simulacrum', where human experience is of a simulation of reality, mediated by signs, rather than reality itself. Roland Barthes' later work was also post-structuralist in thinking and, in *Camera Lucida: Reflections on Photography* (1982), he suggested that the relative innocence which prompted his earlier structuralist essays, such as *Mythologies* (1957, English translation 1970), had passed. Here, he could make fairly stable associations between 'steak and chips' and 'Frenchness' for instance. Later, meanings and signs were seen to be much more unstable.

5   Susan Sontag, Op cit., 98.

6   Bruce Grierson, 'Shock's Next Wave: Advertisers Scramble for New Ways to Shock an Unshockable Generation', in *Adbusters* magazine (Winter 1998). The adverts were designed by Swedish design agency Traktor.

7   Ian MacKinnon, '10 die as Israeli tank shells crowd' in *The Times*, 20 May 2004, 34. Photograph by Kahil Hamra/Associated Press.

8   See Philip Griffiths, *Vietnam Inc.* (London: Phaidon, 2001). Also, The British newspaper, *The Guardian,* offered Iraq photos for sale on its website even as they still appeared in the guise of reportage in the newspaper. One could 'click and own' the photographs. www.guardian.co.uk/iraq

9   These images were distributed to newsrooms world-wide on 1 May 2003. The orchestration of the event, commentary included, was so obvious that reports of its PR manoeuvring accompanied the broadcast of the image.

10 Sufian Abd al-Ghani photographed by Michael Walter on the cover of *The Guardian G2* cover, 15 August 2003.

11 Anne Higonnet, *Pictures of Innocence: The History and Crisis of Ideal Childhood* (London: Thames and Hudson, 1998).

12 Joe Klein, 'The PG-rated War' in *Time*, 7 April 2003, 67.

13 New Arrivals: The US Army's 3rd Infantry Division looking for resistance from Iraqi fighters under airport signs pointing to passport control and baggage claim from 'Destination Baghdad', *Time*, 14 April 2003.

14 Baghdad Ministry of Defence by Simon Norfolk. Printed in 'Afterburn', *The Guardian Weekend*, 24 May 2003, 21. Norfolk also showed work in 'The Sublime Image of Destruction' for 2008

Brighton Photo Biennial curated by Julian Stallabrass.

15 Campaign by Misereor, the overseas development agency of the Catholic Church in Germany.

16 'A Latté – And a Rifle To Go', *The Observer Review* cover, 8 June 2003. Photograph by Alexander Zemilianichenko.

Mediations

After digital... / Sense making?
Digital glass / Digital behaviours
Speech, writing, print... / Serifs and conduits
New reading spaces / Print vs. screen
This page is no longer on this server... / The influence of neighbours

This chapter explores how to incorporate digital media into
design practice and writing: from digital tools to reading;
community to process.

Keywords
Community (304,000,000)
Linguistics (6,140,000)
Nostalgia (3,680,000)

Keywords and their Google hit rate in conjunction with the word design.

After digital...

The Information Super highway is now more than twenty years old and is beginning to show some wear and tear.

Like early Modernist architecture, the Internet has been built on the metaphor of speed, creating a landscape of strip cities made up of Internet servers. Yet, whereas architecture creates a powerful topography – the skyline – digital servers remain anonymous, their presence almost unnoticed, mostly underground, bunkered and sealed from the day to day.

And now...

Speaking to a colleague the other day, he asked, 'What happens when digital technology becomes middle-aged?' And this is the point: in a speeded up digital world the technology has already reached its 'middle-age' crisis. So many of its dreams, offspring and partnerships have either failed, died or taken up lives of their own. What we are seeing (and Limited Language is part of this phenomenon) is a moment of reflection, a wistful interlude where we see a proliferation of blogs which, like Victorian journal entries, try to make sense of the times. Then it was the Industrial revolution, now a more 'velvet' technological one where digital design materialises, as once the Arts and Crafts[1] movement did, in the handmade and the organic, the tactile, the sensual and the interactive.

In the 21st century this is not an attempt to reject, but to humanise, the digital. We are awaiting the outcomes...

See further images here
www.limitedlanguage.org/images

References
1   The Arts & Crafts Movement emerged towards the end of the 19th century into the early years of the 20th century, celebrating craft and quality in an era of mass and cheap reproduction.

Sense making?

After digital... presupposed that digital culture is a culture of speed, invisibility and euphoria at technical innovation. The article spied a moment of reflection, a desire to make it visible and 'real', in order to understand its effects. As Adriana comments in replies to the article on the Limited Language website: '...(finally) [it] starts becoming interesting. Maybe the time of invisibility is over, now that mistakes and frictions start to reveal themselves'.[1]

The original article made a prescient reference to a velvet revolution in the digital realm. Web 2.0 is the result of this revolution. It does not have a single author; it is not a software upgrade, a piece of hardware or a quantifiable commodity. It is a collection of technological ecologies from which cultural developments in digital tool making multiply. Facebook, MySpace and Twitter are examples of this organic development: a social networking ecosystem.

'After', which suggests a passing, is somewhat of a misnomer but it intends to infer a time (now reached) where digital technology is fully embedded in our bodies and in our everyday and, as such, has become 'second nature' to many in a connected world where its networks – from banking to telecommunications – affect everyone. It's in this sense that digital culture has visibly materialised; as a way of thinking, reacting and behaving in the world.

Digital technology has extended our tools of communication and (maybe more radically), how we consume and what we consume. The introduction of the MP3 format for instance, gave rise to the evolution of 'downloading' networks. Napster was the most (in) famous of the Internet sites which introduced the idea of 'sharing' music across networks and

Image: Sandrine by GamonGirls.
http://bit.ly/sandrine

Poladroid is an App which allows the user to
create a digital version of the traditional Polaroid
photograph. The website proclaims: 'Welcome to the
POLADROID world!' The App has an accompanying
group pool on flickr to share and compare users.
creative output.

http://bit.ly/polar_group
http://bit.ly/polardroid

it has radically transformed how we consume music, with iTunes, for instance, being its legitimate, corporate offspring. An important outcome of this use of the World Wide Web is how it has severely questioned the economic model of music consumption: Do you pay? How much do you pay? Do you buy the music outright or pay for access, and simply lease month by month? This shift – from ownership to access – is most radical in a consumer culture and the effects remain to be seen.

Over all, this example might seem to reject Joel's original lament: 'Like all things the Web will reach its "sell by" date, because change is the way of the world'.[11] Whilst it's true that sites like Napster are rebranded to become legitimate business models and, as a result of this, lose popularity and the cache of being against the corporate machine: alternative. What is different from the usual fashion cycle is that it has transformed our way of thinking about music: not simply the technology of its consumption but what music is worth and how we consume from the pick 'n' mix of digital downloads.

We now have the opportunity to make up (and purchase) playlists rather than albums allowing the possibility of a creative act in how we consume music. This can become a performative critical action when mediated through sites like Last.fm (now owned by CBS) which allows users to upload music and create radio stations.

These are essentially playlists that others can access (with the option to purchase tracks). The site promotes itself thus: '...as you use Last.fm, you make it better for you and everyone else. When you recommend some music to a friend, or you tag it, or you write about it – even just listening to it – you shift the song's importance on the site. It'll be recommended to different people, because you've listened to it. It'll move up our music charts and maybe more people will hear it because you thought it was good.'

Isn't it these effects that we need to make visible and real – to understand?

The original article asked whether the effects of digital could appear in the handmade and the organic, the tactile, the sensual and the interactive. Today we would argue that many of these qualities can be found in the patchwork of personal sites created in MySpace and Facebook.

The social networking sites which are popular at the moment aren't the glossy, filmic sites designed by the latest add-ons in Flash, or similar software, but more a cut and past organic interface – a brocage of the sound, vision and interface formats. This sense of the organic is captured in the comment by Mark Zuckerberg the founder/designer of Facebook: 'At Harvard, a few of my friends saw me developing Facebook and they sent it out to a couple of their friends and within two weeks, two thirds of Harvard were using it. Then we started getting emails from people at other schools asking "How do we get Facebook? Could you license us the code so we could run a version of Facebook for our school?" But when I started it, there was no concept of having Facebook across schools'.[1] Based on the idea of a school yearbook, Facebook quickly became a dominant social networking platform because it was facilitated by the 'embedded' nature of Web 2.0; that which seamlessly interacts with our lives.

The Application Programming Interfaces (API) which allow the introduction of third party applications, or Apps, have nurtured Facebook's development. First introduced in 2005 by Facebook, the effect of Apps was immediate; 'The Facebook Platform is a dramatic leap forward for the Internet industry.... Facebook is providing a highly viral distribution engine for applications that plug into its platform'.[2]

Apps have become the dominant development in Web culture – from Firefox to the iPhone – the App or add-on allows us to personalise the user experience.

In just one of the untold number of examples, *Colour Expert* allows you to identify the nearest colour match reference in any photo you have taken in order to use it else-where (in a design?). Although this particular example is released through Apple's App Store (which control what you can download), rival developers[3] are allowing Apps to be developed and distributed by anyone in the original shar-ing/community mode innovated by Web 2.0.

This is part of a broader shift in digitally mediated design, and information design in particular, in which we see a transformation of the traditional model where we simply read and follow instructions. Now we see a more reflective, 'relational' development where a person can 'interact' or engage in dialogue; both as a user and developer.

Instead of, 'data-basing human senses'[III] (as one reply cautioned in responses on the website), it's this 'making sense' that becomes the imperative 'after' digital. As we wrote in our own reply to the original article: 'This is, perhaps, an attempt to help people navigate the 21st century – in the same way the road and motorway signage system designed by Jock Kinneir and Margaret Calvert did in the 1950s and 60s, or the way Harry Beck's 1933 map of the London Underground made real the temporal and invisible realm of travelling. In the digital realm of today, people can both create and experience narrative making in many forms...'[IV]

How designers will engage with these changes is still to be fully realised.

See full responses + carry on the conversation here
http://tiny.cc/chapter6_1

Reader credits

I   Adriana 22/05/2005
II   Joel 16/05/2005
III   Anonymous 15/05/2005 – this comment actually comes out of a disagreement with the original article about whether 'velvet technology' had the capacity for narrative or sense-making; 'I tend to disagree with your [identification of] 'velvet' technology with the Arts and Crafts movement. To me the tactile products of the digital age seem more an abandonment of humanism rather than praise of it. What differentiates humans from animals, in my opinion, is the ability to create a narrative. And this is what lacks in 'velvet' technology. I am imagining

the iPod as a good example of it, for it is invented to 'personalize' the huge amount of tunes produced and consumed...Yet because it has easy access to the Internet, a huge memory you can never fill up and a function that automatically shuffles songs, we end up drawn into the sea of high and low cultures of music...the process of data-basing human senses.'

IV The authors 25/05/2005

References

1   Mark Zuckerberg quoted in Amy Shuen, *Web 2.0: A Strategy Guide* (Beijing; Farnham: O'Reilly, 2008), 93.

2   Marc Andreessen (the founder of Netscape) quoted in Amy Shuen, ibid, 95.

3   For instance, at the time of writing 'Android', Google's competitor to the iPhone is allowing Apps to be developed and distributed by anyone, leveraging the Web community to monitor quality; the model for Wikipedia et al. As reported by Gavin Lucas, 'Killer Apps' in *Creative Review*, December 2008, 28.

Jon Wozencroft
Digital glass

In reference to an earlier post on Limited Language, *After Digital* [this volume p. 249].

After Digital points to the assumption, which in some respects is fairly entrenched already, that we have the hang of digital media: we can sit down, put our feet up in front of the widescreen, its FreeView box and broadband access, and work out what our options are. And yet, if we can agree that for most of the design community, digital software became a modus operandi at the end of the 1980s, then the digital sphere is not 'middle-aged' and still very much in its youth. Digital impacted very quickly on graphic design and print media but, for the rest of the world, it was the age of the Internet and mobile telephony, rather than the graphic design software of the PC and Mac, that had the greater effect, almost a decade later.

I am completely sympathetic with the notion that digital is middle-aged. There is a sense of fatigue, maybe, and the suspicion that the early and quite critical years of 1990-95 have been superseded by a radical conformity. At the outset, there were voices in opposition to the prevailing currents. The climate changed.

To get personal for a moment, Neville Brody and I took the opportunity to end the second book we did in 1994 (*The Graphic Language of Neville Brody* 2),[1] on a note of caution rather than the false optimism characteristic of the early 1990s. However, it was 'out of time' – even when the surface of it was readily taken up as a template for a digital aesthetic. The *FUSE*[2] project, a platform for experimental design and typography launched in 1991, was both misunderstood (possibly our mistake) and widely adopted way beyond its print-run. The Internet was being spoken of as a superhighway but there were no cars on it. The 'End of Print'[3] rhetoric that followed was one take on the 'slacker' aesthetic but there is no movement in the decision to replace text with Zapf

Digital behaviours

'The facility…operates seven days a week from 9 a.m. to 9 p.m., has eight research rooms decorated as living rooms or home offices, with hardwood floors, soft lighting and comfortable furniture. There is also a theatre that allows a dozen people to participate in a simultaneous experiment. … The rooms are built around a central command post, where researchers scrutinize participants via video monitor – one room has 20 cameras – and through one-way mirrors'.[1]

Is the facility an Orwellian scenario from *Nineteen Eighty-Four*? Or *Brave New World*? Maybe even the back-story for the latest Terry Gilliam movie?… Actually it is a Walt Disney facility for research into how we respond to what we see on the Web – more precisely, Web based advertising. A research lab where 'in addition to tracking eye movement, [a] 14-member team use heart-rate monitors, skin temperature readings and facial expressions (probes are attached to facial muscles) to reach conclusions'.[2]

The sci-fi connotations described above are apposite as the title to Wozencroft's original post *Digital Glass*, which was a nod to the Russian novelist, Yevgeny Zamyatin, 1920s dystopian novel *We*.[3] The novel depicts a society, 500 years hence, who live in a glass city – OneState – cut off from nature by a green wall. The main protagonist, D-305 (people's names being replaced by numbers with a letter prefix, vowels for women, consonants for men), a scientist and mathematician, is coerced (seduced) by I-330, a vampish, liberated woman who at one point chides the mathematician by asking him to name the final number – he objects that numbers are infinite and she replies that so is the number of revolutions…

The infinitesimal conundrum is part of

the phenomenom of the World Wide Web – when will the last page be posted?

For us, when thinking of the World Wide Web today, the challenges are tracing its history (and the notion of time) and equally, in Wozencroft's words, 'The work needing to be done (physiologically) on the effects of digital on the mind, body and spirit...' All of these elements inform the original article and the responses it solicited.

You could argue Wozencroft's essay is nostalgic for a non-digital world; of shopping queues, young people and Dessicant Silica Gel. It is a world whose relationship with the digital is still in flux.

But nostalgia helps identify the very changes digital technology has wrought... shopping queues disappear in the online shopping experience ('LET US DO THE WALKNG' one home Internet service proclaims), young people are avatars, surfers or YouTube actor/writer/directors, and Dessicant Silica Gel is redundant because the digitised networks providing warehouse, logistics, inventory management, delivery, courier, and storage distribution services means commodities no longer wait in damp warehouses: welcome to the flows of the digital world (or so the story goes).

But nostalgia is only one way of demarcating history; the catalyst for the original essay was trying to map the time-zones and histories of digital cultures.

In an essay, *Critique of the Instant and the Continuum*, the Italian philosopher Giorgio Agamben, makes explicit the importance of history/time in constituting cultures (both established and emerging): 'Every conception is invariably accompanied by a certain experience of time which is implicit in it, conditions it, and thereby has to be elucidated. Similarly, every culture is first and foremost a particular experience of time, and no new culture is possible without an alteration in this experience. The original task of a genuine revolution, therefore, is never merely to 'change the world', but also – and above all – to change 'time'.[4]

Dingbats, only knowing illiteracy and more hero-designer boredom. This is what we always tried to resist.

Desktop publishing gives way to desktop music, photography and film making, which race towards new compression codes that wish to deliver everything to a screen the size of a credit card. Celebrity and corporate culture looks the same at any size or resolution. It's easy to churn out because it is digital, and copying is encouraged just as long as you don't make copies.

What exactly is 'digital'? It is not as all-pervasive as Nicholas Negroponte's evangelist line of *Being Digital*[4] proposed, nor, for those of an i-Podded perspective, as desperate on a daily basis as Paul Virilio[5] would have it. The reality is split down the middle.

A while ago, I stood in the queue in a camera shop behind a man who had asked for a roll of film to go with his new digital camera. 'Actually, sir, it's a digital camera, it doesn't need film.' After five minutes had elapsed as this point was explained in front of a frustrated queue, he was sent packing with his new purchase, and a roll of 35mm film.

The professions that have their daily lives determined by digital media get very arrogant about its ubiquity compared to the experience of many people, who are both seduced and baffled by speedy technological change. I don't think we've even begun to see the wider consequences, let alone understand what digital means for the human race.

Is it the domain of young people? Is it normal to want your child to be computer literate as early as possible? Economically, yes; developmentally, heaven forbid. You can see young people are both fascinated and terrorised by the demands of the latest mobile phones, the PlayStations; and older people are intimidated by the complexity of choices and swift-fingered techniques. Older people are physically excluded whilst younger children are made competitive over gadgets that quite literally fry their brains.

The work needing to be done (physiologically) on

the effects of digital on the mind, body and spirit will be some time in coming. The mental effects – these, hopefully, being the domain of the artist – seem to have been abandoned in favour of a market game of musical chairs.

The Fine Art scene has yet to come to terms with 'digital'; it mirrors its 'immateriality' in other respects. I got very annoyed about Nicolas Bourriaud's 2002 book *Post Production* because it promised a critique of this tendency, whilst proceeding to proselytise a list of emerging and already successful artists. There was no critical position in relation to their marketing by galleries, the media and critics such as him. 'To make diverse work...that had a lack of desire to control what comes out of it'[5] depends on a degree of invisibility that is anathema to Bourriaud's position.

To refer to another contention of the *After Digital* post – between the Velvet Revolution in the Czech Republic in 1989 and the notion that we are approaching some digital media-equivalent – I have to say that all would agree the human touch is the thing that's missing.

The iPod...it's like Hi-Fi never happened: a Shellac from the pre-stereo era has more presence and vitality than MP3 compression offers. The earlobe/headphones make their users (they are NOT listeners) look like a walking ECG, but countless millions are perfectly content with personal isolation and virtual community. In pre-digital time, Dessicant Silica Gel (a crystalline powder the manufacturers put in a white pouch) was included with packaging for stereos etc., to remove moisture. This would seem to be the effect the digital has on the brain.

Until there's a revolution the likes of which we have little idea about, nothing is going to change. All the weblogs and interactive devices in the world will add to what's already carved up in the computer fabric of those who have, and those who have not. We haven't got to zombie level yet but there is little to shine light on what the real questions should be.

It's obvious to all, I hope, that at this moment we

The revolution in Internet/digital technology is with a small r, but no less radical for that.[5]

The Wozencroft essay was responding to our original contention of a 'velvet revolution in digital use' and our comment on how in a 'speeded up digital world the technology has already reached its "middle-age" crisis; so many of its dreams, offspring and partnerships have either failed, died or taken up lives of their own'.[1] Here we were thinking of the dot.com crash, the corporatisation of peer-to-peer networking with the advent of iTunes, and the evolving use of social networking sites – or as Evan Schwartz dramatically reports in his book *Digital Darwinism*:

'...even as life on the Web flourishes on the surface, danger lurks beneath. With the raw fear largely gone, with the primitive experimentation mostly left behind, with the original novelty of Internet shopping and e-commerce wearing off, with technology no longer appearing futuristic, the digital business environment has taken on an air of indispensability, of inevitability'.[6]

His book clearly defines the corporate sphere, '[a]s an environment that can sustain economic life,'[7] but there is another distinct cultural sphere – the inter-personal: we both consume and communicate through the Internet: from music downloads to blogging, and a network of communication through a range of VoIP* protocols too.

Design uniquely bridges both spheres; it advertises its wares on the Web, alongside any other corporate, commercial concern whilst equally, it will need to create and harness the creative possibilities digital technologies offer to the practice of design: often providing the interface for both corporate and inter-personal communication too.

The design critic, Rick Poynor,[8] has commented on the non-design of many of the inter-personal sites (MySpace for instance) but in one way, this is missing the point as it is the content of these sites (not the corporate style) where we find the creative synapses which will fire future creativity: the music, film, photography found on these sights often captures the visual/sonic zeitgeist. These sites form parasitic relationships to the 'professions' in music, or the more plastic arts like graphic design: all of who have a presence themselves on these sights. The sites are a meeting place between the professional and the vernacular/novice/amateur.

In the 1970s we had the DTP revolution which placed once specialised technology in the hands of the novice – you could now produce your own corporate literature but inevitably much of it was bad – template based – design. What is noticeably different in the way the Web interacts with the amateur is how it allows a space for the exchange of ideas – many to many communication – it is not solely a technical phenomena like DTP but a relational, informative and constructive space. YouTube, amongst all the juvenilia, will, in the future, produce filmmakers; likewise MySpace – musicians; blogs – authors, and so it goes...

See full responses + carry on the conversation here
http://tiny.cc/chapter6_2

Reader credits
I   For discussion on *After Digital*, the original post see:
     www.limitedlanguage.org/discussion/index.php/
     archive/after-digital/

References
1   Brooks Barnes, 'Lab Watches Web Surfers to See
     Which Ads Work' *The New York Times*, 27 July 2009,
     81.
2   Ibid.
3   Yevgeny Zamyatin, *We* (Penguin Books, 1970).
4   Giorgio Agamben, *Infancy and History : On the
     Destruction of Experience* (London; New York: Verso,
     2007), 99.
5   For a study on the political dimension of the Internet
     read James Boham 'Expanding dialogue: the Internet,
     the public sphere and prospects for transnational
     democracy' in Jürgen Habermas, Nick Crossley, and
     John M. Roberts, *After Habermas: New Perspectives
     on the Public Sphere, Sociological Review Monographs*
     (Oxford, UK; Malden, MA: Blackwell Publishing/
     Sociological Review, 2004), 131-55.
6   Evan Schwartz, *Digital Darwinism: Seven
     Breakthrough Strategies for Surviving in the Web
     Economy* (London: Penguin, 1999), 8.

have a surfeit of recording modes and delivery systems that give us an enormous freedom, but which are not currently being developed in a humanistic way...a rare set of extremes operate on automatic.

It wouldn't be beyond the pale to imagine a universal compression code whose speed and 'quality' was stratified rather like the divisions between dial-up, broadband and the not-yet-on-the-market. You can see that at the *Frieze Art Fair* in London – like everything, it goes punter/curator/owner baron. 'Digital' gives the impression that these three poles are interdependent and dynamic. Most of all they are susceptible to Crash, which makes their day-to-day manifestations ever more reactionary.

Can 'digital' ever enter the socialist stage? This is a big question, and one that will possibly only ever be resolved when the system reaches meltdown. To think that because a few people in Africa have laptops and that in India the economy has been turned around to a command economy, everything is going to reach middle-aged maturity is, I think, forgetting the internal schisms. It's also forgetting China and its analogue of corporate America; the need for short term supremacy.

The meltdown hasn't happened yet... Its time-based nature is outside our comprehension and against our nature. There is petrol, there is gas and electricity, there is essence. For the time being, middle age is like a blur from youth – history repeating itself in secret – except you come to appreciate such things and still take them for granted.

Middle age is a state of mind whose digital characteristic can be summarised by one being either 'on' or 'off' the case. It is very much linked to the body and one's ability to survive the immobility.

The glass ceiling that disadvantages women is double-glazed when it comes to old people. Digital makes life triple glazing.[7] You, the one [the dot] and the zero. The surface is read by lasers. My eyes are hurting. I have a bit of a headache. The youthful urge is to say 'show me something new', anything to distract from the current condition. Today's digital technologies are never around for long enough for us to build a true understanding of their nature.

See further images here
www.limitedlanguage.org/images

References

1   Jon Wozencroft, *The Graphic Language of Neville Brody 2* (London: Thames and Hudson, 1994). It had been preceded by *The Graphic Language of Neville Brody 1* (London: Thames and Hudson, 1988).
2   www.researchstudios.com/home/007-fuse/FUSE_about.php
3   This was picked up by Lewis Blackwell's collaboration with graphic designer David Carson in Lewis Blackwell, *The End of Print: The Grafik Design of David Carson* (Chronicle Books, 1995) and David Carson: *2nd Sight: Grafik Design After the End of Print* (Laurence King, 2000). After these books, reference to the 'end of print' and/or a 'slacker' aesthetic, often implies Carson who in one 1994 issue of *Ray Gun* set a Bryan Ferry interview in the typeface Zapf Dingbats because he thought it was a boring interview…
4   Nicholas Negroponte, *Being Digital* (New York: Alfred A. Knopf, 1995).
5   Paul Virilio, *Politics of the Very Worst* (New York: Semiotext[e], 1999).
6   Nicolas Bourriaud, *Postproduction* (New York: Lukas & Sternberg, 2002).
7   The basis for the 'digital glass' metaphor comes from the novel, Yevgeny Zamyatin, *We* (1922), set within a glass-enclosed city. This was the first in the 'trilogy' which included Aldous Huxley, *Brave New World* (1932) and George Orwell, *Nineteen Eighty-Four* (1949).
7   Ibid.
8   Rick Poynor, 'Digital self-expression' in *Eye*, No. 61, Vol. 16 http://www.eyemagazine.com/opinion.php?id=140&oid=353 (accessed 7/7/09).

*   Voice over Internet Protocol (VoIP) is a general term for a family of transmission technologies for delivery of voice communications over IP networks.

Michael Clarke

Speech, writing, print...

Within the context of postmodern theoretical writing, (phonetic) writing is a limiting medium. From Plato to Ferdinand de Saussure[1] and onwards to a bevy of structuralist and post-structuralist writers, words are acknowledged to have only an insecure relationship to the objects or concepts they seek to represent. For Jacques Derrida,[2] the Western philosophical tradition has prioritised the spoken word over the written. This is a conditioning cultural factor he identifies as logocentricism. In the presence of a speaker, we hear not only the author but also the authority of a statement. Written and, even more so, printed texts are denied this authority. For instance, handwriting is so often seen as an authentic representation of the individual (think of the authority invested in an autographic signature), and yet it has been claimed that writing does not possess the same degree of conviction as the spoken word. The printed word is seen to be further removed from the authority of the speaker.

Given this logocentricism, it is not surprising that classical literary criticism has focused attention on identifying the intentions of an author in order to arrive at the authentic interpretation of a text. This has frequently involved the use of extra-textual sources, most usually biographical or anecdotal material. Difficulties arise when there is little or nothing known about the writer. But as Roland Barthes, Michel Foucault, Derrida and others have observed;[3] if language itself lacks any certain hold on what it seeks to represent, there can be no reliable investment of authority in an author. Any possible meanings reside not in the author's intentions but in the text and the interpretations of the readers. Quite clearly, we are all involved in this as writers, readers or both and there are forceful implications for designers.

Writers often seek ways of breaking out of this linguistic straightjacket. In the early 20th century, a number of these sidestepped the expected semantical

Serifs and conduits

The linguistic straightjacket has not gone away...warns Michael Clarke in his essay exploring the unstable relationship between language and type: the interiority of the former opposed to the exteriority of the latter. But should typography, and by extension design, be ashamed of its naked world-li-ness: its out-there-ness?

Typography is the visible conduit to design meaning: a point made clear again, and again in design writing. Look at Steven Heller on *Designing Hate*[1] or more latterly the documentary *Helvetica* where Rick Poynor comments, 'Type is saying things to us all the time. Typefaces express a mood, an atmosphere. They give words a certain colouring...'[2]

The above are investigations of cultural semiosis rather than the art of typography itself: the ink that keys to the page to make our thoughts readable, or the pixels we manipulate to bring text into flickering existence on the computer screen.

The semiosis, or symbolism, of type is encountered – often unconsciously – every day. The German Gothic typeface, for instance, when used today – from WWII cinema posters to Goth T-shirts – uses the type style in such a way that historicises, creating symbolic meaning. This process obscures the pivotal role played by German design culture in the development of the sans serif (from which is born Helvetica): 'In Germany at the end of the 19th century, the Grotesk (the German name for sans serif) gained popularity fast. These Grotesks turned out to be the most influential faces in the history of the sans serif, much more so than their English counterparts'.[3]

But back to the question, how do we free ourselves from the linguistic straightjacket of deconstructionist thinking (or any other ist or ism for that matter). The conundrum has been eloquently addressed by Ellen Lupton when commenting on Deconstructionism: 'Rather than viewing it as a style, I see it as a process – an act of questioning'.[4] And this, in a nutshell, is the relationship between theory and practice – theory provides an opportunity to inform process, it provides tools for asking and formulating questions rather than a material end-in-itself: it provides a methodology rather than style alone.

Stephen Styles' opening response to Clarke's essay immediately circumvents the original's trajectory to one about processes by asking for a, 'reinvestigation of the phonocentric world' and by extension, the haptic world too: with a '...need to rebalance between ear and eye'.[1]

This rebalancing, in fact, is central to some of the examples already cited by Clarke. The Futurists, for example, were early protagonists in placing the sonic realm into artistic/ cultural discourse: from the use of a sound cannon to visceral poetry readings, they placed the experiential alongside the purely visual.[5]

The letterpress-produced poetry of Marinetti was an expression not of typography as an art form alone (if at all?), but rather the 'multilinear lyricism'[6] of industrial processes, synethesia and the onomatopoeic.

To counter the Futurist enthusiasm for change (but remaining on the trajectory of the sensorial) one can look at the typographer/ artist Eric Gill, who in 1931 wrote *Essay on Typography*. Reading it today, what is prescient is his worries concerning the tactile nature of typography (and its perceived corrosion):

'...the history of printing has been the history of the abolition of the impression. A print is properly a dent made by pressing; the history of letterpress printing has been the abolition of that dent... But the very smooth paper and the mechanically very perfect presses required for printing which shall show no "impression" can only be produced in a world which cares for such things, and such a

use of words and gave emphasis, instead, to the sounds themselves. Dadaists Raoul Hausmann and Kurt Schwitters recited and printed phonetic poems, for instance, *Sonate* of 1923. Ronald Firbank invented pataspeak to provide dialogue between marginal characters in his novel, *Valmouth* of 1919:

'Yahya!'
'Wazi jahm?'
'Ah didadididacti, didadidiacti.'
'Kataka mukha?'
'Ah mawardi, mawardi.'
'Jelly.'

Firbank's text, like most Dadaist texts, is a literary device. On other occasions, writers have gone beyond the issue of the literary alone to embrace the graphic and typographic too. This is spectacularly the case with the Italian Futurists such as Filippo Marinetti's 1919 *ScABrrRrraaNNG*. Firbank's application of typographic nuance operated in a much less aggressive, but equally disruptive way. For instance, in *The Flower Beneath The Foot* from 1923, he represented the response of one of two characters in a short stretch of dialogue entirely by typographical and punctuational means.

Whilst phonetic speech can be spoken, these examples by Firbank and Marinetti exist only on the printed page. Likewise with Stéphane Mallarmé's 1897 *Un Coup de Dés*,[4] where the literary and typographic become inseparable. To hear someone speak this text is to severely limit the richness of the printed page. Mallarmé's language is consistently indirect; it aims to suggest, not state. The speaker can give only one interpretation whilst the printed text's use of upper and lower case, italics, flexible spacing and the entire mise-en-page, invite multiple readings.

Mallarmé's poem is usually referred to in most discussions of Derrida's 1974 book *Glas*.[5] In French, glas means a tolling or passing bell; 'to toll the knell'.[6] However, Derrida's text is an open onslaught upon Western logocentricism and its phonetic bias. Its mise-en-page is

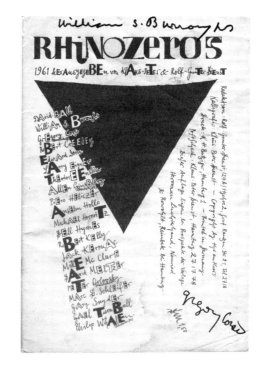

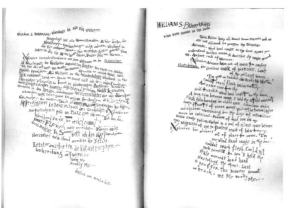

Cover of *Rhinozero5,* 1961, which included *Wind Hand Caught in the Door* by William Burroughs (page spread). This is an example of visual poetry in the tradition of Mallarmé, Apollinaire and the Dadaists up to the concrete poetry of the 1960s.
Photograph by Jed Birmingham RealityStudio.org

Zang Tumb Tumb by Filippo Marinetti on the wall in Leiden.
Photograph by Rienk Mebius (2003).
http://bit.ly/Rienk_Mebius

world is of its nature inhuman. The industrial world of to-day is such, and it has the printing it desires and deserves'.[7]

Gill believes design aesthetics are a sham when based solely upon the bottom-line of commercial interest and enterprise alone.

What Eric Gill foretells is the erasure of the tactile, the haptic dimension in typography and by extension a deskilling in design (brought about by a technological imperative focused on commercial gain).

Today, increasingly design ends up on-screen, on workstations and laptop desktops: a Web-based mediated world.

Just as the MP3 format changed how we consume music, the advent of Amazon's Kindle and similar products will change our relationship with printed material (not the end of the book but an end to its exclusivity). This technological progress leads to people increasingly losing touch with the tactile world.

Many of these anxieties have grown incrementally since the Futurist valediction to tradition, in favour of speed and technology. At the end of the 1940s, a series of talks on the subject of Graphic Form featuring leading designers of the day, including Paul Rand (who attacked the taboo against the use of black in design), reiterated the concerns already heard in the Gill comment, namely a loss of the sensual and sensorial, one presentation by György Kepes[8] is both eloquent and contemporary in its tone when he observes: 'Today's obsession for speed and quantity has profoundly influenced the ways in which we think and feel. Mass production and mass communication, with the characteristic standardized thoughts and vision, have overworked ideas, making of them exhausted stereotypes.'... He continues, 'Vigilance is needed not only in the spheres where we [designers] are vaguely aware of the intentional misuse and manipulation of words and ideas, as in political propaganda or the cheaper aspects of advertising. It is needed also in the fields where we assume that we know what we are talking about, in our own profession. Here we

a continuous series of parallel, opposing commentaries and inset paragraphs without any hierarchy.[7] No single definitive interpretation is possible. This bricolage of texts easily demonstrates how printed writing can resist any claims to universal truth.

Post-1968 writers, graphic designers and typographers have frequently embraced the challenge of postmodern theoretical writing. If David Carson and Neville Brody[8] quickly became familiar in the 1980s, they are far from being alone.

What now and beyond? The linguistic straightjacket has not gone away. Might an enterprising publisher commission a typographical re-setting of Virginia Woolf's 1931 novel, *The Waves?*[9] To date, the reflections of the six characters, which are intercut with poetic invocations, have been printed consecutively rather then in parallel. More topically, how might the political rhetoric of so much media print today be exposed?

See further images here
www.limitedlanguage.org/images

References
1 Ferdinand de Saussure, *Course in General Linguistics* (English translation 1974).
2 Jacques Derrida, *Of Grammatology* (Original French 1967, English translation 1976).
3 Roland Barthes, 'Death of The Author' (English translation in 'Image-Music-Text', 1977) and Michel Foucault, 'What is an Author'? (Original French 1969, English translation 1979).
4 Stéphane Mallarmé, *Un Coup de Dés* (English translation, 1994).
5 Jacques Derrida, *Glas* (Original French 1974, English translation 1986). Glas has spawned many offspring and Ellen Lupton and J. Abbot Miller discuss several of these in their essay 'Deconstruction and Graphic Design' in *Design Writing Research* (Kiosk Books, 1996).
6 *The Concise Oxford French Dictionary* (Edition 1993).
7 The principal sources of these parallel texts are taken from the writings of Georg Friedrich Hegel (philosopher of absolute reason, the state, Christianity and the bourgeois family) and Jean Genet (convicted criminal, writer, atheist and homosexual).
8 See Lewis Blackwell, *The End of Print: The Grafik Design of David Carson* (Chronicle Books, 1995) and *David Carson: 2nd Sight: Grafik Design After the End of Print* (London: Laurence King, 2000) and also Jon Wozencroft, *The Graphic Language of Neville Brody 1 & 2* (London: Thames and Hudson, 1988 and 1994).
9 Virginia Woolf, *The Waves* (London: Hogarth Press, 1931).

must be doubly alert, for we lack the perspective that distance offers'.[9]

Now, 50 years on, we have the benefit of that critical perspective: speed has been reduced to the instantaneous, typography to a series of Bézier curves, screen manipulations or semantic codes.

Some graphic designers have attempted to address this notion of erasure, both historical and cultural.

The typographer Martin Majoor is conscious of working within the historical context of his art form. In 1993 he redesigned the telephone directory for the Dutch telecommunications company KPN. In the existing directory he inherited the sterile plains of a Univers landscape, barren of any fidelity to anything bar its mechanical discipline. His answer was to design a typeface, Telefont List and Telefont Text, which were created within the technical parameters of the commission yet not reduced to a formulae but something more organic; creating a typeface with cultural inflections, which build upon, rather than erase, a visual cultural form. Majoor, when creating the typeface, was aware of the typeface in context of the design project as a whole, it allows a relationship between utilitarian use (of the phonebook) and the overall design thinking: the typefaces responded to how he designed the page layouts. Majoor has commentated on the process as a form of 'interactive design'. Majoor's typefaces build upon established typographic precedents (histories), layer upon layer, each layer always translucent to the one beneath – not the exhausted stereotypes feared by the generation of designers before, going back to Gill and Goudy before him. One enriched with typographic knowledge: a synthesis of technology, culture and craft.

See full responses + carry on the conversation here
http://tiny.cc/chapter6_3

Reader credits
| Stephen Styles 27/07/2005

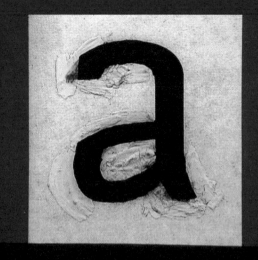

'Majoor's typefaces build upon established typographic precedents (histories), layer upon layer, each layer always translucent to the one beneath...'

The sketch of the a for Seria was to Majoor like a 2D sculpture, adding white and black-in layers.

Scala started out in 1988, and these are some of the early drawings of the font.

Photography Luc Devroye.

فإن الجمعية العامة تنادي
بهذا الإعلان العالمي لحقوق
الإنسان على أنه المستوى
المشترك الذي ينبغي أن
تستهدفه الشعوب والأمم
حتى يسعى كل فرد وهيئة

'FF Seria® Arabic originally called Sada,
by designer Pascal Zoghbi, is an Arabic
type companion to FF Seria®, designed
in the 1990s by Martin Majoor. The Arabic
type family was part of the *Typographic
Matchmaking 01* project organised by the
Khatt Foundation'. http://www.khtt.net/
http://bit.ly/fontfont
http://bit.ly/29letters

References

1   See *Designing Hate* by Steven Heller where he
    comments, 'Symbols of power and violence are
    common in the lexicon of hate' in Steven Heller
    and Philip B. Meggs, *Texts on type: critical writings
    on typography* (New York: Allworth Press, 2001) or
    Roy R. Behrens, 'The Swastika: Symbol Beyond
    Redemption', *Leonardo,* Vol. 34, No. 3 (June 2001),
    280.

2   *Helvetica* (2007) Dir: Gary Hustwit.

3   Martin Majoor, 'Inclined to be dull' in *Eye, No. 63, Vol.
    16* (Spring 2009).

4   Ellen Lupton, 'A Postmortem on Deconstruction'
    in Philip B. Meggs and Steven Heller. *Texts on Type:
    Critical Writings on Typography* (New York: Allworth
    Press, 2001), 45.

5   see Luigi Russolo, *The Art of Noises*
    http://shrinkify.com/108f

6   '…In addition, I have conceived multilinear lyricism,
    …On several parallel lines, the poet will throw
    out several chains of colour, sound, smell, noise,
    weight, thickness, analogy.' Destruction of Syntax
    – Imagination without strings – Words-in-Freedom
    (1913) F.T. Marinetti http://www.unknown.nu/
    futurism/destruction.html

7   Eric Gill and Rene Hague, *An essay on typography*
    (London: Sheed & Ward, 1931), 120.

8   György Kepes, was painter, designer, author and
    educator who founded and directed the Center for
    Advanced Visual Studies at MIT, he died in 2002.

9   György Kepes and Bruce Shapiro, Bruce Rogers
    Collection (Library of Congress), *Graphic forms: the
    arts as related to the book* (Cambridge, MA: Harvard
    University Press, 1949), 128.

Max Bruinsma
New reading spaces

In 1998 I addressed an audience of typographers at the
ATypI conference in Lyon, France, with a question: why
do type designers invest so little research and creative energy in the computer screen as a medium and
in designing fonts for it? The usual answer was that
the screen is not worthy of their detailed skills until it
can match the high definition and resolution of printed
matter – which won't happen in their lifetime. While
that remains to be seen, it was in my view not the only or
even the most pressing problem. The problem was, and is,
that forms in ink on paper are quite different beasts than
similar forms projected by electrons on the back of light-
emitting screens. Ten years have passed, and although
content that is meant for the screen these days often
actually looks like it's made for it rather than for paper,
the typefaces we are supposed to read in this medium
have not changed much. A case in point is Limited Language's screen typeface, Monaco, a monospace font that
works pretty well in fairly large sizes in print but is literally an eyesore when used for reading on screen.[1]

But there's more: how these typefaces behave in the
versatile and interactive environment they live in has
hardly been addressed in terms of typographic design.
Yes, one can click on words and something will happen,
type is twisting and turning in animated headlines,
and you can change its size in Web texts for better
reading. But that's not exactly what I meant, although
some of it helps. Designing typefaces that are tailored
to the peculiarities of the screen is a growing concern
for designers, and some are doing an excellent job
making them work. But typographing texts in a way that
addresses the actual potential of the medium they are
published in is something else.

There have emerged new 'reading spaces', that are
incomparable with the traditional paper ones, but still
behave like they were made by Gutenberg. New port-

Print vs. screen

Max Bruinsma's article on typographic design
for new reading spaces challenges typographers
to make reading on screen rewarding instead of
eye soaring. This goes beyond type and form to
the structure of the reading experience itself:
the relationship between reader and typography
as they interact in the space of the screen.

The relationship between reading, text
and space has been traced by Walter Ong in
Orality and Literacy. 'Writing had reconstituted the originally oral, spoken word in visual
space. Print embedded the word in space more
definitively'.[1] The way print 'lays out' words
for the perusal of the eye, Ong suggests, can
be seen from lists to 'the use of abstract typographic space to interact geometrically with
printed words in a line of development that
runs from Ramism[2] to concrete poetry...'[3]

The abstract 'typographic space' of concrete
poetry plays with typographical arrangement to
convey – extrapolate – the meaning and rhythm
of words in a poem or prose.

Alternatively, the experiments of Vito
Acconci (at the same time as the 1960s concrete
poets), were '...more in a relation between reader
and page. I was interested in movement more
than meaning, movement from left margin to
right margin, movement from top of the page
to bottom. I didn't want to transform/reduce
words to a visual thing: rather, I wanted words
to contradict themselves and subvert meaning so
that there would be nothing left, only movement,
movement over a page and from page to page'.[4]

For Acconci, typography is a series of
movements and the page a performative space
around which the reader navigates. In these
works, 'Words ...[are] obstacles, lures, street
signs, prompts. Instead of describing the
actions of a fictional character, they provoked
the actions of a real one: the reader'.[5]

Acconci's 1969 poem *READ THIS WORD* starts; 'READ THIS WORD THEN READ THIS WORD READ THIS WORD NEXT READ THIS WORD NOW'.[6]

The performative is evident in Bruinsma's thinking too. In *Deepsites*, published in 2003, he observed that in a digital era, 'users are performers of the content'.[7] However, he warns typographers they have to entice the reader into the performative possibilities of screen-based typography.

In Bruinsma's interactive experiment, *Usetext*, it's only when you click (and hold the mouse button down), on a line that more content is revealed on the screen.

Like Acconci, Bruinsma's interest in typography is not its visual structure alone, but its relationship to access. In response to discussions on the website, Bruinsma set *READ THIS WORD* in Usetext.[8]

In contrast to Acconci's setting of the text in print, on screen it becomes a temporal – moving – space. It is the performative relationship between the lines of the text and their reading (not the spatial relationship alone), which draws attention to the act of reading.

On the website, Ruth Ellery, provided context: 'Anja Rau[9] is interesting here...she's a writer of hyper fiction and she reminds us of the "active reader"...[commenting that]... "Hypertext (fictional or non-fictional) is said to activate the reader who has to realize the text in reading it."'[1]

Rau calls the new screen-based reader/user a 'wreader'. 'The active, in control reader-become-writer, the wreader, is a welcome guest of hypertext...'[10] Rau argues use activates a greater psychological engagement in reading (the screen only mimics the immersion of the imagination and reading of a book).

Could investigations today ask how to activate the reader differently? And, what different forms of control does the reader have? The 'in control' 'wreader' of hypertext culture (as on the Limited Language website!) can click to 'read' and 'reply'.

A phenomenological investigation of

able 'e-readers' like Amazon's Kindle or the iLiad are state-of-the-art gizmos that still mimic a paper page's format, albeit of a one-page-fits-all kind. The notion that one can manipulate the appearance and behaviour of text on screen still has had no serious consequences in any generally distributed medium, including the Web. The simple idea that text, not necessarily the content it carries, but its formal structure and the way it is accessed, can be laid-out in variable ways to be triggered situatively by the reader, has been only marginally worked out in mainstream on-screen media, in what we could call 'template culture'. What we see as 'interactive text' is mostly functional text, i.e. text that functions in verbal wayfinding within websites and on-screen forms and menus. You click a word, and a list of subcategories appears. You mouse over a word or an image, and an explanatory line or paragraph pops up.

Such ubiquitous functionality could be used for richer purposes than mere informational messages; it could be used as an integral part of a text, and of the reading experience it offers. The standard hierarchies of text in print media (headline, chapeau, introduction, main text, footnotes, captions) can function in a totally different way in on-screen media. There, if need be, and if the author sees it as an interesting way of communicating, each letter could spawn an endless variety of text formats. A summary statement could give access to deeper layers of argumentation and reference within the same 'page'. An image could morph into its own description, or vice-versa. A question or argument could become surrounded by answers or counter arguments. A text could give more or less detail, depending on the reader's behaviour.

There are, of course experiments that explore such new functionality and new reading spaces. In 2003, I initiated a few of them with designer and JavaScript maverick Joes Koppers. Usetext (usetext.com) was an attempt to make use of the specific potential of on-screen text: A short text is readable as such, but each line also

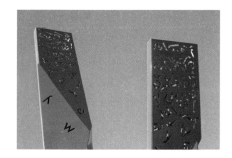

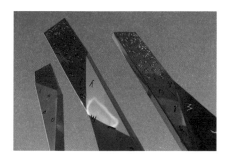

We All Fly public art project, Sanjeev Shankar (2009). The steel wings are composed of alphabets which congregate at the top to become the words *we*, *all* and *fly*. The concept was part of a design initiative with students and the community near Brisbane, Australia. www.sanjeevshankar.com

traditional book reading reveals it is not totally without a performative action because, 'there is a constant dynamic interplay between parts and wholes and the way they are interconnected and [...] the bounds of any of these items emerge in the activity of reading itself'.[11]

Design can investigate and utilise the gaps and indeterminacies that the shift of register between screen based and traditional reading creates.

In the public art project *We All Fly*, one shift is between book reading and of an urban sculpture, who's steel wings are composed of letters which congregate at the top becoming the words of the title. As it is a community design initiative, another reward might be returning reading (and writing!) to a communal activity.

Beyond more and more typefaces, what will be the rewards of the typographic experiments in these new interpretation practices – and these coalitions of reading spaces?

See Max Bruinsma's setting of READ THIS WORD by Vito Acconci (1969): http://bit.ly/bruinsma

See full responses + carry on the conversation here http://tiny.cc/chapter6_4

Reader credits
| Ruth Ellery 28/03/2009

References
1   Walter J. Ong, *Orality and Literacy: The Technologising of the Word* (London: Routledge, 1991), 123.
2   16th century theories on rhetoric, logic and pedagogy.
3   Walter J. Ong, Op cit.
4   Email exchange (2009).
5   Shelley Jackson talks with Vito Acconci in *The Believer*, December 2006/January 2007.
6   Vito Acconci, READ THIS WORD in Craig Dworkin (ed.), *Language to Cover a Page: The Early Writings of Vito Acconci* (Cambridge, MA: MIT, 2006).
7   Max Bruinsma, *Deepsites: Intelligent Innovation in Web Design* (London: Thames and Hudson, 2003), 161.
8   We can't represent the work properly in print for, as Bruinsma wrote in an email exchange; 'it rather misses the point, don't you think?' (2009). See link above.
9   Anja Rau, 'Wreader's Digest' in *Journal of Digital Information*, Vol. 1, Issue 7 (2000).
10 Ibid.
11 Annamaria Carusi, 'Textual Practitioners' in *Arts & Humanities in Higher Education*, Vol. 5, No. 2, 177.

functions as an interface into what's, literally, behind the lines. I used the application for instance to write my introduction to an online story by Young-Hae Chang Heavy Industries', *View Plan of Seoul*. The introduction, 'Starbucks with Victoria', is both an appetizer and a critique of sorts, as well as a pastiche of Chang's signature style in a different medium. And in the Web version of my editorial for *Items* magazine no.1, 2009, I used another Koppers script to realize the movement of the quotes bursting out of the main text, which could only be suggested by the layout of the printed magazine spread.

While such experiments remain modest in scope and design, they do, in my view, give an indication of the potential of the screen as an interesting and engaging medium for reading. Readers, of course, will have to do their part: actively 'feeling' a text for an interactive response, rather than duly clicking links. But readers won't move a finger until designers present them with an invitation: to explore a text's behaviour and expect it to answer in ways that are unthinkable on paper. In other words, designers should explore the medium to find reasons for readers to not print out a text they find online. Reading on screen can be a rewarding experience instead of an eye soaring exercise.

See further images here
www.limitedlanguage.org/images

References
1   Bruinsma's alternatives for the Limited Language's screen typeface:
    www.limitedlanguage.org/discussion/index.php/archive/typographic-design-for-new-reading-spaces/#more-82
2   Young-Hae Chang Heavy Industries' *View and Plan of Seoul*, www.yhchang.com/VAPOS_TRAILER.html
3   Introduction to Young-Hae Chang Heavy Industries' *View and Plan of Seoul*, by Max Bruinsma, set in Usetext: http://usetext.com/users/maxb/browse.php?tool=01&text=25&window=1&admin=1
4   Editorial for Items, No. 1, 2009, set in Usetext: http://items.nl/pages/redactioneel.html

This page is no longer on this server...

The theorist George Landow, writing on digital hypertext, urges us to forget the usual conceptual elements which hold language together and, instead, use new substitutes 'such as multilinearity, nodes, links, or networks'.[1] Elements of syntax – and, when, so, or – are now converted to a range of physical manoeuvres; mouse up, mouse over, mouse down etc. A click now links us to our mediated world.

In this new world the Internet is often described as a virtual landscape without a horizon. However, with the average lifespan of a website measured in months rather than years, in practice it has surprisingly many broken links and dead-ends. Although the Web links us to snapshots of 'history' in unlimited supply, it has no memory, just a post saying 'this page is no longer on this server...'. When going 'back' is really going sideways, we can only link, in endless configurations of synchronicity, to the present.

This change to narrative structures is not a new phenomenon. Technology has always influenced the way we visually navigate our world. The narratives of story telling, songs and pictograms were gradually outmoded by the technological developments of the 19th century. Walter Benjamin, writing at the time, describes a moving away from the traditional links of language.[2] The narratives of storytelling, for instance, were being replaced by the mechanically reproduced image which, like 'mini explosions', were displayed as photographs, cinema clips and so on.

Perhaps the link on the webpage is today's mini explosion? Each click takes us into a new realm; a new page, image or sonic experience. Web artist Peter Luining created a site, Click Club,[3] which was without content except link buttons. Another Web artist produced a faux porn site where, upon entering, you were shown a provocative image of a naked body with the genitals

The influence of neighbours

In the 1990s the American playwright John Guare popularised the theory of the Human Web of relationships in his play *Six Degrees of Separation*. Today, with the World Wide Web, this interrelated chain of relationships has become more literal, and not simply inter-personal, but a network of communities and user groups. A chain of no more than six acquaintances does not only connect individuals but communities too are only a few links away: a news article on the BBC can take you to a Wikipedia entry on the axis of Evil to rogue states; to an Iranian portal page; to a specialist Asian pornography site. You click from community to community; The Right wing politics of John R. Bolton and *The Continuing Threat of Weapons of Mass Destruction*, to an escort agency homepage declaring: Welcome to the BOLTON escorts page in GREATER MANCHESTER.

The world is shrinking thanks to the 'global village' we now inhabit and this notion of 'communities' on the Web is further defined by scientist Albert-Laszlâo Barabâas who explains, 'there are no sharp boundaries between various communities...indeed, the same Website can belong simultaneously to different groups'.[1]

Our original article looked at how the Web was breaking down and reconfiguring the reading experience. The uncanny nature of surfing the Web – link to link – is an element of this process. Today, a casual chit chat with a colleague on the war in Afghanistan, say, arises again as an anonymous image of a bloody child, woman or soldier on a Web page inadvertently arrived at when surfing – likewise child pornography, clearly morally repugnant is only a click away on the office workstation, or laptop.

The desultory nature of the mouse click; clicking from anonymous link to anonymous link mimics Freud's uncanny experience where:

A poster of President Obama as Heath Ledger's Joker from the film *The Dark Knight* began to appear in inner city areas of the USA in the summer of 2009. The *LA Times* reported: '… the image of President Obama in Heath Ledger's Joker-face is especially disturbing because it is completely devoid of context -- literary, political or otherwise. The image seems to have emerged from nowhere and was created by no one. Deracinated from authorial intent, Obama-as-Joker becomes a free-floating cipher that can be appropriated and re-appropriated by everyone'. *LA Times* 5 August 2009, http://bit.ly/obama_latimes

The 'Joker' poster campaign is an example of the factional and anonymous flipside of 'community' and the WWW, and how vernacular language does not have the 'fixity' of time, place or ideology that a modernist visual language might lay claim to.

Design for Obama. This is a website which collates Obama posters and rates them. The founders write; 'Many artists including Shepard Fairey have already proven that poster art is not a dead medium in the United States and have also shown how much of an impact a single poster can have… At such a turbulent (yet exciting) time in our nation's history, collaboration has never been more important.'
http://designforobama.org/

The Obama poster by the artist Shepard Fairey. He is most well known for his *Obey Giant* street poster series. The *Obey* campaign has been described by Fairey as an 'experiment in Phenomenology' which attempts to 'reawaken a sense of wonder about one's environment'.
http://obeygiant.com/about

'it is only this factor of involuntary repetition which surrounds us with an uncanny atmosphere what would be otherwise innocent enough, and forces upon us the idea of something fateful and inescapable where otherwise we should have spoken of "chance" only'.[2]

One of the comments to our original piece asked: 'I can see the theory behind the new worlds of the WWW, but I am yet to find a distinct methodological tool to open it up, as a site for experimentation and creative experience.'[1]

One answer, outside the more theoretical rhetoric of Web cultures, is that of community.

If there is a central theme to the new writing on design it is the role of community: the relationship of communication and consumption.

Discussions on design and community are not new, but have often been overlooked in favour of more fashionable rhetoric on the authentic, the auteur and the practitioner.

Victor Papanek's *Design for the Real World,* is a case in point. When first published in 1971 it was not universally welcomed: an ecology of design was seen as an *alternative* rather than a mainstream conceptual framework. Today, ecology and ecosystems are dominant metaphors in critical thinking on design. Similarly, his call for a non 'sexed-up' design which focused upon process rather than surface alone, was a precursor to the sea-of-change in design writing today.

Increasingly, design writing is moving away from simple interpretation and historical timeline – it addresses a more holistic approach that calls upon anthropological, relational dialogue to interrogate meaning(s) and use value in design culture.

Papanek remarks in his introduction: 'Design must become an innovative, highly creative, cross-disciplinary tool responsive to the true needs of men [sic]. It must be more research orientated, and we must stop defiling the earth itself with poorly designed objects and structures'.[3]

Today we read this as a call for community – a design community where ideas can be covered by a link button[4]. Each time you clicked on the button you opened another window with increasingly fractured images of naked bodies and more buttons... And of course, you never got to the fully naked body. On this site, the frustration was two-fold. It reminds us of how we consume the visual image and how, like channel surfing, the link has become the fetish itself... constantly zapping to capture what we might be missing.

The question is, in our broadband, Wi-Fi, Bluetooth linked world...is there anything left to miss?

See further images here
www.limitedlanguage.org/images

References
1   George P. Landow, Hypertext 3.0: *Critical Theory and New Media in an Era of Globalization*, 3rd ed. (Baltimore, MD; London: Johns Hopkins University Press, 2006). See Introduction.
2   Susan Buck-Morss, *The Dialectics of Seeing: Walter Benjamin and the Arcades Project* (Cambridge, MA.; London: MIT Press, 1989), 244. Walter Benjamin used the tem 'now-time' (Jetztzeit) to describe a revolutionary break in the continuity of history, a moment when 'truth is laden with time to the point of explosion'.
3   Peter Luining's *PC Click Club* (1995-2000). See also www.luining.com
4   This faux porn site was created by Dutch group DEPT, who ceased operation in 2001.

Garth Walker (Mister Walker Design, and founder of Orangejuice
Design Studios in Durban South Africa) in 2004 was commissioned
to create the signage for the entrance to the new South African
Constitutional Court. The final installation drew upon the vernacular
signage already found in the area providing a 'new' typographic
representation of the local style. The project reflects his claim that
his 'true passion is vernacular design from South Africa's streets and
townships'.

shared with not only the design world, but a wider non-specialist public (Papanek is critical of literature on design, which he bemoans is written for and by designers).

The need for a broader design education informs Aaris Sherin's thinking in her essay *Escape From the Tyranny of Things* (this Volume p. 99), where an educated public might consume with greater awareness of good design allowing, in the words of Virginia Postrel, a 'democratization of design' which has been informed by the WWW and an increasing access to design discourse. Postrel is indirectly addressing the 'literal and metaphorical' language of graphic design – good and bad – as mediated through Web design; allowing a greater public (and professional) awareness and appreciation of graphic design. The interface is often our first engagement with how graphic design works: hierarchies, colour and how they influence how we navigate the page.

But we feel, by extension, sites like Design Boom, Design Observer, Core 77 and Limited Language in the main, address those-in-the-know, but also allow (consciously or not) a breaking down between disciplines. They provide a day-to-day view of disciplinary thinking – rhetorically and visually.

These websites are individual communities but because of the matrix structure of the Web, they also facilitate the cross-disciplinary thinking advocated by Papanek in a pre-Internet age. Today you are only six clicks away from another design discipline.

But in conclusion, the communities thus described are in a global context, parochial at best; homogenising systems at worst. Designers like Garth Walker, founder of the South African agency, Orangejuice Design; are vigilant to the nature of the Web and reaffirm the vernacular in their work whilst participating in the pragmatics of a global economic market: whether in the signage of public buildings or tobacco branding. The vernacular acts like a Google map in identifying where we are in a design, and designed, world.

Our original article asked: is there

anything left to miss?... And this is an increasing anxiety, not least because, 'The speed and intensity with which both material and ideological elements now circulate across national boundaries have created a new order of uncertainty in social life'.[5]

As such, we have never needed design, and design writing more to help make sense of our world.

See full responses + carry on the conversation here
http://tiny.cc/chapter6_5

Reader credits
1   Dylan Hopson 19/11/2008

References
1   Albert-Laszlâo Barabâasi, *Linked: The New Science of Networks* (Cambridge, MA: Perseus Pub., 2002), 171.
2   Freud quoted in Julie Rivkin and Michael Ryan. *Literary Theory: An Anthology* (Revised ed. Malden, MA: Oxford: Blackwell, 1998), 427.
3   Victor J. Papanek, *Design for the Real World: Human Ecology and Social Change* (2nd, completely rev. ed. New York: Van Nostrand Reinhold Co., 1984), x.
4   Virginia I. Postrel, *The Substance of Style: How the Rise of Aesthetic Value Is Remaking Commerce, Culture, and Consciousness* (New York, NY: HarperCollins, 2003), 55.
5   Arjun Appadurai, *Fear of Small Numbers: An Essay on the Geography of Anger* (Public Planet Books. Durham, NC; London: Duke University Press, 2006), 5.

Collaborators' biographies

Monica Biagioli is an artist, writer and curator. She lectures at the University of the Arts London and recent projects include *Sound Proof*, a series of yearly sound exhibitions focusing on the Olympics site in London, hosted at E:vent Gallery (2008) and by v22 Presents (2009); *Venus Rising*, a series of events hosted by the Science Museum's Dana Centre and the Institute of Contemporary Art (2005); and participation in the 50th *Venice Biennale* (2003).

Max Bruinsma is Editor in Chief of *Items* design magazine, the Netherlands, and Editorial Director of *ExperimentaDesign*, Portugal. His publications include *Deep Sites: Intelligent Innovation in Contemporary Web Design* (2003).

Angus Carlyle is a sound artist, lecturer, writer and co-director of CRISAP, Creative Research into Sound Arts Practice.

Michael Clarke is a writer and lecturer and was for more than twenty-five years the art and design critic for the *Times Educational Supplement* in Britain. His most recent publication is *Verbalising the Visual: Translating Art and Design into Words* (2007).

David Crowley is a writer, lecturer and curator based at the Royal College of Art in London. He has published widely on Polish culture and he was co-curator of *Cold War Modern: Design 1945-1970* at the Victoria and Albert Museum, London (2008).

Johnny Hardstaff is a moving graphic imagemaker represented internationally by Ridley Scott Associates and Central Illustration Agency. He writes and lectures in his field, and has screened works at Tate Modern (London), Laforet Museum (Tokyo), Museum of Contemporary Art (Chicago), MOMA (San Francisco) and Palace of Fine Arts (San Francisco).

Adam Kossoff is a filmmaker/artist and writer based in London. He is also Senior Lecturer in Video at the School of Art and Design, University of Wolverhampton. His book *On Terra Firma; Space, Place and the Moving Image* (2008) is published by Vdm Verlag.

Esther Leslie is Professor of Political Aesthetics at Birkbeck, University of London. Publications include *Hollywood Flatlands: Animation, Critical Theory and the Avant Garde* (2002), *Synthetic Worlds: Nature, Art and the Chemical Industry* (2005) and *Walter Benjamin* (2007).

Tom McCarthy is a writer and artist living in London. His books include *Men in Space* (2007), *Tintin and the Secret of Literature* (2006) and *Remainder* (2005), the last of which won the 2007 Believer Book Award and is currently being adapted for cinema by Film4. He is also General Secretary of the International Necronautical Society, a 'semi-fictitious avant-garde organisation'.

Julia Moszkowicz is a writer and Senior Lecturer in The History and Theory of Graphic Communication at Bath Spa University in the UK. She has published in *Screen, Eye* magazines and the *Journal of Visual Arts Practice.*

Mario Moura is a design writer and lecturer at the Porto Academy of Art, Portugal. He trained as a graphic designer and is vibrant in the Portuguese design world, including the design blog Texto and his collaboration on the publication, *Barbara Says* (2006). He has published a selection of short texts on design, politics and ethics; *Design em Tempos de Crise* (Design in Times of Crisis) (2008).

John Russell is an artist who exhibits Internationally. He is a founder member of the art group BANK (1990-2000) He is Reader in Contemporary Art&Theory and Director of Research at the University of Reading, England.

Nicky Ryan lectures in visual culture and theory at the London College of Communication. Nicky has delivered conference papers and published widely in relation to art and business, corporate patronage, museums, and the role of culture in regeneration. She is a regular reviewer for the *Museums Journal.*

David Phillips is an architect, designer and writer based in London. He teaches information design at the London College of Communication.

Aaris Sherin is an Associate Professor of Graphic Design at St. John's University in Queens, New York. She writes and lectures on the history of women, design and social and environmental issues and is author of the book, *SustainAble: A Handbook of Materials and Applications for Graphic Designers and their Clients* (2008) and co-author of *Forms, Folds and Sizes: 2nd Edition* (2009).

Ezri Tarazi is an industrial designer and writer. He is Head of the Masters Program for Industrial Design at Bezalel Academy of Art and Design in Jerusalem. In 2005, with Ellen Lupton, he co-curated *New Design from Israel* at the Cooper Hewitt National Design Museum. He set up the Design Center of Israel.

Jon Wozencroft is a writer, designer and photographer who set up the music publishing company Touch in 1982. He wrote *The Graphic Language of Neville Brody 1 and 2* (1988 & 1994) and collaborated with Brody on the *FUSE* project (1991 onwards).

Joanna Zylinska is a cultural theorist based at Goldsmiths, University of London and Reviews Editor for *Culture Machine.* Selected books include *Bioethics in the Age of New Media* (2009), *The Ethics of Cultural Studies* (2005) and *The Cyborg Experiments: The Extensions of the Body in the Media Age* (2002).

Biographies

Limited Language co-founders

Colin Davies writes and teaches about design history. He has three kids and a manic depressive dog.

Monika Parrinder is based in London and writes and teaches about design history. She has two kids and trained as a graphic designer.

Designers

Sofia Andersson assistant designer; Sofia works as a freelance illustrator/designer and has worked with the Swedish magazine *SEX* and *Amelia* magazine, among other clients. She studied Fine Art Foundation at Central Saint Martins/Byam Shaw School of Art in 2003/2004 and graduated from Forsbergs School of Graphic Design in 2007.

Amalie Borg-Hansen assistant designer; Amalie recently graduated from BA Graphic and Media Design at the London College of Communication, specialising in Information Design. She will continue her studies in Switzerland, starting on the MA at the Basel School of Design. Amalie has worked as an editorial assistant and researcher at *Eye* magazine, and as a designer for Dorling Kindersley, ico Design and Misha Anikst Ltd.

Oskar Karlin concept and design for the Limited Language website and book; Oskar is a graphic designer and cartographer who graduated from BA Graphic and Media Design at the London College of Communication in 2004. As well as freelance designing, he works in the Human Geography department at Stockholm University as a research assistant and GIS teacher.

Sub-editors

Emma Angus is currently studying for a PhD in image classification at the University of Wolverhampton after completing her first degree in Publishing with English at Loughborough University.

Michael Clarke is a writer and lecturer and was for more than twenty-five years the art and design critic for the *Times Educational Supplement* in Britain. His most recent publication is *Verbalising the Visual: Translating Art and Design into Words* (2007).

Index